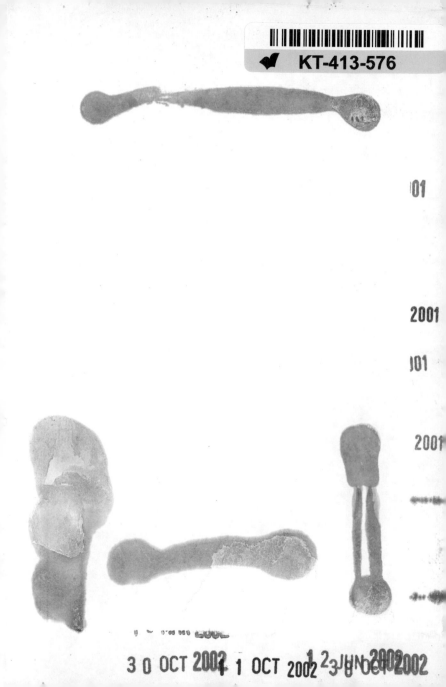

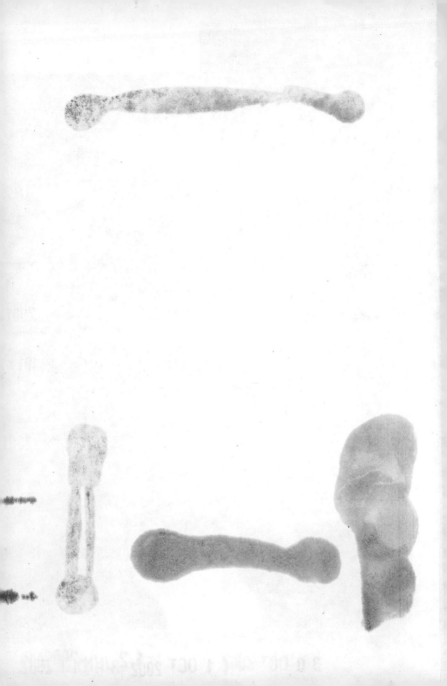

FILM TECHNIQUE AND
FILM ACTING

PUDOVKIN IN THE CUTTING ROOM

PHOTO. D. SHOLOMOVICH, DECEMBER 1949

V. I. PUDOVKIN

FILM
TECHNIQUE
AND
FILM ACTING

TRANSLATED AND EDITED BY IVOR MONTAGU

MEMORIAL EDITION

with Portrait, Memoir and a revised and completed
record of the author's film work

VISION

VISION PRESS LIMITED

157 KNIGHTSBRIDGE
LONDON SW1X 7PA

Pudovkin on Film Technique first published in English by
Victor Gollancz Ltd., October 1929
2nd Impression, January 1930

Enlarged Edition by George Newnes Ltd., 1933
2nd Impression, 1935

Film Acting, first published in English by George Newnes, Ltd., 1937

Film Technique and Film Acting, Lear (U.S.A.), 1949
Reprinted by Vision Press Ltd., 1954
Memorial Edition, revised and enlarged, 1958
2nd Impression 1968
3rd Impression 1974
ISBN 0 85478 121 8
MCMLXXIV

PRINTED IN GREAT BRITAIN
BY PHOTOLITHOGRAPHY
CLARKE, DOBLE & BRENDON LTD.,
PLYMOUTH,

CONTENTS

PREFACE TO
THE MEMORIAL EDITION

THIS reprinting, by Vision Press, is now the only form in which are available to the public the two major written works of V. I. Pudovkin, *Film Technique* and *Film Acting* in any language.

The selected edition of the author's writings* published three years ago in his home country contain only extracts, drastically abbreviated in the case of the former.

During the later years of his life, Pudovkin hesitated to authorize republication of his earlier works, modestly believing that, as his ideas had become modified and broadened in the light of experience, his mature views might be misunderstood should these first writings reappear without qualification. He need not have worried. Everybody can understand that these books, written thirty and twenty years ago, do not and could not say the last word about film creation. They do spell out its A.B.C. As Lewis Jacobs wrote, in an introduction to the last American edition: "So sound are their points of view, so valid their tenets, so revelatory their analyses, that they remain to day, twenty years after their initial appearance, the foremost books of their kind." The ideas set out in *Film Technique* remain basic to any philosophy of the film, to appreciation of the relation of real material to film appearance, to any understanding of

* Izbrannyiye Statyi, see p. 388.

7

exactly what we are doing when we create an effect upon the screen, and they will so remain as long as cinema continues.

It is hard to overestimate the influence that *Pudovkin on Film Technique* has had on the development, not just of film theorizing, but of practical film-making. This influence has no doubt been greater abroad than in the author's own country where, in the 'twenties, argument and speculation about film was a commonplace and Pudovkin, acclaimed as a director of genius, was as writer seen only as a popularizer of ideas already current. But in England and Hollywood above all, where so many splendid films had been made for years without their authors having leisure to think in face of the time-pressure of chasing the weekly pay-cheque, these ideas arrived with the thunder-clap simplicity of Columbus' egg. Makers of film were inarticulate in those days, theorizing the domain of high-brow, long-hair, egg-head. In a moment these books became, and for a generation they have remained, film "bibles". The established dipped surreptitiously. The young—our present established—absorbed them with their milk. The amateur found sudden illumination. Today's critics were bred on them. Their contents are the grammar and the syntax upon which all present-day film thinking and film working are indirectly founded. It is time that they be removed from the hazards of the second-hand barrow and re-presented with the dignity they deserve.

In now making them available, therefore, the publishers have merited well not only of the film world and its outskirts, but of all who are interested in aesthetics and the science of analysis of the creative process in any art form. The texts are published as those of classics deserve, exactly in their original form, and to bring their author nearer to the reader we have added a portrait and a personal memoir, as well as brought up-to-date and made complete the "Iconography" that lists his film career.

I.M.

PREFACE TO SECOND PRINTING OF THE MEMORIAL EDITION

TEN years ago, when the Memorial Edition first appeared, the present writer commented that the works included here retained an evergreen freshness and applicability. The proof of this is shown by the concomitance that now, ten years later, almost forty years since the first of them was written, a new printing has been called for.

This is an extraordinary thing when you come to think of it. Film-making itself is hardly 75 years old. And for more than half of this time Pudovkin's classic has held the field, teaching generations of beginners the elementary bases on which rest all the ramifications of the film-making craft or art.

In most branches of art it is the custom from time to time to speak of the latest fashions current as having superceded everything that has gone before. There is little harm in this, and much good, for it is healthy that each generation should feel a glow of discovery and not be constricted unduly by the frameworks of the past. Nevertheless, it is of course only modes of presentation and styles that change, to fit the novel interests corresponding to the changing life that surrounds each fresh artistic wave. The basic laws of method deriving from the technical nature of each art do not change but remain as consistently applicable in practice as do simple mathematics to any novel calculation.

Pudovkin, though a great creative artist, was not a profoundly original theoretician. The principles he sets out in his writings were less his own discoveries than generalisations he learned from his own teachers and verified in practice. But such was his enthusiastic and straightforward nature that, as he grasped them, he set them out with an energy that still carries everyone forward and a simplicity that enables everyone to understand.

When I used the word "beginners" in this context, be it understood that I meant not only the youth on whom continuity and perpetual renewal of cinema depends, but the hardened professional veteran of a hundred battles with front-office, the greybeard versed in other disciplines of culture—just anybody to whom it has not hitherto occurred to *think* about the cinema. Begin with Pudovkin, you start on the right tack. Everything that follows, the boundless possibilities of sound-film, the technical refinements made feasible by delicate modern instrumentation, falls into place because you came with the right approach.

OCTOBER 1967   I.M.

PERSONAL MEMOIR BY
IVOR MONTAGU

V SEVOLOD ILLARIONOVICH PUDOVKIN was one of the three top great men in the Soviet cinema: Eisenstein, the self-conscious genius and intellectual, satirist, creator of unforgettable patterns and researches; Pudovkin, naïve and rugged countryman from Penza, whose simple dramatic sincerity aroused shattering emotion; and Dovzhenko, poet and artist from the Ukraine, touching the timeless, digging deep beneath the skin.

Now that Pudovkin has died suddenly at the age of 60, the last is the only one left.* Certainly, there are other wonderful national screen personalities in the USSR, but for the most part the height of their medium is character, rendered in dialogue and other touches of characterization which need a share of native culture for full perception, and cannot wholly cross language and social barriers. These three alone were so essentially graphic in their spheres that anyone, of any land, could sense all their power.

Pudovkin achieved at least four films that will for ever remain classics of the cinema: *Mother*, *The End of St. Petersburg*, *Storm Over Asia*, and *Suvorov*. The first three of these were made while he and others were still treating actors as "types". In none of these could one really say that he created character, or in the first, for example, that the mother or son had the roundness and depth of

* Dovzhenko died in November, 1956.

11

the persons created by Gorky. Yet such was the power
of his own feeling that, through these films, he depicted
social injustice, and the revolt against it, the injustice of
imperialist war, and the revolt against it, the injustice of
colonialism, and the revolt against it, with a force and
emotional impact that have never been excelled. In the
fourth, when talk was beginning to preoccupy the Soviet
cinema with problems of character, he created the
historical figure of the name part so vividly that it is
impossible for anyone who has not seen the film to read
of that general and not see him always in every line,
action and gesture exactly as he was portrayed.

Pudovkin made plenty of other pictures, stamped with
his personality and of the highest class. It was entirely
characteristic of him, his simplicity, directness and lack
of introspection, that he also threw himself readily and
enthusiastically into yet a number of other subjects that
were not really suited to him, and proved failures, being
outside his special qualities.

Comparatively speaking, he was not a great theorist,
not a great innovator. Yet precisely because of this,
because he was not an intellectual, the theory he set out—
inferences from Griffith, digested through Kuleshov;
undigested scraps of Eisenstein; scraps of Stanislavsky;
all harmonized and rearranged into a coherent framework pattern by his own simple, direct enthusiasm—has
had a far greater influence than the often subtler,
profounder analyses of his mentors.

His first two little books—two tiny paper pamphlets
in Russian, long read and read to bits and fallen apart
and entirely lost in their country of origin, then put into

German, and finally translated by me as *Pudovkin on Film Technique*—have educated a whole generation of film makers. They are part of general film grammar, and even today convey truths that still remain basic— whatever qualifications they now need—despite all technical improvements. Amateurs read them. The greatest in contemporary British cinema brought them selves up on them. And the other day a perfect stranger on an aeroplane, catching sight of my passport, intro- duced himself to me as the Hollywood producer of a current festival prizewinner and avowed his own entry- ticket and bible in the industry to have been that all- arousing book. The secret, the author's heartfelt absorp- tion and transmission of essentials, plus the infection of his own keenness.

Himself he remained always unstudied. I remember discussing with him once his then latest and far from successful picture *Deserter*. He was describing with excitement his making of the early ship-welding scenes— in themselves, certainly, exceeding well done. My inter- jections were reserved, and presently I criticized his treatment of the scenes, quoting as authority his own remarks—set out in his book and taken to heart by all of us—about the necessity of visualizing each film as a whole and not allowing hypertrophy of a section to disturb the general balance. He looked at me with the utmost astonishment. "Did I write that?" he said.

It was the same with his relationship to acting. What he wrote about acting was simple and true, and written with such conviction, as a reflection of his own effort at the time to grasp the truth, that it stimulated hundreds of good minds all over the world. Yet, loving acting himself, on the screen he was an impossible ham. This was equally true whether he was directed by another (the principal in Otsep's *The Living Corpse*) or self-directed (the Nazi general in *The Russians*); whether in a leading part as in these two films, or in a tiny cameo, such as the fop with the sunshade in Kozintsev and Trauberg's *New Babylon* or the mad preacher in Eisenstein's *Ivan the Terrible* (this last, I fear, was a not very obscure joke played by Eisenstein on his friend). He was eager to try anything, and not at all a self-judge. If it was wrong, he neither noticed nor grieved over it. If it happened to be right. it came off, and became immortal.

There was never a more loyal and enthusiastic son of the Soviet Union. He was proud of his decorations. Neither my wife nor I will ever forget his shining eyes as he retailed to her stories illustrating Lenin's coolness and wisdom in revolutionary crises, simple legends that had fired him so that he could convey their fire, exactly the quality of dramatic transmission that made his films so tremendous when they hit their target. Pudovkin also liked the English. He learned the language from fellow prisoners of war in a p.o.w. camp in Germany during 1914–18. When he first came to London his smattering enabled him to read a speech to the Film Society of which we had carefully marked the accentuation. Later, Marie Seton helped to polish him, and in the end he spoke extremely well, though with rather a plum in his mouth, and held his own splendidly among the great concourse that came to honour him and Picasso in Felix

Topolski's studio on the occasion of the battered-by-authority Sheffield Peace Conference.* I remember his defending, at the Film Society discussion, his British imperial types in *Storm Over Asia* against the charge of being overdrawn, urging fiercely that they were no more caricatured than Dickens' figures. And then a few hours later, as we sat in an office soliciting from the authorities a prolongation of his visa, he pointed out to me an official who in every exterior feature and movement exactly duplicated one of the personages in the film. (But he would often seize on such details. Calling at a hotel to find a friend, we were guided along the corridor by an English boots; as our guide knocked on the door and bent to listen, Pudovkin gripped my shoulder with iron fingers to point out the man's bent posture, hand cupped to ear, assumed unaffectedly in nature, and yet so seeming-exaggerated beyond convention that any audience would have called it caricature in a film. Precisely such a mind's eye notebook is the indispensable baggage of every gifted film director.) I remember his joy at discovering how easy it was to speak to his wife in Moscow by the telephone at my flat, his delight in shopping to buy English clothes—not in the least from snobbery, but because they were exotic and English, as a London visitor to Moscow might buy an embroidered cap or shirt.

A charming photograph that I have shows him wearing a sweater from Fair Isle that I brought and asked him to pass on to a friend, but which, like a child, he simply could not resist intercepting (of course with

* On that occasion he found himself, rather unflatteringly, one of the only two Soviet delegates out of the lot regarded by the Home Office as "safe".

15

open and plentiful apologies to the friend). I know how happy he was to preside over the British film festival in wartime Moscow, and I do not forget, either, how he would come to me at peace conferences, in order to make sure, at least as far as he could by consultation, that, where criticizing British government policy when he thought it right to do so, this should never be done in phrases that were exaggerated, or unjust to the British people.

He was so frank and affectionate that it was impossible not to respond with like affection. His was what is called in the cliché a *large* nature. I remember my last sight of him at work. It was in 1949. I had motored from Moscow along the road the Germans came. Some distance beyond their first trenches, we turned off suddenly to the left. The motor bumped along incredible ruts and splashed up mud. The fields wore the green of an exceptionally wet summer. Somewhere farther on we turned off left and jolted past the cows on to a big prairie. Round one edge were set tents. I made my way across to them, peered inside and called. He sprang up, emerged, screwed up his eyes and folded me in giant arms. We sat down in the gloom of the tent and recalled old friends, old times. Presently there rose a hubbub. The showers had suddenly ceased, and the sun was struggling through a gap in the clouds, glistening on the raindrops. At once all kinds of apparatus and all kinds of people pushed out across the meadow. In the centre was a full-size model of a Farman plane. The camera was set up, we all took our places, the pilot lay full length, invisible wires brought the plane into motion and to a halt, far in the back of the shot rode angry and futile gendarmes, shouting in scarlet and blue. We retook again and again, once because a line of collective cows appeared on the horizon, once for mechanical defects. A gendarme got off his horse and took Farman's place and cap. Suddenly, I noticed behind yet in the midst of us a short-sleeved boy and a girl, uncaring for anyone, under an umbrella, engrossed in each other. Vsevolod Illarionovich beamed, catching my line of glance, "Aren't they sweet?" he said. "Assistant camera and continuity. We don't like to disturb them. They've got to know each other on this unit and now they're going to be married . . ."

He had a big, athletic frame. He won the badge "Ready for Labour and Defence". Run a mile, swim a mile, ride a mile, parachute jump and the rest, all to certain standards. It means a good deal. At the Wroclaw Conference we got into an argument. It was the usual trouble, agreeing a text. It had occurred to me that we few film people there should not let ourselves be swamped but should take the chance of coming together from so many countries to issue our own appeal to work for peace, to film people. All were keen. Now Pudovkin and I were supposed to draft it. There was no difference of substance, but a hell of a row on form. As always when arguing with a Russian, a Frenchman, or indeed almost any continental European, the Englishman complained that the other fellow's text was windy, rhetorical, bunk. Equally, as always when arguing with an Englishman, the continental complained that my text was dry, un-inspiring, impossible. We both refused to give way. We were strolling round a huge pool in a pleasure ground outside the building where the conference had its restaurant. Suddenly Pudovkin put down his brief-case. "Let's run", he said, without any other preliminary. I agreed and put down mine. We set off. The distance was at least 400 metres. At first we jogged together. I am fat sometimes, but my low blood-pressure gives me a good wind. He had the badge, but was ten years older than I. From time to time I caught him glancing at me out of the side of his eye to see if it was safe to sprint or whether, if he did, I had enough in hand to pass him. Finally we both sprinted and arrived in a perfect dead-heat to much handkerchief waving by Moussinac and others in the style of miners encouraging whippets. But here is the point. Resuming our brief-cases, we almost at once reached agreement. We were far too out of breath to have any left to waste on further conflict. I have often though there must be a moral somewhere to this ridiculous episode.

Now his physical powers have gone back on him. All eager for his next film, Pudovkin died suddenly on vacation, struck down by a heart attack, after too strenuous lawn tennnis and a swim. A loss to wife, friend the cinema, the Soviet Union, peace, mankind. They do not come like him very often. However, in life he gave us very much.

First published in the *Anglo-Soviet Journal*, vol. xiv, No. 3, Autumn, 1953.

FILM TECHNIQUE

FILM TECHNIQUE

INTRODUCTION TO THE
GERMAN EDITION

THE foundation of film art is *editing*. Armed with this watchword, the young cinema of Soviet Russia commenced its progress, and it is a maxim that, to this day, has lost nothing of its significance and force.

It must be borne in mind that the expression " editing " is not always completely interpreted or understood in its essence. By some the term is naïvely assumed to imply only a joining together of the strips of film in their proper time-succession. Others, again, know only two sorts of editing, a fast and a slow. But they forget—or they have never learnt—that rhythm (i.e., the effects controlled by the alternation in cutting of longer or shorter strips of film) by no means exhausts all the possibilities of editing.

To make clear my point and to bring home unmistakably to my readers the meaning of editing and its full potentialities, I shall use the analogy of another art-form—literature. To the poet or writer separate words are as raw material. They have the widest and most variable meanings which only begin to become precise through their position in the sentence. To that extent to which the word is an integral part of the composed phrase, to that extent is its effect and meaning variable until

23

it is fixed in position, in the arranged artistic form.

To the film director each shot of the finished film subserves the same purpose as the word to the poet. Hesitating, selecting, rejecting, and taking up again, he stands before the separate takes, and only by conscious artistic composition at this stage are gradually pieced together the " phrases of editing," the incidents and sequences, from which emerges, step by step, the finished creation, the film.

The expression that the film is " shot " is entirely false, and should disappear from the language. The film is not *shot*, but *built*, built up from the separate strips of celluloid that are its raw material. If a writer requires a word—for example, *beech*—the single word is only the raw skeleton of a meaning, so to speak, a concept without essence or precision. Only in conjunction with other words, set in the frame of a complex form, does art endow it with life and reality. I open at hazard a book that lies before me and read " the tender green of a young beech "—not very remarkable prose, certainly, but an example that shows fully and clearly the difference between a single word and a word structure, in which the beech is not merely a bare suggestion, but has become part of a definite, literary form. The dead word has been waked to life through art.

I claim that every object, taken from a given viewpoint and shown on the screen to spectators, is a *dead object*, even though it has moved before the camera. The proper movement of an object before the camera is yet no movement on the screen, it is no more than raw material for the future building-up, by editing, of the movement that is conveyed by the assemblage of the various strips of film. Only if the object be placed together among a number of separate objects, only if it be presented as part of a synthesis of different separate visual images, is it endowed with filmic life. Transformed like the word " beech " in our analogy, it changes itself in this process from a skeletal photographic copy of nature into a part of the filmic *form*.

Every object must, by editing, be brought upon the screen so that it shall have not *photographic*, but *cinematographic* essence.

One thus perceives that the meaning of editing and the problems it presents to the director are by no means exhausted by the logical time-succession inherent in the shots, or by the arrangement of a rhythm. Editing is the basic creative force, by power of which the soulless photographs (the separate shots) are engineered into living, cinematographic form. And it is typical that, in the construction of this form, material may be used that is in reality of an entirely different character from that in the guise of which it eventually appears. I shall take an example from my last film, *The End of St. Petersburg*.

At the beginning of that part of the action that represents war, I wished to show a terrific explosion. In order to render the effect of this explosion with absolute faithfulness, I caused a great mass of dynamite to be buried in the earth, had it blasted, and shot it. The explosion was veritably colossal—but filmically it was nothing. On the screen it was merely a slow, lifeless movement. Later, after much trial and experiment, I managed to " edit " the explosion with all the effect I required—moreover, without using a single piece of the scene I had just taken. I took a *flammenwerfer* that belched forth clouds of smoke. In order to give the effect of the crash I cut in short flashes of a magnesium flare, in rhythmic alternation of light and dark. Into the middle of this I cut a shot of a river taken some time before, that seemed to me to be appropriate owing to its special tones of light and shade. Thus gradually arose before me the visual effect I required. The bomb explosion was at last upon the screen, but, in reality, its elements comprised everything imaginable except a real explosion.

Once more, reinforced by this example, I repeat that editing is the creative force of filmic reality, and that nature provides only the raw material with which it works. That, precisely, is the relationship between reality and the film.

These observations apply also in detail to the *actors*. The man photographed is only raw material for the future composition of his image in the film, arranged in editing.

When faced with the task of presenting a captain of industry in the film *The End of St. Petersburg*, I sought to solve the problem by cutting in his figure with the equestrian statue of Peter the Great. I claim that the resultant composition is effective with a reality quite other than that produced by the posing of an actor, which nearly always smacks of Theatre.

In my earlier film, *Mother*, I tried to affect the spectators, not by the psychological performances of an actor, but by plastic synthesis through editing. The son sits in prison. Suddenly, passed in to him surreptitiously, he receives a note that next day he is to be set free. The problem was the expression, filmically, of his joy. The photographing of a face lighting up with joy would have been flat and void of effect. I show, therefore, the nervous play of his hands and a big close-up of the lower half of his face, the corners of the smile. These shots I cut in with other and varied material—shots of a brook, swollen with the rapid flow of spring, of the play of sunlight broken on the water, birds splashing in the village pond, and finally a laughing child. By the junction of these components our expression of " prisoner's joy " takes shape. I do not know how the spectators reacted to my experiment—I myself have always been deeply convinced of its force.

Cinematography advances with rapid stride. Its possibilities are inexhaustible. But it must not be forgotten that its path to a real art will be found only when it has been freed from the dictates of an art-form foreign to it—that is, the Theatre. Cinematography stands now upon the threshold of its own methods.

The effort to affect from the screen the feelings and ideas of the public by means of editing is of crucial importance, for it is an effort that renounces theatrical method. I am firmly convinced that it is along this path that the great international art of cinematography will make its further progress.

(Published in *Filmregie und Filmmanuskript*, translated by Georg and Nadia Friedland, Lichtbildbuehne, Berlin, 1928, and re-translated from German by I. M., in *The Film Weekly*, London, October 29, 1928.)

I

THE FILM SCENARIO AND ITS THEORY

FOREWORD

THE scenarios usually submitted to production firms are marked by a specific character. Almost all represent the primitive narration of some given content, their authors having apparently concerned themselves only with the relation of incident, employing for the most part literary methods, and entirely disregarding the extent to which the material they propose will be interesting as subject for cinematographic treatment. The question of special cinematographic treatment of material is highly important. Every art possesses its own peculiar method of effectively presenting its matter. This remains true, of course, for the film. To work at a scenario without knowing the methods of directorial work, the methods of shooting and cutting a film, is as foolish as to give a Frenchman a Russian poem in literal translation. In order to communicate to the Frenchman the correct impression, one must rewrite the poem anew, with knowledge of the peculiarities of French verse-form. In order to write a scenario suitable for filming, one must know the methods by which the spectator can be influenced from the screen.

The opinion is often met with that the scenarist has

only to give a general, primitive outline of the action. The whole work of detailed " filmic " adaptation is an affair of the director. This is entirely false. It should be remembered that in no art can construction be divided into stages independent of one another. Already that very general approach involved in the fact of a work being thought out as a substantial future presupposes attention to possible particularities and details. When one thinks of a theme, then inevitably one thinks simultaneously, be it hazily and unclearly, of the treatment of its action, and so forth. From this it follows that, even though the scenarist abstain from laying down detailed instructions on what to shoot and how to shoot it, what to edit and how to edit it, none the less a knowledge and consideration of the possibilities and peculiarities of directorial work will enable him to propose material that *can* be used by the director, and will make possible to him the creation of a *filmically expressive* film. Usually the result is exactly the opposite—usually the first approach of the scenarist to his work implies in the best cases uninteresting, in the worst insurmountable, obstacles to filmic adaptation.

The purpose of this study is to communicate what is, it is true, a very elementary knowledge of the basic principles of scenario work in their relation to the basic principles of directorial work. Apart from those considerations specifically filmic, the scenarist, especially in the field of general construction, is confronted with the laws governing creation in other allied arts. A scenario may be constructed in the style of a playwright, and will then be subject to the laws that determine the construction of a play. In other cases it may approach the novel, and its construction will consequently be conditioned by other laws. But these questions can be treated only superficially in the present sketch, and readers especially interested in them must turn to specialised works.

PART I

THE SCENARIO

THE MEANING OF THE " SHOOTING-SCRIPT "

IT is generally known that the finished film consists of a whole series of more or less short pieces following one another in definite sequence. In observing the development of the action the spectator is transferred first to one place, then to another ; yet more, he is shown an incident, even sometimes an actor, not as a whole, but consecutively by aiming the camera at various parts of the scene or of the human body. This kind of construction of a picture, the resolving of the material into its elements and subsequent building from them of a filmic whole, is called " constructive editing," and it will be discussed in detail in the second part of this sketch. As a preliminary it is necessary only for us to note the fact of this basic method of film-work.

In shooting a film, the director is not in a position to do so consecutively—that is, begin with the first scene and thence, following the scenario, proceed in order right up to the last. The reason is simple. Suppose, for argument's sake, you build a required set—it nearly always happens that the scenes taking place in it are spread throughout the whole scenario —and suppose the director take it into his head, after shooting a scene on that set, to proceed immediately with the scene next following in the order of the action of the developing scenario, then it will be necessary to build a new set without demolishing the first, then another, and so forth, accumulating a whole series of structures without being able to destroy the preceding ones. To work in this way is impracticable for simple technical reasons. Thus both director and actor are deprived of the possibility of continuity in the actual process of shooting ; but, at the same time, continuity is essential. With the loss of continuity, we lose the unity of the work— its style and, with that, its effect. From this derives the inevitable necessity of a detailed preliminary overhauling of the scenario. Only then can a director work with confidence, only then can he attain significant results, when he treats each piece carefully according to a filmic plan, when, clearly visualising to himself a series of screen images, he traces and fixes the whole course of development, both of the scenario action and of the work of the separate characters. In this preliminary paper-work must be created that style, that unity, which conditions the value of any work of art. All the various positions of the camera—such as long-shot, close-up, shot from above, and so forth ; all the technical means—such as " fade," " mask," and " pan "—that affect the relation of a shot to the piece of celluloid preceding and following it ; everything that comprises or strengthens the inner content of a scene, must be exactly considered ; otherwise in the shooting of some scene, taken at random from the middle of the scenario, irreparable errors may arise. Thus this overhauled " working "—that is, ready for shooting—form of scenario provides in itself the detailed description of each, even the smallest, piece, citing every technical method required for its execution.

Certainly, to require the scenarist to write his work in such a form would be to require him to become a director ; but all this scenario work must be done, and, if he cannot deliver a " cast-iron " scenario, ready for shooting, nevertheless, in that degree in which he provides a material more or less approaching the ideal form, the scenarist will provide the director not with a series of obstacles to be overcome, but with a series of impulses that can be used. The more technically complete his working-out of the scenario, the more chance the scenarist has to see upon the screen the images shaped as he has visualised them.

THE CONSTRUCTION OF THE SCENARIO

If we try to divide the work of the scenarist into, as it were, a succession of stages, passing from the general to the particular, we get the following rough scheme :

1. The theme.
2. The action (the treatment).*
3. The cinematographic working-out of the action (filmic representation).

Certainly, such a scheme is the result of the dissection of an already completed scenario. As already remarked, the creative process can take place in other sequence. Separate scenes can be imagined and simultaneously find their position in the process of growth. But, none the less, some final overhaul of the work on the scenario must take into account all these three stages in their sequence. One must always remember that the film, by the very nature of its construction (the rapid alternation of successive pieces of celluloid), requires of the spectator an exceptional concentration of attention. The director, and consequently the scenarist also, leads despotically along with him the attention of the spectator. The latter sees only that which the director shows him ; for reflection, for doubt, for criticism, there is neither room nor time, and consequently the smallest error in clearness or vividness of construction will be apprehended as an unpleasant confusion or as a simple, ineffective blank. Remember, therefore, that the scenarist must always take care to secure the greatest simplicity and clarity in the resolution of each separate problem, at whatever moment in his work it may confront him. For convenience in

* I combine these two as one for the purposes of a short sketch, but this is not technically exact. (*Author's note.*)

34

elucidation we will discuss separately in order each of the separate points of the scheme outlined, that we may establish the specific requirements set by the film in the selection and application of different materials and the different methods of their treatment.

THE THEME

The theme is a supra-artistic concept. In fine, every human concept can be employed as a theme, and the film, no more than any other art, can place bounds to its selection. The only question that can be asked is whether it be valuable or useless to the spectator. And this question is a purely sociological one, the solution of which does not enter the scope of this sketch. But mention must be made of certain formal requirements, conditioning the selection of the theme, if only because of the present-day position of film-art. The film is yet young, and the wealth of its methods is not yet extensive ; for this reason it is possible to indicate temporary limitations without necessarily attributing to them the permanence and inflexibility of laws. First of all must be mentioned the scale of theme. Formerly there ruled a tendency, and in part it exists to-day, to select such themes as embrace material spreading extraordinarily widely over time and space. As example may be quoted the American film *Intolerance*, the theme of which may be represented as follows : " Throughout all ages and among all peoples, from the earliest times to the present day, stalks intolerance, dragging in its wake murder and blood." This is a theme of monstrous extent ; the very fact that it spreads " throughout all ages and among all peoples " already conditions an extraordinary breadth of material. The result is extremely characteristic. In the first place, scarcely compressed into twelve reels, the film became so ponderous that the tiredness it created largely effaced its effect. In the second place, the abundance of matter forced the director to work the theme out quite generally, without touching upon details, and consequently there was a strong discrepancy between the depth of the motif and the superficiality of its form. Only the part played in the present day, in which the action was more concentrated, produced the necessary, effective impression. It is especially necessary to pay attention to this forced superficiality. At the present moment film-art, still in its infancy, does not possess means enabling it to embrace so wide a material.

Note that most good films are characterised by very simple themes and relatively uncomplicated action. Bèla Balàzs, in his book " Der Sichtbare Mensch," quite correctly remarks that the failure of the majority of film adaptations of literary works is to be ascribed mainly to the fact that the scenarists concerned strove to compress a superabundance of material into the narrow confines of the picture.

Cinematography is, before anything else, limited by the definite length of a film. A film more than 7,000 feet long already creates an unnecessary exhaustion. There is, it is true, a method of issuing a long film in several so-called serial parts. But this method is possible only to films of a special kind. Adventure-films, their content consisting chiefly of a series of extraordinary happenings in the career of the hero, little connected with one another after all, and always having each an independent interest (stunts—either acrobatic or directorial), can naturally be shown to the spectator in several episodes of a single cycle. The spectator, losing nothing in impression, can see the second part without acquaintance with the first, the content of which he gathers from an opening title. The relationship between the episodes is attained by crude play upon the curiosity of the spectator ; for example, at the end of the first part the hero lands into some inextricable situation, solved only at the beginning of the second, and so forth. But the film of deeper content, the value of which lies always in the impression it creates as a whole, can certainly not be thus divided into parts for the spectator to see separately, one each week.[1] The influence of this limitation of film length is yet increased by the fact that the film technician, for the effective representation of a concept, requires considerably more material than, let us say, the novelist or playwright. In a single word often a whole complex of images is contained. Visual images having an inferential significance of this nature are, however, very rare, and the film technician is therefore forced to carry out a detailed representation if he desire to achieve an effective impression. I repeat that the necessity to limit the scale of the theme is perhaps only a temporary one, but, having regard to our actual store of means of filmic representation, it is unavoidable.

Meanwhile, the other requirement, conditioned by the basic character itself of filmic spectacle, will probably exist for ever—the necessity for *clarity*. I have already mentioned above the necessity for absolute clarity in the resolution of every problem met with in the process of working on the film ; this holds true, of course, for the work on the theme. If the basic idea that is to serve as backbone to the scenario be vague and indefinite, the scenario is condemned to miscarry.[2] True that in the examination of the written representation, it is possible, by careful study, to disentangle one's way among the hints and unclarities, but, transposed upon the screen, such a scenario becomes irritatingly confusing.

I give an example ; a scenario-writer sent us an already completed scenario on the life of a factory workman in the days before the Russian revolution. The scenario was written round a given hero, a workman. In the course of the action he came into contact with a series of persons—hostile and friendly : the enemies harmed him, the friends helped him. At the beginning of the scenario the hero was depicted as a rough, ungoverned man ; at the end he became an honest, class-conscious workman. The scenario was written in well-drawn, naturalistic environmental colours, it undoubtedly contained interesting, live material witnessing to the powers of observation and the knowledge of its author, yet none the less it was turned down. A series of slices of life, a series of chance meetings and encounters bound together by no more than their sequence in time, is, after all, no more than a group of episodes. The theme as basic idea, uniting in itself the meaning of all the events depicted—that is what was lacking. Consequently the separate characters were without significance, the actions of the hero and the people round him as chaotic and adventitious as the movements of pedestrians on a street, passing by before a window.

But the same author went through his scenario, altering it in accordance with the remarks made to him. He carefully reconstructed the line of the hero, guided by a clearly formulated theme. As basis he set the following idea : " It is not sufficient to be revolutionarily inclined ; to be of service to the cause one must possess a properly organised consciousness of reality." The merely blustering workman of the opening was changed to a reckless anarchist,[3] his enemies thus stood in a clear and definite front, his contacts with them and with his future friends assumed clear purpose and clear meaning, a whole series of superfluous complications fell away, and the modified scenario was transformed to a rounded and convincing whole. The idea defined above can be termed that theme the clear formulation of which inevitably organises the entire work and results in a clearly effective creation. Note as rule : formulate the theme clearly and exactly—otherwise the work will not acquire that essential meaning and unity

39

that conditions every work of art. All further limitations influencing the choice of theme are connected with the action-treatment. As I have already said, the creative process never takes place in schematic sequence ; thinking of the theme involves, nearly simultaneously, thinking of the action and its treatment.

THE ACTION-TREATMENT OF THE THEME

The scenarist, in the very first stages of his work, already possesses a given material later to be disposed in the framework of his future creation. This material is provided for him by knowledge, experience, and, finally, imagination. Having established the theme, as basic idea conditioning the selection of this material, the scenarist must begin its grouping. Here the persons of the action are introduced, their relations to one another established, their various significance in the development of the plot determined, and, finally, here are indicated given proportions for the distribution of the entire material throughout the scenario.

In entering the province of the action-treatment of the theme, the scenarist first comes into contact with the requirements of creative work. Just as the theme is, by definition, a supra-artistic element, so, contrastingly, the work on the action is conditioned by a whole series of requirements peculiar to the given art.

Let us first approach the most general aspect—let us determine the character of the work on the action.

ON FILM TECHNIQUE

A writer, when he plans out a future work, establishes always a series of, as it were, key-stones, significant to the elucidation of the theme and spread over the whole of the work in preparation. These key-stones, as it were, mark the general outline ; to them belong the elements characteristic of the various persons, the nature of the events that bring these persons together, often the details conditioning the significance and strength of the elements of crescendo and diminuendo, often even just separate incidents selected for their power and expressiveness.

Exactly the same process occurs certainly in the work of the scenarist. To consider the action abstractly is impossible. It is impossible to plan merely that at the beginning the hero is an anarchist and then, after meeting with a series of mishaps in his efforts at revolutionary work, becomes a conscious communist. A scheme of this kind is no advance on the theme and brings us no nearer the essential treatment. Not only *what* happens must be perceived, but also *how* it happens ; in the work on the action the *form* must already be sensible. Imagining a reform in the cosmic philosophy of the hero is still very far from creating a climax in the scenario. Before the discovery of a definite concrete form that, in the scenarist's opinion, will affect the spectator from the screen, the abstract idea of a reform has no creative value and cannot serve as a key-stone in the constitution of the action ; but these key-stones are necessary ; they establish the hard skeleton and remove the danger of those blank gaps that may always occur if some important stage in the development of the scenario be treated carelessly and abstractly. Neglect of this element in the work of final filmic polishing may occasion inexpressive material, unsuitable for plastic treatment, and thus may destroy the whole construction.

The novelist expresses his key-stones in written descriptions, the dramatist by rough dialogue, but the scenarist must think in plastic (externally expressive) images. He must train his imagination, he must develop the habit of representing to himself whatever comes into his head in the form of a sequence of images upon the screen. Yet more, he must learn to command these images and to select from those he visualises the clearest and most vivid ; he must know how to command them as the writer commands his words and the playwright his spoken phrases.[4]

The clarity and vividness of the action-treatment directly depends on the clear formulation of the theme. Let us take as an example an American film, naïve, certainly, and not especially valuable, issued under the name *Saturday Night*. Though its content is slight, it affords an excellent model of a theme clearly outlined and action simply and vividly treated. The theme is as follows : " Persons of different social class will never be happy when intermarried." The construction of the action runs so. A chauffeur spurns the favours of a laundress, for he falls in love with a capitalist's daughter whom he drives every day in his car. The son of another capitalist, chancing to see the young laundress in his house, falls in love with her. Two marriages are celebrated. The narrow garret of the chauffeur seems an absurd dog-kennel to the daughter of the mansion. The natural desire of the chauffeur to find a meal at home ready for him after a hard day's work encounters an invincible obstacle in the fact that his wife has no idea how to make a fire or manage the cooking utensils ; the fire is too hot, the crockery dirties her hands, and the half-cooked food flies all over the floor. When friends of the chauffeur visit him to spend a jolly evening, they behave themselves so crudely, by the standards of the spoilt lady, that she stalks demonstratively out of the room and bursts into an unexpected fit of hysterics.

Meanwhile, no better fares the ex-laundress in the mansion of the rich. Surrounded by scornful servants, she plumps from one embarrassment into another. She marvels at the lady's-maids who help her to dress and undress, she looks clumsy and absurd in her long-trained gown, at a dinner-party she becomes an object of ridicule, to the distress of her husband and his relatives. By chance the chauffeur and the former laundress meet. It is obvious that, influenced by disappointment, their former mutual inclination re-awakens. The two unhappy couples part, to reunite themselves in new and happier combinations. The laundress is brilliant in the kitchen, and the capitalist's new wife wears her dresses faultlessly and is marvellous at the fox-trot.

The action is as primitive as the theme, but none the less the film can be regarded as highly successful in its clear, well-thought out construction. Every detail is in place and directly related to the pervading idea. Even in this superficial sketch of its content one senses the presence of vivid, externally expressed images : the kitchen, the chauffeur's friends, the elegant clothes, the guests at dinner, and, again, the kitchen and the clothes in another form. Every essential element in the development of the scenario is characterised by clear, *plastic* material.

As counter-model I shall reproduce an extract from one of the many scenarios that pour in every day : " The Nikonov family is reduced to direst poverty, neither the father nor Natasha can find work —refusals everywhere. Often Andrei visits them, and seeks with fervent words to encourage the despairing Natasha. At last, in despair, the father goes to the contractor and offers to make peace with him, and the contractor agrees on condition that he shall receive the daughter in marriage, and so forth." This is a typical example of filmic colourlessness and helplessness in representation. There is nothing but meetings and talkings. Such expressions as " *Often* Andrei visits them," " with fervent words he *seeks to encourage* " " refusals *everywhere*," and so forth, show a complete lack of any connection between the work on the action and that filmic form the scenario is later to assume. Such incidents may serve, at best, as material for titles, but never for shots. For the word " often " means, in any case, several times, and to show Andrei making his visit four or five times would seem absurd even to the author of this scenario ; the same applies to the expression " refusals everywhere."

What is said here is not being pedantic about a word. It is important to realise that even in the preparatory general treatment of the scenario must be indicated nothing that is impossible to represent, or that is inessential, but only that which can be established as clear and plastically expressive keystones. To express externally the character of a scene showing direst poverty, to find acts (not words) characterising the relationship of Andrei to Natasha —this is what will provide such key-stones. It may be argued that work on plastic form belongs already to the next stage and can be left to the director, but to this I emphasise once again that it is always important to have the possible plastic form before one's eyes even in the general approach to the work, in order to escape the possibility of blank gaps in the subsequent treatment. Remember, for example, the word " often," already mentioned as one entirely unnecessary and incapable of plastic expression.

Thus we have established the necessity for the scenarist always to orientate himself according to the plastic material that, in the end, must serve as form for his representation. We now turn to the general questions of concentration of the action as a whole. There is a whole series of standards that regulate the construction of a narrative, of a novel, of a play. They stand all, undoubtedly, in close relation to scenario work, but their transcription cannot be compressed into the narrow limits of this sketch.[5]

Of the questions of general construction of the scenario, mention must be made here only of one. During work on the treatment the scenarist must always consider the varying degree of *tension* in the action. This tension must, after all, be reflected in the spectator, forcing him to follow the given part of the picture with more or less excitement. This excitement does not depend from the dramatic situation alone, it can be created or strengthened by purely extraneous methods.[6] The gradual winding-up of the dynamic elements of the action, the introduction of scenes built from rapid, energetic work of the characters, the introduction of crowd scenes, all these govern increases of excitement in the spectator, and one must learn so to construct the scenario that the spectator is gradually engrossed by the developing action, receiving the most effective impulse only at the end. The vast majority of scenarios suffer from clumsy building up of tension. As example one may quote the Russian film *The Adventures of Mr. West*. The first three reels are watched with ever-growing interest. A cowboy, arrived in Moscow with the American visitor West, lands into and escapes from a series of exceedingly complicated situations, the interest steadily increasing with his dexterity. The dynamically saturated earlier reels are easy to look at and grip the spectator with ever-increasing excitement. But after the end of the third reel, where the cowboy's adventures came to an unexpected end, the spectator experiences a natural reaction, and the continuation, in spite of the excellent directorial treatment, is watched with much diminished interest. And the last reel, containing the weakest material of the whole (a journey through the streets of Moscow and various empty factories), completely effaces the good impression of the film and lets the spectator go out unsatisfied.

As an interesting example of opposite and correct regulation of increasing elements of tension in the action may be instanced the films of the well-known American director, Griffith. He has created a type of film-ending, even distinguished by his name, that is used by the multitude of his successors up to the present day. Let us take the present-day part of the film *Intolerance*, already instanced. A young workman, discharged owing to participation in a strike, comes to New York, and falls in straightway with a band of petty thieves ; but, after meeting the girl he loves, he decides to seek honest employment. Yet the " villains " do not leave him in peace. Finally they involve him in a trial for murder and he gets into prison. The proofs seem so incontestable to the judge and jury that he is condemned to death. At the end of the picture his sweetheart, meanwhile become his wife, unexpectedly discovers the real murderer. Her husband is already being prepared for execution ; only the governor has power to intervene, and he has just left the town on an express train.

There ensues a terrific chase to save the hero. The woman rushes after the train on a racing-car whose owner has realised that a man's life depends upon his speed. In the cell the man receives unction. The car has almost reached the express. The preparations for the execution are nearing their end. At the very last moment, when the noose is being laid round the neck of the hero, comes the pardon, attained by the wife at the price of her last energy and effort. The quick changes of scene, the contrasting alternation of the tearing machines with the methodical preparations for the execution of an innocent man, the ever-increasing concern of the spectator—" will they be in time, will they be in time ? "—all these compel an intensification of excitement that, being placed at the end, successfully concludes the picture. In the method of Griffith are combined the inner dramatic content of the action and a masterly employment of external effort (dynamic tension).

His films can be used as models of correctly contrasted intensification. A working out of the action of the scenario in which all the lines of behaviour of the various characters are clearly expressed, in which all the major events in which the characters take part are consecutively described, and in which, last but not least, the tension of the action is correctly considered and constructed in such a way that its gradual intensification rises to a climactic end—this, in fine, is a treatment already of considerable value and useful to the director in representation. Written though it may be in purely literary phraseology, such a treatment will provide the libretto, as it were, of the scenario ; and, in the hands of the specialist director, it will be transformable into a working script the more easily the more that orientation on plastic material, of which I spoke above, has been taken into consideration in working out the action.

Already the next stage in the work of the scenarist is the specific cinematographic overhaul of the action. The scenario must be divided into sequences, these into scenes, and the scenes into the separate shots (script-scenes)[7] that correspond to the separate pieces of celluloid from which the film is ultimately joined together. A reel must not exceed a certain length— its average length works out at from 900 to 1,200 feet. The film consists usually of from six to eight reels, and the scenario-writer desirous of endowing his work with specific filmic treatment must learn to *feel* its length. In order correctly to feel it he should take into consideration the following facts. The projector at normal speed runs through about one foot per second. Consequently a reel runs through in under fifteen minutes, and the whole film in about an hour and a half. If one try to visualise each separate scene as a component of a reel, as it appears upon the screen, and consider the time each will take up, one can reckon the quantity required as content of the whole scenario.[8]

A scenario worked out to the elementary and preliminary extent of division into a series of reels, sequences, and separate scenes looks as follows[9] :

REEL ONE

Scene 1.—A peasant waggon, sinking in the mud, slowly trails along a country road. Sadly and reluctantly the hooded driver urges on his tired horse. A figure cowers into the corner of the waggon, trying to wrap itself in an old soldier's cloak for protection against the penetrating wind. A passer-by, coming towards the waggon, pauses, standing inquisitively. The driver turns to him.

Title :
" Is it far to Nakhabin ? "

The pedestrian answers, pointing with his hand. The waggon sets onward, while the passer-by stares after it and then continues on his way.

Scene 2.—A peasant hut. In the corner on a bench lies an old man covered with rags ; he breathes with difficulty. An old woman is busying herself about the hearth and irritably clattering among the pots. The sick man turns himself round painfully and speaks to her.

Title :
" It sounds as if some one were knocking."

The old woman goes to the window and looks out.

Title :
" Imagination, Mironitch ; the door rattles in the wind."

A scenario written in this way, already divided into separate scenes and with titles, forms the first phase of filmic overhaul. But it is still far from the working-script, referred to above, already fully prepared for immediate shooting. Note that there is a whole series of details characteristic for the given scene and emphasised by their literary form, such as, for example, " sinking in the mud," " sadly the driver," " a passenger, wrapped in a soldier's cloak," " the piercing wind "—none of these details will reach the spectator if they are introduced merely as incidentals in shooting the scene as a whole, just as it is written. The film possesses essentially specific and highly effective methods by means of which the spectator can be made to notice each separate detail (mud, wind, behaviour of driver, behaviour of fare), showing them one by one, just as we should describe them in separate sequence in literary work, and not just simply to note " bad weather," " two men on a waggon." This method is called constructive editing.[10] Something of the kind is used by certain scenario-writers in *interpolating* into their description of a scene a so-called "close-up"—thus, "a village street on a church holiday. An animated group of peasants. In the centre speaks a Comsomolka [11] (close-up). New groups come up. The elders of the village. Indignant cries are heard from them."

Such " interpolated close-ups " had better be omitted—they have nothing to do with constructive editing. Terms such as " interpolation " and " cut-in " are absurd expressions, the remnants of an old misunderstanding of the technical methods of the film. The details organically belonging to scenes of the kind instanced must not be interpolated into the scene, but the latter must be built out of them. We will turn to editing, as the basic method of influencing the spectator effectively from the screen, when we have given the necessary explanations of the basic sorts and selection of plastic material.

CONCLUSION

If the scenarist wish to communicate to the spectator from the screen the entirety of his concepts, he must approximate his work as closely as possible to its final shooting form, that is to say, he must consider, use, and perhaps even partly discover, all those specific methods that the director can later employ. He must watch films attentively, and, after seeing them, must try to express various sequences, endeavouring to represent their editing construction. By such attentive observation of the work of others can the necessary experience be gained, I will give an example of an already prepared scenario sequence, its editing constructed and ready for shooting.

REEL ONE

Title :

The rising of the workers is crushed.

1. *Slow fade-in.*—The ground strewn with empty cartridge-cases. Rifles lying about.

2. *Slow panorama.*—A long barricade passes the lens, on it lie strewn the corpses of workmen.

3. Part of the barricade. The corpses of workmen. A woman with her head hanging over backwards lies among them. From a broken flagstaff hangs a torn flag. *Mix.*

4. *Closer.*—The woman with her head hanging back, her eyes staring at the lens. *Mix.*

5. The torn flag flutters in the wind. *Slow fade-out.*

This is an example of a slow, solemn, introductory sequence. The mixes are used to emphasise the slowness. The " pan " gives the same effect, and the fades separate the sequence into a separate independent motif.

Now an example of a dynamic sequence in heightened editing tempo.

1. From the corner rushes a crowd of workmen. They run towards the lens ; the figures flee rapidly past it.

2. A workman leaps over a great crowbar and runs on. He suddenly stops, and calls :

Title :

" *Save the first shop !* "

3. A second workman clambers on to a crane.

4. Steam streams upwards. A frenzied siren shrieks.

5. The workman on the crane bends over and looks downwards.

6. The running crowd of workpeople (*taken from above*).

7. The workman on the crane calls with all his strength :

Title (in large letters) :

" SAVE THE FIRST SHOP ! "

8. *Shot from above.*—The running crowd stops, stands for a moment, and then rushes on anew.

9. A section of the running crowd knocks over a woman.

10. *Close-up.*—The woman who fell raises herself, and clasps her head, swaying.

11. The running mass.

Here is shown the editing of quickly alternating pieces, creating the desired excitement by their rhythm. The increase in size of the title emphasises the increasing panic.

Of course, this form of scenario requires thorough, special training, but I repeat once again that only determined effort on the part of the scenarist to reach as near as possible to this technically correct form will turn him into a writer able to give in a general treatment material even *usable* in film work.

A scenario will only be good if its writer shall have mastered a knowledge of specific methods, if he know how to use them as weapons for the winning of effect ; otherwise the scenario will be but raw material that must, to an extent of ninety per cent, be subordinated to the treatment of a specialist.

Part II

THE PLASTIC MATERIAL

The scenario-writer must bear always in mind the fact that every sentence that he writes will have to appear plastically upon the screen in some visible form. Consequently, it is not the words he writes that are important, but the externally expressed plastic images that he describes in these words. As a matter of fact, it is not so easy to find such plastic images. They must, before anything else, be clear and expressive. Anyone familiar with literary work can well represent to himself what is an expressive word, or an expressive style ; he knows that there are such things as telling, expressive words, as vividly expressive word-constructions—sentences. Similarly, he knows that the involved, obscure style of an inexperienced writer, with a multitude of superfluous words, is the consequence of his inability to select and control them. What is here said of literary work is entirely applicable to the work of the scenarist, only the word is replaced by the plastic image. The scenarist must know how to find and to use plastic (visually expressive) material : that is to say, he must know how to discover and how to select, from the limitless mass of material provided by life and its observation, those forms and movements that shall most clearly and vividly express in images the *whole content* of his idea.[12]

Let us quote certain illustrative examples.

In the film *Tol'able David* there is a sequence in which a new character—an escaped convict, a tramp—comes into the action. The type of a thorough scoundrel. The task of the scenarist was to give his characteristics. Let us analyse how it was done, by describing the series of following shots.

1. The tramp—a degenerate brute, his face overgrown with unshaven bristles—is about to enter a house, but stops, his attention caught by something.

2. Close-up of the face of the watching tramp.

3. Showing what he sees—a tiny, fluffy kitten asleep in the sun.

4. The tramp again. He raises a heavy stone with the transparent intention of using it to obliterate the sleeping little beast, and only the casual push of a fellow, just then carrying objects into the house, hinders him from carrying out his cruel intention.

In this little incident there is not one single explanatory title, and yet it is effective, clearly and vividly. Why? Because the plastic material has been correctly and suitably chosen. The sleeping kitten is a perfect expression of complete innocence and freedom from care, and thus the heavy stone in the hands of the huge man immediately becomes the symbol of absurd and senseless cruelty to the mind of the spectator who sees this scene. Thus the end is attained. The characterisation is achieved, and at the same time its abstract content wholly expressed, with the help of happily chosen plastic material.

Another example from the same film. The context of the incident is as follows : misfortune is come upon a family of peasants—the eldest son has been crippled by a blow with a stone ; the father has died of a heart-attack ; the youngest son (the hero of the film), still half a boy, knows who is responsible for all their ills—the tramp, who had treacherously attacked his brother. Again and again in the course of the picture the youngster seeks to be revenged upon the blackguard. The weapon of revenge—an old flint-lock. When the disabled brother is brought into the house, and the family, dazed with despair, is gathered round his bed, the boy, half crying, half gritting his teeth, secretly loads the flint-lock. The sudden death of the father and the supplications of the mother, clinging in despair to the feet of her son, restrain his outbreak. The boy remains the sole hope of the family. When, later, he again reaches secretly for the flint-lock and takes it from the wall, the voice of his mother, calling him to go and buy soap, compels him to hang the gun up again and run out to the store. Note with what mastery the old, clumsy-looking flint-lock is here employed. It is as if it incarnated the thirst for revenge that tortures the boy. Every time the hand reaches for the flint-lock the spectator knows what is passing in the mind of the hero. No titles, no explanations are necessary. Recall the scene of soap fetched for the mother just described. Hanging up the flint-lock and running to the store implies forgetfulness of self for the sake of another. This is a perfect characterisation, rendering on the one hand the naïve directness of the man still half a child, on the other his awakening sense of duty.

Another example, from the film *The Leather Pushers*. The incident is as follows. A man sitting at a table is waiting for his friend. He is smoking a cigarette, and in front of him on the table stand an ash-tray and a glass half empty of liquid, both filled with an enormous number of cigarette ends. The spectator immediately visualises the great space of time the man has been waiting and, no less, the degree of excitement that has made him smoke nearly a hundred cigarettes.

From the examples quoted above it will be clear what is to be understood by the term : expressive plastic material. We have found here a kitten, a tramp, a stone, a flint-lock, some cigarette ends, and not one of these objects or persons was introduced by chance ; each constitutes a visual image, requiring no explanation and yet carrying a clear and definite meaning.

Hence an important rule for the scenarist : in working out each incident he must carefully consider and select each visual image ; he must remember that for each concept, each idea, there may be tens and hundreds of possible means of plastic expression, and that it is his task to select from amongst them the clearest and most vivid. Special attention, however, must be paid to the special part played in pictures by objects. Relationships between human beings are, for the most part, illuminated by conversations, by words ; no one carries on conversation with objects, and that is why work with them, being expressed by visual action, is of special interest to the film technician, as we have just seen in these examples. Try to imagine to yourself anger, joy, confusion, sorrow, and so forth expressed not in words and the gestures accompanying them, but in action connected with objects, and you will see how images saturated with plastic expression come into your mind. Work on plastic material is of the highest importance for the scenarist. In the process of it he learns to imagine to himself what he has written as it will appear upon the screen, and the knowledge thus acquired is essential for correct and fruitful work.

One must try to express one's concepts in clear and vivid visual images. Suppose it be a matter of the characterisation of some person of the action—this person must be placed in such conditions as will make him appear, by means of some action or movement, in the desired light (remember the tramp and the kitten). Suppose it be a matter of the representation of some event—those scenes must be assembled that most vividly emphasise visually the essence of the event represented.

In relation to what we have said, we must turn to the question of sub-titles. The usual view of titles as an invading, adventitious element, to be avoided wherever possible, is fundamentally erroneous. The title is an organic part of the film and, consequently, of the scenario. Naturally a title can be superfluous, but only in the sense in which a whole scene can be superfluous. According to their content titles can be divided into two groups :

CONTINUITY TITLES

Titles of this kind give the spectator a necessary explanation in short and clear form, and thus sometimes replace a whole episode of the action in the development of the scenario. Let us take an example from *Tol'able David*. Three tramps, needed by the scenarist to create an opposing evil influence to the hero of the scenario, are introduced. Before their appearance on the screen comes a title : " Three convicts escaped from the nearest prison." Naturally the escape itself could be shown instead of the title, but, as it is not the escape, but the tramps that are important to the scenarist, he replaces the whole incident of the escape, as having no basic importance in the development of the action, by a title. The essential action—the appearance of the tramps —is shown on the screen preceded by a continuity title. This is correct construction. It is an entirely different matter for a title to replace an essential element of the scenario, where the subsequent action is, so to say, its result. For example : after the title " Olga, unable to endure the character of her hardhearted husband, resolved to leave him," Olga is shown walking out of the front door. This is no good at all. The action is weaker than the title, and shows inability to resolve the plastic problem concerned.

To the group " continuity titles " must also be referred such titles as indicate an hour or place of the action—for example : " in the evening," " at Ivan's," replacing by words those parts of the scenario the visual representation of which would uselessly spin out and burden the development of the action. To summarise what has been said about continuity titles we must emphasise once again the following : the continuity title is only good if it removes the superfluous from the scenario, if it shortly explains essentials to the spectator and prepares him for clearer apprehension of the subsequent action (as in the example with the tramps). A continuity title must never be stronger than the subsequent image of the action (as in the example of Olga leaving her husband).[13]

SPOKEN TITLES

This kind of title introduces living, spoken speech into the picture. Of their significance not much need be said. The main consideration affecting them is : good literary treatment and, certainly, as much compression as possible.[14] One must consider that, on the average, every line of title (two to three words) requires three feet of film.[15] Consequently a title twelve words long stays on the screen from twelve to eighteen seconds, and can, by a temporal interruption of this kind, destroy the rhythm, and with it the sequence and impression, of the current shots.

Clarity is as important for the spoken as for the continuity title. Superfluous words that may enhance the literary beauty of the sentence but will complicate its rapid comprehension are not permissible. The film spectator has no time to savour words. The title must " get " to the spectator quickly—in the course of the process of being read.

To what has been said must be added that in construction of the scenario one must be careful of the distribution of the titles. A continual, even interruption of the action by titles is not desirable. It is better to try to distribute them (this is especially important with continuity titles) so that by concentrating them in one part of the scenario the remainder is left free for development of the action. Thus work the Americans, giving all the necessary explanations in the early reels, strengthening the middle by use of more spoken titles, and at the end, in quicker tempo, carrying through the bare action to the finish without titles.

It is interesting to note that, apart from its literal content, the title may have also a plastic content. For example, often large, distinct lettering is used, the importance of the word being associated with the size of the letters with which it is formed. An example—in the propaganda film *Famine* there was an end title as follows : first appeared in normal size the first word " Comrades " ; it disappeared and was replaced by a larger " Brothers " ; and finally appeared the third—filling the whole screen— " Help ! " Such a title was undoubtedly more effective than an ordinary one. Consideration of the plastic size of the title is undoubtedly very interesting, and this the scenarist should remember.[16] Yet more important than the plastic aspect of a title is its rhythmic significance. We have already said that too long titles must not be used. This is not all ; it must be borne in mind that with the length of a title must be considered the speed of the action in which it appears. Rapid action demands short, abrupt titles [17] ; long-drawn-out action can be linked only with slow ones.

THE SIMPLEST SPECIFIC METHODS OF SHOOTING

Having learned the nature of plastic material, we must gain a knowledge of some of the purely formal methods used by the director and cameraman in shooting the picture. The simplest of these are as follows :

Fade-in [18] *:* The screen is entirely dark ; as it becomes lighter the picture is disclosed.

Fade-out : The reverse process—the darkening of the picture until it has disappeared.

The fade has mainly a rhythmic significance. The slow withdrawal of the picture from the view-field of the spectator corresponds, in contradistinction to its usual sudden breaking-off, to the slow withdrawal of the spectator from the scene. One usually ends a sequence with a fade-out, especially when the scene itself has been carried out in retarded tempo. For example : a man exhaustedly approaches an armchair, lowers himself into it, drops his head in his hands—pause—slowly the shutter closes.

The fade-in is, on the contrary, equivalent to the purposeful introduction of the spectator to a new environment and new action. It is used to begin a film, or a separate sequence. In determining the general rhythm of the action one should indicate the speed of the fade : quick, slow. Often shots are bounded by a fade-in and fade-out—that is to say, the scene begins with the opening and ends with the closing of the shutter. By the use of this method is achieved the emphasis of an incident divorced from the general line of the scenario—very often, for example, this method is used for a refrain (*leit-motif*) or a flash-back. The fade can take various forms. A common form, now old-fashioned, is the round iris. At an iris-in there appears upon the dark screen a spot of light, disclosing the picture as it broadens.[19] Other forms of shutter are, for example, an iris like a widening or narrowing slit, a falling or rising horizontal shutter, vertical side shutters, and so forth. It should be mentioned, however, that the frequent use of various irises and shutters [20] is unnecessarily trying to the spectator.

Shots in iris or in mask.—The screen is darkened except for a light opening in the centre, round or otherwise in shape. The action takes place in this opening. This is a so-called " mask." Its employment has various meanings. The most common is its use to let the spectator see from the viewpoint of the hero—for example, the hero looks through a keyhole ; there appears what he sees, shown in a mask shaped like a keyhole. A field-glass-shaped mask can also be used, and so forth.

It is interesting to note the special use of a small, round mask (a stationary iris), often used in American films. For example : (*a*) The hero stands on a hill and gazes into the distance. (*b*) A road taken from far off is shown in a little round mask ; along the road gallops a horse. A dual object is attained with this kind of shot : in the first place, by the narrowing of the field of view the attention of the spectator becomes concentrated on that which the hero is looking at ; in the second place, the small scale by which the impression of distance is maintained is not lost.

The Mix.—The transition from one section of the film to another is effected not by the usual cut, but gradually—that is to say, one image disappears slowly and another appears in its place. This method has also a mainly rhythmic significance. Mixes involve a slow rhythm. Often they are used in the representation of a flash-back, as if imitating the birth of one idea from another.

It is necessary to warn the scenarist against overuse of mixes. Technically, in making a mix, the cameraman, after having taken the one shot, must immediately begin to take the other, which is not always possible. If, for example, in a scenario the action is indicated as follows : the Spasskaia Tower (Moscow) *mix* to the Isaakievski Cathedral (Leningrad), it means that after taking the tower the cameraman must proceed immediately to Leningrad.[21]

The Panorama (Pan).—In shooting, the camera is given an even movement sideways, upwards, or downwards.[22] The lens of the camera turns to follow the object shot as it moves before it, or glides along the object showing various parts of it one after the other. This is a purely technical method, and its significance is obvious.

Forward or Backward Movement (*Tracking or Trolleying*).—The camera approaches or becomes distant from the object during the shot. This method is nowadays scarcely ever used.[23] It gives a gradual transition from long-shot to close-up, and the reverse.

Shots Out of Focus.—In the latest American films one often notices sections (especially faces in close-up) taken so that the outlines appear slightly indistinct.[24] This method undoubtedly gives a special colour of softness and " tenderness," especially in scenes of lyric character, but it must be considered as a specific æsthetic method devoid of general application.

Everything said here regarding simple methods of taking shots has certainly only information value. What particular method of shooting is to be used, only his own taste and his own finer feelings can tell the scenarist. Here are no rules ; the field for new invention and combination is wide.

METHODS OF TREATMENT OF THE MATERIAL

(*Structural Editing*)

A cinematograph film, and consequently also a scenario, is always divided into a great number of separate pieces (more correctly, it is built out of these pieces). The sum of the shooting-script is divided into sequences, each sequence into scenes,[25] and, finally, the scenes themselves are constructed from a whole series of pieces (script-scenes) shot from various angles. An actual scenario, ready for use in shooting, must take into account this basic property of the film. The scenarist must be able to write his material on paper exactly as it will appear upon the screen, thus giving exactly the content of each shot as well as its position in sequence. The construction of a scene from pieces, a sequence from scenes, and reel from sequences, and so forth, is called *editing*. Editing is one of the most significant instruments of effect possessed by the film technician and, therefore, by the scenarist also. Let us now become acquainted with its methods one by one.

EDITING OF THE SCENE

Everyone familiar with a film is familiar with the expression " close-up." The alternating representation of the faces of the characters during a dialogue ; the representation of hands, or feet, filling the whole screen—all this is familiar to everyone. But in order to know how properly to use the close-up, one must understand its significance, which is as follows : the close-up directs the attention of the spectator to that detail which is, at the moment, important to the course of the action. For instance, three persons are taking part in a scene. Suppose the significance of this scene consist in the *general* course of the action (if, for example, all three are lifting some heavy object), then they are taken simultaneously in a *general* view, the so-called long-shot. But suppose any one of them change to an independent action having significance in the scenario (for example, separating himself from the others, he draws a revolver cautiously from his pocket), then the camera is directed on him alone. His action is recorded separately.

What is said above applies not only to persons, but also to separate parts of a person, and objects. Let us suppose a man is to be taken apparently listening calmly to the conversation of someone else, but actually restraining his anger with difficulty. The man crushes the cigarette he holds in his hand, a gesture unnoticed by the other. This hand will always be shown on the screen separately, in close-up, otherwise the spectator will not notice it and a characteristic detail will be missed. The view formerly obtained (and is still held by some) that the close-up is an " interruption " of the long-shot. This idea is entirely false. It is no sort of interruption. It represents a proper form of construction.

In order to make clear to oneself the nature of the process of editing a scene, one may draw the following analogy. Imagine yourself observing a scene unfolded in front of you, thus : a man stands near the wall of a house and turns his head to the left ; there appears another man slinking cautiously through the gate. The two are fairly widely distant from one another—they stop. The first takes some object and shows it to the other, mocking him. The latter clenches his fists in a rage and throws himself at the former. At this moment a woman looks out of a window on the third floor and calls, " Police ! " The antagonists run off in opposite directions. Now, how would this have been observed ?

1. The observer looks at the first man. He turns his head.

2. What is he looking at ? The observer turns his glance in the same direction and sees the man entering the gate. The latter stops.

3. How does the first react to the appearance on the scene of the second ? A new turn by the observer ; the first takes out an object and mocks the second.

4. How does the second react ? Another turn ; he clenches his fists and throws himself on his opponent.

5. The observer draws aside to watch how both opponents roll about fighting.

6. A shout from above. The observer raises his head and sees the woman shouting at the window.

7. The observer lowers his head and sees the result of the warning—the antagonists running off in opposite directions.

The observer happened to be standing near and saw every detail, saw it clearly, but to do so he had to turn his head, first left, then right, then upwards, whithersoever his attention was attracted by the interest of observation and the sequence of the developing scene. Suppose he had been standing farther away from the action, taking in the two persons and the window on the third floor simultaneously, he would have received only a general impression, without being able to look separately at the first, the second, or the woman. Here we have approached closely the basic significance of editing. Its object is the showing of the development of the scene in relief, as it were, by guiding the attention of the spectator now to one, now to the other separate element. The lens of the camera replaces the eye of the observer, and the changes of angle of the camera—directed now on one person, now on another, now on one detail, now on another—must be subject to the same conditions as those of the eyes of the observer. The film technician, in order to secure the greatest clarity, emphasis, and vividness, shoots the scene in separate pieces and, joining them and showing them, directs the attention of the spectator to the separate elements, compelling him to see as the attentive observer saw. From the above is clear the manner in which editing can even work upon the emotions. Imagine to yourself the excited observer of some rapidly developing scene. His agitated glance is thrown rapidly from one spot to another. If we imitate this glance with the camera we get a series of pictures, rapidly alternating pieces, creating a *stirring scenario editing-construction*. The reverse would be long pieces changing by mixes, conditioning a calm and slow editing-construction (as one may shoot, for example, a herd of cattle wandering along a road, taken from the viewpoint of a pedestrian on the same road).

We have established, by these instances, the basic significance of the constructive editing of scenes.

It builds the scenes from separate pieces, of which each concentrates the attention of the spectator only on that element important to the action. The sequence of these pieces must not be uncontrolled, but must correspond to the natural transference of attention of an imaginary observer (who, in the end, is represented by the spectator). In this sequence must be expressed a special logic that will be apparent only if each shot contain an impulse towards transference of the attention to the next. For example (1) A man turns his head and looks ; (2) What he looks at is shown.

EDITING OF THE SEQUENCE

The guidance of the attention of the spectator to different elements of the developing action in succession is, in general, characteristic of the film. It is its basic method. We have seen that the separate scene, and often even the movement of one man, is built up upon the screen from separate pieces. Now, the film is not simply a collection of different scenes. Just as the pieces are built up into scenes endowed, as it were, with a connected action, so the separate scenes are assembled into groups forming whole sequences. The sequence is constructed (edited) from scenes. Let us suppose ourselves faced with the task of constructing the following sequence : two spies are creeping forward to blow up a powder magazine ; on the way one of them loses a letter with instructions. Someone else finds the letter and warns the guard, who appear in time to arrest the spies and save the magazine. Here the scenarist has to deal with simultaneity of various actions in several different places. While the spies are crawling towards the magazine, some-one else finds the letter and hastens to warn the guard. The spies have nearly reached their objec-tive ; the guards are warned and rushing towards the magazine. The spies have completed their preparations ; the guard arrives in time. If we pursue the previous analogy betwen the camera and an observer, we now not only have to turn it from side to side, but also to move it from place to place. The observer (the camera) is now on the road shadowing the spies, now in the guardroom recording the confusion, now back at the magazine showing the spies at work, and so forth. But, in combination of the separate scenes (editing), the former law of sequence succession remains in force. A consecutive sequence will appear upon the screen only if the attention of the spectator be transferred correctly from scene to scene. And this correctness is conditioned as follows : the spectator sees the creeping spies, the loss of the letter, and finally the person who finds the letter. The person with the letter rushes for help. The spectator is seized with inevitable excitement—Will the man who found the letter be able to forestall the explosion ? The scenarist immediately answers by showing the spies nearing the magazine—his answer has the effect of a warning " Time is short." The excitement of the spectator—Will they be in time ?—continues ; the scenarist shows the guard turning out. Time is very short—the spies are shown beginning their work. Thus, transferring attention now to the rescuers, now to the spies, the scenarist answers with actual impulses to increase of the spectator's interest, and the construction (editing) of the sequence is correctly achieved.

There is a law in psychology that lays it down that if an emotion give birth to a certain movement, by imitation of this movement the corresponding emotion can be called forth. If the scenarist can effect in even rhythm the transference of interest of the intent spectator, if he can so construct the elements of increasing interest that the question, " What is happening at the other place ? " arises and at the same moment the spectator is transferred whither he wishes to go, then the editing thus created can really excite the spectator. One must learn to understand that editing is in actual fact a compulsory and deliberate guidance of the thoughts and associations of the spectator. If the editing be merely an uncontrolled combination of the various pieces, the spectator will understand (apprehend) nothing from it ; but if it be co-ordinated according to a definitely selected course of events or conceptual line, either agitated or calm, it will either excite or soothe the spectator.

EDITING OF THE SCENARIO [26]

The film is divided into reels. The reels are usually equal in length, on an average from 900 to

1,200 feet long. The combination of the reels forms the picture. The usual length of a picture should not be more than from 6,500 to 7,500 feet. This length, as yet, involves no unnecessary exhaustion of the spectator. The film is usually divided into from six to eight reels. It should be noted here, as a practical hint, that the average length of a piece (remember the editing of scenes) is from 6 to 10 feet, and consequently from 100 to 150 pieces go to a reel. By orientating himself on these figures, the scenarist can visualise how much material can be fitted into the scenario. The scenario is composed of a series of sequences. In discussing the construction (editing) of the scenario from sequences, we introduce a new element into the scenarist's work—the element of so-called dramatic continuity of action that was discussed at the beginning of this sketch. The continuity of the separate sequences when joined together depends not merely upon the simple transference of attention from one place to another, but is conditioned by the development of the action forming the foundation of the scenario. It is important, however, to remind the scenarist of the following point : a scenario has always in its development a moment of greatest tension, found nearly always at the end of the film. To prepare the spectator, or, more correctly, preserve him, for this final tension, it is especially important to see that he is not affected by unnecessary exhaustion during the course of the film. A method, already discussed, that the scenarist can employ to this end is the careful distribution of the titles (which always distract the spectator), securing compression of the greater quantity of them into the first reels, and leaving the last one for uninterrupted action.

Thus, first is worked out the action of the scenario, the action is then worked out into sequences, the sequences into scenes, and these constructed by editing from the pieces, each corresponding to a camera angle.

EDITING AS AN INSTRUMENT OF IMPRESSION

(*Relational Editing*)

We have already mentioned, in the section on editing of sequences, that editing is not merely a method of the junction of separate scenes or pieces, but is a method that controls the " psychological guidance " of the spectator. We should now acquaint ourselves with the main special editing methods having as their aim the impression of the spectator.

Contrast.—Suppose it be our task to tell of the miserable situation of a starving man ; the story will impress the more vividly if associated with mention of the senseless gluttony of a well-to-do man.

On just such a simple contrast relation is based the corresponding editing method. On the screen the impression of this contrast is yet increased, for it is possible not only to relate the starving sequence to the gluttony sequence, but also to relate separate scenes and even separate shots of the scenes to one another, thus, as it were, forcing the spectator to compare the two actions all the time, one strengthening the other. The editing of contrast is one of the most effective, but also one of the commonest and most standardised, of methods, and so care should be taken not to overdo it.

Parallelism.—This method resembles contrast, but is considerably wider. Its substance can be explained more clearly by an example. In a scenario as yet unproduced a section occurs as follows: a working man, one of the leaders of a strike, is condemned to death ; the execution is fixed for 5 a.m. The sequence is edited thus : a factory-owner, employer of the condemned man, is leaving a restaurant drunk, he looks at his wrist-watch : 4 o'clock. The accused is shown—he is being made ready to be led out. Again the manufacturer, he rings a door-bell to ask the time : 4.30. The prison waggon drives along the street under heavy guard. The maid who opens the door—the wife of the condemned—is subjected to a sudden senseless assault. The drunken factory-owner snores on a bed, his leg with trouser-end upturned, his hand hanging down with wrist-watch visible, the hands of the watch crawl slowly to 5 o'clock. The workman is being hanged. In this instance two thematically unconnected incidents develop in parallel by means of the watch that tells of the approaching execution. The watch on the wrist of the callous brute, as it were connects him with the chief protagonist of the approaching tragic *dénoue-ment*, thus ever present in the consciousness of the spectator. This is undoubtedly an interesting method, capable of considerable development.

Symbolism.—In the final scenes of the film *Strike* the shooting down of workmen is punctuated by shots of the slaughter of a bull in a stockyard. The scenarist, as it were, desires to say : just as a butcher fells a bull with the swing of a pole-axe, so, cruelly and in cold blood, were shot down the workers. This method is especially interesting because, by means of editing, it introduces an abstract concept into the consciousness of the spectator without use of a title.

Simultaneity.—In American films the final section is constructed from the simultaneous rapid development of two actions, in which the outcome of one depends on the outcome of the other. The end of the present-day section of *Intolerance*, already quoted, is thus constructed.[27] The whole aim of this method is to create in the spectator a maximum tension of excitement by the constant forcing of a question, such as, in this case : Will they be in time ?—will they be in time ?

The method is a purely emotional one, and nowadays overdone almost to the point of boredom, but it cannot be denied that of all the methods of constructing the end hitherto devised it is the most effective.

Leit-motif (*reiteration of theme*).—Often it is interesting for the scenarist especially to emphasise the

77

basic theme of the scenario. For this purpose exists the method of reiteration. Its nature can easily be demonstrated by an example. In an anti-religious scenario that aimed at exposing the cruelty and hypocrisy of the Church in employ of the Tsarist régime the same shot was several times repeated : a church-bell slowly ringing and, superimposed on it, the title : " The sound of bells sends into the world a message of patience and love." This piece appeared whenever the scenarist desired to emphasise the stupidity of patience, or the hypocrisy of the love thus preached.

The little that has been said above of relational editing naturally by no means exhausts the whole abundance of its methods. It has merely been important to show that constructional editing, a method specifically and peculiarly filmic, is, in the hands of the scenarist, an important instrument of impression. Careful study of its use in pictures, combined with talent, will undoubtedly lead to the discovery of new possibilities and, in conjunction with them, to the creation of new forms.

(First published as Number Three of a series of popular scientific film handbooks by Kinopetchat, Moscow and Leningrad, 1926.)

II

FILM DIRECTOR AND FILM MATERIAL

PART I

THE PECULIARITIES OF FILM MATERIAL

THE FILM AND THE THEATRE

IN the earliest years of its existence the film was no more than an interesting invention that made it possible to record movements, a faculty denied to simple photography. On the film, the appearances of all possible movements could be seized and fixed. The first films consisted of primitive attempts to fix upon the celluloid, as a novelty, the movements of a train, crowds passing by upon the street, a landscape seen from a railway-carriage window, and so forth. Thus, in the beginning, the film was, from its nature, only " living photography." The first attempts to relate cinematography to the world of art were naturally bound up with the Theatre. Similarly only as a novelty, like the shots of the railway-engine and the moving sea, primitive scenes of comic or dramatic character, played by actors, began to be recorded. The film public appeared. There grew up a whole series of relatively small, specialised theatres in which these primitive films were shown.

The film now began to assume all the characteristics of an industry (and indeed a very profitable

one). The great significance was realised of the
fact that from a single negative can be printed
many positives, and that by this means a reel of film
can be multiplied like a book, and spread broadcast
in many copies.[28] Great possibilities began to open
themselves out. No longer was the film regarded
as a mere novelty. The first experiments in recording serious and significant material appeared. The
relationship with the Theatre could not, however,
yet be dissolved, and it is easy to understand how,
once again, the first steps of the film producer
consisted in attempts to carry plays over on to
celluloid. It seemed at that time to be especially
interesting to endow the theatrical performance—
the work of the actor, whose art had hitherto been
but transitory, and real only in the moment of
perception by the spectator—with the quality of
duration.

The film remained, as before, but living photography. Art did not enter into the work of him who
made it. He only photographed the " art of the
actor." Of a peculiar method for the film actor, of
peculiar and special properties of the film or of technique in shooting the picture for the director, there
could as yet be no suspicion. How, then, did the
film director of that time work ? At his disposal was
a scenario, exactly resembling the play written for
the Theatre by the playwright ; only the words of
the characters were missing, and these, as far as
possible, were replaced by dumb show, and sometimes by long-winded titles. The director played the

scene through in its exact theatrical sequence ; he recorded the walkings to and fro, the entrances and exits of the actors. He took the scene thus played-through as a whole, while the cameraman, always turning, fixed it as a whole upon the celluloid. The process of shooting could not be conceived of otherwise, for as director's material served these same real persons—actors—with whom one worked also in the Theatre ; the camera served only for the simple fixation of scenes already completely arranged and definitely planned. The pieces of film shot were stuck together in simple temporal sequence of the developing action, just as the act of a play is formed from scenes, and then were presented to the public as a picture. To sum up in short, the work of the film director differed in no wise from that of the theatrical producer.

A play, exactly recorded upon celluloid and projected upon a screen, with the actors deprived of their words—that was the film of those early days.

THE METHODS OF THE FILM

The *Americans* were the first to discover in the film-play the presence of peculiar possibilities of its own. It was perceived that the film can not only make a simple record of the events passing before the lens, but that it is in a position to reproduce them upon the screen by special methods, proper only to itself.

Let us take as example a demonstration that files by upon the street. Let us picture to ourselves an observer of that demonstration. In order to receive a clear and definite impression of the demonstration, the observer must perform certain actions. First he must climb upon the roof of a house, to get a view from above of the procession as a whole and measure its dimensions ; next he must come down and look out through the first-floor window at the inscriptions on the banners carried by the demonstrators ; finally, he must mingle with the crowd, to gain an idea of the outward appearance of the participants.

Three times the observer has altered his viewpoint, gazing now from nearer, now from farther away, with the purpose of acquiring as complete and exhaustive as possible a picture of the phenomenon under review. The Americans were the first to seek to replace an active observer of this kind by means of the *camera*. They showed in their work that it was not only possible to record the scene shot, but that by manœuvring with the camera itself—in such a way that its position in relation to the object shot varied several times—it was made possible to reproduce the same scene in far clearer and more expressive form than with the lens playing the part of a theatre spectator sitting fast in his stall. The camera, until now a motionless spectator, at last received, as it were, a charge of *life*. It acquired the faculty of movement on its own, and transformed itself from a *spectator* to an active *observer*. Henceforward the camera, controlled by the director, could not merely enable the spectator to see the object shot, but could induce him to apprehend it.

It was at this moment that the concepts *close-up*,

mid-shot, and *long-shot* first appeared in cinematography, concepts that later played an enormous part in the creative craft of editing, the basis of the work of film direction. Now, for the first time, became apparent the difference between the theatrical producer and his colleague of the film. In the beginning the material with which both theatrical producer and film director worked was *identical*. The same actors playing through in their same sequence the same scenes, which were but shorter, and, at the most, unaccompanied by words. The technique of acting for the films differed in no respect from that of stage-acting. The only problem was the replacement, as comprehensibly as possible, of words by gestures. That was the time when the film was rightly named " a substitute for the stage."

FILM AND REALITY

But, with the grasping of the concept *editing*, the position became basically altered. The real material of film-art proved to be not those actual scenes on which the lens of the camera is directed. The theatrical producer has always to do only with *real* processes—they are his material. His finally composed and created work—the scene produced and played upon the stage—is equally a real and actual process, that takes place in obedience to the laws of *real space* and *real time*. When a stage-actor finds himself at one end of the stage, he cannot cross to the other without taking a certain necessary number of paces. And crossings and intervals of this kind are a thing indispensable, conditioned by the laws of real space and real time, with which the theatrical producer has always to reckon, and which he is never in a position to overstep. In fact, in work with real processes, a whole series of *intervals* linking the separate significant points of action are unavoidable.

If, on the other hand, we consider the work of the film director, then it appears that the active raw material is no other than those *pieces of celluloid* on which, from various viewpoints, the separate movements of the action have been shot. From nothing but these pieces is created those appearances upon the screen that form the filmic representation of the action shot. And thus the material of the film director consists not of real processes happening in real space and real time, but of those pieces of celluloid on which these processes have been recorded. This celluloid is entirely subject to the will of the director who edits it. He can, in the composition of the filmic form of any given appearance, eliminate all points of interval, and thus concentrate the action in time to the highest degree he may require.

This method of *temporal concentration*, the concentration of action by the elimination of unnecessary points of interval, occurs also, in a more simplified form, in the Theatre. It finds its expression in the construction of a play from acts. The element of play-construction by which several years are made to pass between the first and second act is, properly, an analogous temporal concentration of the action. In the film this method is not only pursued to a maximum, it forms the actual *basis* of filmic representation. Though it is possible for the theatrical producer temporally to approach two neighbouring acts, he is, none the less, unable to do the same with separate incidents in a single scene. [29]

The film director, on the contrary, can concentrate in time not only separate incidents, but even the movements of a single person. This process, that has often been termed a " film trick," is, in fact, nothing other than the characteristic method of filmic representation.

In order to show on the screen the fall of a man from a window five stories high, the shots can be taken in the following way :

First the man is shot falling from the window into a net, in such a way that the net is not visible on the screen [30] ; then the same man is shot falling from a slight height to the ground. Joined together, the two shots give in projection the desired impression. The catastrophic fall never occurs in reality, it occurs only on the screen, and is the resultant of two pieces of celluloid joined together. From the event of a real, actual fall of a person from an appalling height, two points only are selected : the beginning of the fall and its end. The intervening passage through the air is eliminated. It is not correct to call the process a trick ; it is a method of filmic representation exactly corresponding to the elimination of the five years that divide a first act from a second upon the stage.

From the example of the observer watching the

demonstration pass by on the street, we learned that the process of film-shooting may be not only a simple *fixation* of the event taking place before the lens, but also a *peculiar form* of representation of this event. Between the natural event and its appearance upon the screen there is a marked difference. It is *exactly this difference that makes the film an art*. Guided by the director, the camera assumes the task of removing every superfluity and directing the attention of the spectator in such a way that he shall see only that which is significant and characteristic. When the demonstration was shot, the camera, after having viewed the crowd from above in the long-shot, forced its way into the press and picked out the most characteristic details. These details were not the result of chance, they were selected, and, moreover, selected in such a way that from their sum, as from a sum of separate elements, the image of the whole action could be assembled. Let us suppose, for instance, that the demonstration to be recorded is characterised by its component detail : first Red soldiers, then workmen, and finally Pioneers.[31] Suppose the film technician try to show the spectator the detail composition of this demonstration by simply setting the camera at a fixed point and letting the crowd go by unbroken before the lens, then he will force the spectator to spend exactly as much time in watching the representation as he would have needed to let the crowd itself go by. By taking the procession in this way he would force the spectator to apprehend the mass of detail as it streamed past. But, by the use of that method peculiar to films, three short pieces can be taken separately : the Red soldiers, the workmen, and the Pioneers. The combination of these separate pieces with the general view of the crowd provides an image of the demonstration from which no element is lacking. The spectator is enabled to appreciate both its composition and its dimension, only the time in which he effects that appreciation is altered.

FILMIC SPACE AND TIME

Created by the camera, obedient to the will of the director—after the cutting and joining of the separate pieces of celluloid—there arises a new *filmic* time ; not that real time embraced by the phenomenon as it takes place before the camera, but a new *filmic* time, conditioned only by the speed of perception and controlled by the number and duration of the separate elements selected for filmic representation of the action.

Every action takes place not only in time, but also in space. Filmic time is distinguished from actual in that it is dependent only on the lengths of the separate pieces of celluloid joined together by the director. Like time, so also is filmic space bound up with the chief process of film-making, editing. By the junction of the separate pieces the director builds a filmic space entirely his own. He unites and compresses separate elements, that have perhaps been recorded by him at differing points of real, actual space, into one *filmic* space. By virtue of the possibility of eliminating points of passage and interval, which we have already analysed and which obtains in all film-work, filmic space appears as a synthesis of real elements picked out by the camera.

Remember the example of the man falling from the fifth floor. That which is in reality but a ten-foot fall into a net and a six-foot further leap from a bench appears upon the screen as a fall from a hundred feet high.

L. V. Kuleshov assembled in the year 1920 the following scenes as an experiment :

1. A young man walks from left to right.

2. A woman walks from right to left.

3. They meet and shake hands. The young man points.

4. A large white building is shown, with a broad flight of steps.

5. The two ascend the steps.

The pieces, separately shot, were assembled in the order given and projected upon the screen. The spectator was presented with the pieces thus joined as one clear, uninterrupted action : a meeting of two young people, an invitation to a nearby house, and an entry into it. Every single piece, however, had been shot in a different place ; for example, the young man near the G.U.M. building, the woman near Gogol's monument, the handshake near the Bolshoi Teatr, the white house came out of an American picture (it was, in fact, *the* White House), and the ascent of the steps was made at St. Saviour's

ON FILM TECHNIQUE

Cathedral. What happened as a result? Though
the shooting had been done in varied locations, the
spectator perceived the scene as a whole. The parts
of real space picked out by the camera appeared
concentrated, as it were, upon the screen. There
resulted what Kuleshov termed " creative geo-
graphy." By the process of junction of pieces of
celluloid appeared a new, filmic space without
existence in reality. Buildings separated by a distance of thousands of miles were concentrated to a
space that could be covered by a few paces of the
actors.

THE MATERIAL OF FILMS

We have now established the chief points in the
difference between the work of the film director and
that of the theatrical producer. This difference lies
in the distinction of material. The theatrical producer works with real actuality, which, though he
may always remould, yet forces him to remain bound
by the laws of real space and real time. The film
director, on the other hand, has as his material
the finished, recorded celluloid. This material from
which his final work is composed consists not of
living men or real landscapes, not of real, actual
stage-sets, but only of their images, recorded on
separate strips that can be shortened, altered, and
asembled according to his will. The elements of
reality are fixed on these pieces ; by combining them
in his selected sequence, shortening and lengthening
them according to his desire, the director builds up
his own " filmic " time and " filmic " space. He

89

does not adapt reality, but uses it for the creation of a new reality, and the most characteristic and important aspect of this process is that, in it, laws of space and time invariable and inescapable in work with actuality become tractable and obedient. The film assembles the elements of reality to build from them a new reality proper only to itself; and the laws of space and time, that, in work with living men, with sets and the footage of the stage, are fixed and fast, are, in the film, entirely altered. Filmic space and filmic time, the creation of the technician, are entirely subject to the director. The basic method of filmic representation, this construction of the unity of a film from separate pieces or elements, the superfluous among which can be eliminated and only the characteristic and significant retained, offers exceptional possibilities.

Everyone knows that the nearer we approach a regarded object, the less material appears simultaneously in our view-field; the more clearly our investigating glance examines an object, the more details we perceive and the more limited and sectional becomes our view. We no longer perceive the object as a whole, but pick out the details with our glance in order, thus receiving by association an impression of the whole that is far more vivid, deeper, and sharper than if we had gazed at the object from a distance and perceived the whole in a general view, inevitably missing detail in so doing. When we wish to apprehend anything, we always begin with the general outlines, and then, by intensifying our examination to the highest degree, enrich the apprehension by an ever-increasing number of details. The particular, the detail, will always be a synonym of intensification. It is upon this that the strength of the film depends, that its characteristic speciality is the possibility of giving a clear, especially vivid representation of detail. The power of filmic representation lies in the fact that, by means of the camera, it continually strives to penetrate as deeply as possible, to the mid-point of every image. The camera, as it were, forces itself, ever striving, into the profoundest deeps of life ; it strives thither to penetrate, whither the average spectator never reaches as he glances casually around him. The camera goes deeper ; anything it can see it approaches, and thereafter eternalises upon the celluloid. When we approach a given, real image, we must spend a definite effort and time upon it, in advancing from the general to the particular, in intensifying our attention to that point at which we begin to remark and apprehend details. By the process of editing the film removes, eliminates, this effort. The film spectator is an ideal, perspicuous observer. And it is the director who makes him so. In the discovered, deeply embedded detail there lies an element of perception, the creative element that characterises as art the work of man, the sole element that gives the event shown its final worth.

To show something as everyone sees it is to have accomplished *nothing*. Not that material that is embraced in a first, casual, merely general and superficial glance is required, but that which discloses itself to an intent and searching glance, that can and will see deeper. This is the reason why the greatest artists, those technicians who feel the film most acutely, deepen their work with details. To do this they discard the general aspect of the image, and the points of interval that are the inevitable concomitant of every natural event. The theatrical producer, in working with his material, is not in a position to remove from the view of the spectator that background, that mass of general and inevitable outline, that surrounds the characteristic and particular details. He can only underline the most essential, leaving the spectator himself to concentrate upon what he underlines. The film technician, equipped with his camera, is infinitely more powerful. The attention of the spectator is entirely in his hands. The lens of the camera is the eye of the spectator. He sees and remarks only that which the director desires to show him, or, more correctly put, that which the director himself sees in the action concerned.

ANALYSIS

In the disappearance of the general, obvious outline and the appearance on the screen of some deeply hidden detail, filmic representation attains the highest point of its power of external expression. The film, by showing him the detail without its background, releases the spectator from the unnecessary task of eliminating superfluities from his view-field.

By eliminating distraction it spares the spectator's energy, and reaches thereby the clearest and most marked effect. As example we shall take some instances from well-known films in which notable directors have attained great strength of expression.

As example, the trial scene in Griffith's *Intolerance*. Here there is a scene in which a woman hears the death sentence passed on her husband, who is innocent of the crime. The director shows the face of the woman : an anxious, trembling smile through tears. Suddenly the spectator sees for an instant her hands, only her hands, the fingers convulsively gripping the skin. This is one of the most powerful moments in the film. Not for a minute did we see the whole figure, but only the face, and the hands. And it is perhaps by virtue of this fact that the director understood how to choose and to show, from the mass of real material available, only these two characteristic details, that he attained the wonderful power of impression notable in this scene. Here once more we encounter the process, mentioned above, of clear selection, the possibility of the elimination of those insignificances that fulfil only a transition function and are always inseparable from reality, and of the retention only of climactic and dramatic points. Exactly upon this possibility depends the essence of the significance of editing, the basic process of filmic creation. Confusion by linkage and wastage by intervals are inevitable attributes of reality. When a spectator is dealing with actuality he can overcome them only by a given effort of attention. He rests his glance on a face, then lets it glide down the body until finally it rests attentively on the hands—this is what a spectator has to do when looking at a real woman in real surroundings.

The *film* spares this work of stopping and downward-gliding. Thus the spectator spends no superfluous energy. By elimination of the points of interval the director endows the spectator with the energy preserved, he charges him, and thus the appearance assembled from a series of significant details is stronger in force of expression from the screen than is the appearance in actuality.

We now perceive that the work of the film director has a double character. For the construction of filmic form he requires proper material ; if he wishes to work filmically, he cannot and must not record reality as it presents itself to the actual, average onlooker. To create a filmic form, he must select those elements from which this form will later be assembled. To assemble these elements, he must first find them. And now we hit on the necessity for a special process of analysis of every real event that the director wishes to use in a shot. For every event a process has to be carried out comparable to the process in mathematics termed " differentiation "— that is to say, dissection into parts or elements. Here the technique of observation links up with the creative process of the selection of the characteristic elements necessary for the future finished work. In order to represent the woman in the court scene,

Griffith probably imagined, he may even have actually seen, dozens of despairing women, and perceived not only their heads and hands, but he selected from the whole images only the smile through tears and the convulsive hands, creating from them an unforgettable filmic picture.

Another example. In that filmically outstanding work, *The Battleship " Potemkin,"* [32] Eisenstein shot the massacre of the mob on the great flight of steps in Odessa.[33] The running of the mob down the steps is rendered rather sparingly and is not especially expressive, but the perambulator with the baby, which, loosed from the grip of the shot mother, rolls down the steps, is poignant in its tragic intensity and strikes with the force of a blow. This perambulator is a detail, just like the boy with the broken skull in the same film. Analytically dissected, the mass of people offered a wide field for the creative work of the director, and the details correctly discovered in editing resulted in episodes remarkable in their expressive power.

Another example, simpler, but quite characteristic for film-work : how should one show a motor-car accident ?—a man being run over.

The real material is thoroughly abundant and complex. There is the street, the motor-car, the man crossing the street, the car running him down, the startled chauffeur, the brakes, the man under the wheels, the car carried forward by its impetus, and, finally, the corpse. In actuality everything occurs in unbroken sequence. How was this material

worked out by an American director in the film
Daddy ? The separate pieces were assembled on the
screen in the following sequence :

   1. The street with cars in movement : a pedestrian crosses the street with his back to the camera ;
a passing motor-car hides him from view.

   2. Very short flash : the face of the startled
chauffeur as he steps on the brake.

   3. Equally short flash : the face of the victim,
his mouth open in a scream.

   4. Taken from above, from the chauffeur's seat :
legs, glimpsed near the revolving wheels.

   5. The sliding, braked wheels of the car.

   6. The corpse by the stationary car.

The separate pieces are cut together in short, very
sharp rhythm. In order to represent the accident
on the screen, the director dissected analytically
the whole abundant scene, unbroken in actual
development, into component parts, into elements,
and selected from them—sparingly—only the six
essential. And these not only prove sufficient, but
render exhaustively the whole poignancy of the event
represented.

In the work of the mathematician there follows
after dissection into elements, after " differentiation,"
a combination of the discovered separate elements
to a whole—the so-called " integration."

In the work of the film director the process of
analysis, the dissection into elements, forms equally
only a point of departure, which has to be followed by

the assemblage of the whole from the discovered parts. The finding of the elements, the details of the action, implies only the completion of a preparatory task. It must be remembered that from these parts the complete work is finally to emerge, for, as said above, the real motor-car accident might be dissected by the onlooker into dozens, perhaps indeed hundreds, of separate incidents. The director, however, chooses only six of them. He makes a selection, and this selection is naturally conditioned in advance by that filmic image of the accident—happening not in reality but on the screen—which, of course, exists in the head of the director long before its actual appearance on the screen.

EDITING : THE LOGIC OF FILMIC ANALYSIS

The work of the director is characterised by thinking in filmic pictures ; by imagining events in that form in which, composed of pieces joined together in a certain sequence, they will appear upon the screen ; by considering real incidents only as material from which to select separate characteristic elements ; and by building a new filmic reality out of them. Even when he has to do with real objects in real surroundings he thinks only of their appearances upon the screen. He never considers a real object in the sense of its actual, proper nature, but considers in it only those properties that can be carried over on to celluloid. The film director looks only *conditionally* upon his material, and this conditionality is extraordinarily specific ; it arises from a whole series of properties peculiar only to the film. Even while being shot, a film must be thought of already as an editable sequence of separate pieces of celluloid. The filmic form is never identical with the real appearance, but only similar to it. When the director establishes the content and sequence of the separate elements that he is to combine later to filmic form, he must calculate exactly not only the content, but the length of each piece, or, in other words, he must regard it as an element of filmic space and filmic time. Let us suppose that before us lie, haphazard on the table, those separate pieces of material that were shot to represent that scene of the motor-car accident described above. The essential thing is to unite these pieces and to join them into one long strip of film. Naturally we can join them in any desired order. Let us imagine an intentionally absurd order—for example, the following :

Beginning with the shot of the motor-car, we cut into the middle of it the legs of the man run over, then the man crossing the street, and finally the face of the chauffeur. The result is a senseless medley of pieces that produces in the spectator an impression of chaos. And rational order will only be brought into the alternation of pieces when they are at least conditioned by that sequence with which a chance observer would have been able to let his glance and attention wander from object to object ; only then will relation appear between the pieces, and their combination, having received organic unity, be effective on the screen. But it is not sufficient that the pieces be united in definite order. Every event takes place not only in space, but in time, and, just as filmic space is created, as we saw, by the junction in sequence of selected pieces, so must also be created, moulded from the elements of real time, a new filmic time. Let us suppose that, at the junction of the pieces shot to represent the accident, no thought has been given to their proportionate lengths ; in result the editing is as follows :

1. Someone crosses the street.

2. Long : the face of the chauffeur at his brake.

3. Equally long : the screaming, wide-open mouth of the victim.

4. The braked wheel and all the other pieces shown similarly in very long strips.

A reel of film cut in this way would, even in correct spacial sequence, appear absurd to the spectator. The car would appear to travel slowly. The inherently short process of running-over would be disproportionately and incomprehensibly drawn out. The *event* would disappear from the screen, leaving only the projection of some chance material. Only when the right length has been found for every piece, building a rapid, almost convulsive rhythm of picture alternation, analogous to the panic glance, thrown this way and that, of an observer mastered by horror, only then will the screen breathe a life of its own imparted to it by the director. And this is because the appearance created by the director is enclosed, not only in filmic space, but also in filmic time, integrated from elements of real time picked from actuality by the camera. Editing is the language of the film director. Just as in living speech, so, one may say, in editing : there is a word—the piece of exposed film, the image ; a phrase—the combination of these pieces. Only by his editing methods can one judge a director's individuality. Just as each writer has his own individual style, so each film director has his own individual method of representation. The editing junction of the pieces in creatively discovered sequence is already a final and completing process whose result is the attainment of a final creation, the finished film. And it is with this process in mind that the director must attend also to the formation of these most elementary of pieces (corresponding to the words in speech), from which later the edited phrases—the incidents and sequences—will be formed.

THE NECESSITY TO INTERFERE WITH MOVEMENT

The organising work of the director is not limited to editing. Quite a number of film technicians maintain that editing should be the only organising medium of the film. They hold that the pieces can be shot anyhow and anywhere, the images must only be interesting ; afterwards, by simply joining them according to their form and kind, a way will be found to assemble them to a film.[34] If any unifying idea be taken as basis of the editing, the material will no doubt be organised to a certain degree. A whole series of shots taken at hazard in Moscow can be joined to a whole, and all the separate shots will be united by their place of taking—the town of Moscow. The spacial grasp of the camera can be narrowed to any desired degree ; a series of figures and happenings can be taken on the market-place and then finally in a room where a meeting is being held, and in all these shots there will undoubtedly be an organising embryo, but the question is how deeply it will be developed. Such a collection of shots can be compared to a newspaper, in which the enormous abundance of news is divided into sections and columns. The collection of news of all the happenings in the world, given in the newspaper, is organised and systematised. But this same news, used in an article or a book, is organised in an even higher degree. In the process of creating a film, the work of organisation can and must extend more widely and deeply than the mere establishment of a hard and fast editing scheme of representation. The separate pieces must be brought into organic relation with each other, and for this purpose their content must be considered in the shooting as a deepening, as an advancement, of the whole editing construction into the inner depth of each separate element of this construction.

In considering certain of our examples, we have had to deal with events and appearances that take place before the camera independent of the will of the director. The shooting of the demonstration was, after all, only a selection of scenes of real actuality, not created by the director, but picked out by him from the hurly-burly flow of life. But, in order to produce an edited representation of a given action, in order to take some piece of reality not specially arranged by him in editable form, the director must none the less, in one way or another, subordinate this action to his will. Even in the shooting of this demonstration we had, if we wished to render as vivid as possible a scenic representation of it, to insinuate ourselves with the camera into the crowd itself and to get specially selected, typical persons to walk past the lens just for the purpose of being taken, thus arbitrarily interfering with the natural course of events in order to make them serve for subsequent filmic representation.[35]

If we use a more complex example we shall see even more clearly that in order to shoot and filmically represent any given action we must subject it to our control—that is, it must be possible for us to bring it to a standstill, to repeat it several times, each time shooting a new detail, and so forth. Suppose we wish editably to shoot the take-off of an aeroplane. For its filmic representation we select the following elements :

1. The pilot seats himself at the controls.
2. The hand of the pilot makes contact.
3. The mechanic swings the propeller.
4. The aeroplane rolls towards the camera.
5. The take-off itself shot from another position so that the aeroplane travels away from the camera as it leaves the ground.

In order to shoot in editable form so simple an action as a take-off, we must either stop after the first movement of the aeroplane, and, having quickly changed the position of the camera, placing it at the tail-end of the machine, take the continuation of the movement, or we must unavoidably repeat the movement of the aeroplane twice ; once let it travel towards the camera, and, the second time, changing the set-up, away from the camera.

In both cases we must, in order to obtain the filmic representation desired, interrupt the natural course of the action, either by stopping or by repetition. Almost invariably, in shooting a dynamically continuous action, we must, if we wish to obtain from it the necessary details, either stop it by interruption or repeat it several times. In such a way we must always make our action dependent on the will of the director, even in the shooting of the simplest events that have nothing to do with " artistic " direction. If we chose not to interfere with the natural unfolding of the real event, then we should be knowingly making the film impossible. We should have left nothing but a slavish fixation of the event, excluding all possibility of using such advantages of filmic representation as the particularisation of details and the elimination of superfluous transitory points.

ORGANISATION OF THE MATERIAL TO BE SHOT

We now turn to a new side of directorial work—namely, the methods of organisation of the material to be shot. Suppose the director to be concerned only in making an industrial film (the work of a factory, large workshop, or institution), a subject which would appear to consist only in the fixation of a number of processes not requiring his interference as director, even so his work consists of something more than the simple setting up of the camera and shooting the machines and people at work from various angles. In order to finish up with a really filmically clear, editable representation, the director is, with each separate process he shoots, inevitably compelled to interrupt and interfere, guided by a clear perception of that editing sequence in which he will later project the pieces on the screen. The director must introduce into his work the element of direction, the element of a special organisation of every action shot, the goal of which organisation is the clearest and most exact possible recording of characteristic details.

But when we go on to the shooting of so-called "dramatic" subjects, then naturally the element of direction, the element of organisation of the material to be shot, becomes yet more important and indispensable. In order to shoot all the essentials of the filmic representation of the motor-car accident, the director had many times to alter the position of his camera ; he had to make the motor-car, the chauffeur, and the victim carry out their separate and essential movements many times. In the direction of a dramatic film very often an event shown on the screen never had existence as a whole in reality. It has been present only in the head, in the imagination of the director, as he sought the necessary elements for the later filmic form.

Here we come to the consideration of that which must be shot in the limits of one uninterrupted piece of celluloid, in the limits of one " shot," as the technical term has it. Work in the limits of one shot is naturally dependent on real space and real time ; it is work with single elements of *filmic* space and *filmic* time ; and is naturally directly conditioned by the cutting later to be carried out. In order to arouse in the spectator the necessary excited impression, the director, in editing the motor-car accident, built up a disturbed rhythm, effected by the exceptionally short lengths of each single piece. But remember, the desired material cannot be got by merely cutting or abruptly shortening the pieces of celluloid ; the necessary length into which the content of each piece had to fit must have been borne in mind when it was shot. Let us suppose that it is our task to shoot and edit a disturbed, excited scene, that accordingly makes necessary quick change of the short pieces. In shooting, however, the scenes and parts of scenes are acted before the lens very slowly and lethargically. Then, in selecting the pieces and trying to edit them, we shall be faced by an insuperable obstacle. Short pieces must be used, but the action that takes place in the limits of each separate piece proves to be so slow that, to reach the necessary shortness of each piece, we must cut, remove part of the action ; while, if

we preserve the shots entire, the pieces prove
too long.

Let us imagine that the camera, embracing in its
view-field a wide area, for example two persons
talking to one another, suddenly approaches one of
the characters and shows some detail important
to the development of the action and, at the
given moment, particularly characteristic. Then the
camera withdraws once more and the spectator sees
the further development of the scene in long-shot
as previously, both persons of the action being found
again in the field of view. It must be emphasised
that the spectator only derives an impression of
unbroken development of the action when the transition from long-shot to close-up (and reverse) is
associated with a movement common to the two
pieces. For example, if as detail concerned is
selected a hand drawing a revolver from a pocket
during the conversation, the scene must infallibly
be shot as follows : the first long-shot ends with a
movement of the hand of the actor reaching for
his pocket ; in the following close-up, showing the
hand alone, the movement begun is completed and
the hand gets out the revolver ; then back to the
long-shot, in which the hand with the revolver,
continuing the movement from the pocket begun
at the end of the close-up, aims the weapon at its
adversary. Such linkage by movement is the essential desideratum in that form of editing construction

in which the object taken is not removed from the view-field at a change of set-up. Now, all three pieces are shot separately (technically, more correctly, the whole of the long-shot is taken uninterruptedly, from the hand-movement to the threat to the adversary ; the close-up is taken separately). It is naturally obvious that the close-up of the hand of the actor, cut into the long-shot of the hand-movement, will only be in the right place and only blend to a unity if the movements of the actor's hand at both moments of actual recording are in exact external correspondence.[36]

The example given of the hand is extremely elementary. The hand-movement is not complicated and exact repetition not hard to achieve. But the use of several set-ups in representing an actor's work occurs very frequently in films. The movements of the actors may be very complicated. And in order to repeat in the close-up the movements made in long-shot, to conform to the requirements of great spacial and temporal exactness, both director and actor must be technically highly practised. Yet another property of films conditions exactness of spacial directorial construction. In the preparation of the material to be shot, in the construction of the work before the camera, in the choice and fixation of one or other movement form—or, in other words, in the organisation of these tasks—not only are bounds set to the director by the considerations of his editing plan, but he is limited also by the specific view-field of the camera itself, which forces all the material shot into the well-known rectangular contour of the cinematograph screen. During his work the film director does not see what takes place in front of him with the eye of a normal spectator—he looks at it with the eye of the lens.[37] The normal human gaze, widely embracing the area in front of him, does not exist for the director. He sees and constructs only in that conditioned section of space that the camera can take in ; and yet more—this space is, as it were, delimited by fast, fixed boundaries, and the very definite expression of these boundaries themselves inevitably conditions an inflexibility of composition in the spacial construction. It is obvious that an actor taken with a fairly close approximation of the camera will, in making a movement too wide in relation to the space he occupies, simply disappear from the view-field of the camera. If, for example, the actor sit with bended head, and must raise his head, at a given approximation of the camera, an error on his part of only an inch or two may leave only his chin visible to the spectator, the rest of him being outside the limits of the screen, or, technically, " cut off." This elementary example broadly emphasises once again the necessity of an exact spacial calculation of every movement the director shoots. Naturally this necessity applies not only to close-ups. It may be a gross mistake to take instead of the whole of somebody, only two-thirds of him. To distribute the material shot and its movements in the rectangle of the picture in such a way that everything is clearly and sharply apprehensible, to construct every composition in such a way that the right-angled boundaries of the screen do not disturb the composition found, but perfectly contain it—that is the achievement towards which film directors strive.

THE ORGANISATION OF CHANCE MATERIAL

Anyone who knows anything of painting knows how the shape of the canvas on which the picture is painted conditions the composition of the design. The forms presented upon the canvas must be organically enclosed in the boundaries of its space. The same is true of the work of the film director. No movement, no construction is thinkable for him outside that piece of space, limited by a rectangular contour and technically termed the " picture."[38] It is true that not always does a film director happen to deal with subordination as direct as that of actors receiving orders easily obeyed. He often encounters happenings and processes that cannot be directly subordinated to his will. For the director strives ever to seize and use everything that the world around can offer him. And far from everything in this world obeys the shouting of a director. For instance, the shooting of a sea, a waterfall, a storm, an avalanche : all this is often brought into a film, and, forming a firmly integral part of the subject, must consequently be organised exactly as any other material prepared for editing. Here the director is completely submerged in a mass of chance happenings. Nothing is directly obedient to his will. The movements before the camera develop in accordance with their own laws. But the material required by the director —that is, out of which the film can be made—must none the less be organised. If the director finds himself confronted with a phenomenon that is chance in this sense, he cannot and must not give in to it, for otherwise his work will change itself to a simple, unregulated record. He must employ the adventitious phenomenon, and he does so by constantly inventing a series of special methods. Here comes to his help that possibility of disregarding the natural development of the action in *real* time, of which I have already spoken above. The director, alertly watching with his camera, finds it possible to pick out the material required and to unite the separate shots on the screen, even though they may in reality be separated from one another by wide temporal intervals. Suppose he require for a film a small stream, the bursting of a dam, and the flood consequent on the catastrophe, he can shoot the stream and the dam in autumn, the river when in spate in spring, and secure the required impression by combination of the two sections. Suppose the action take place on the shores of a sea with a continuous and tempestuous breaking of the surf, the director can only take his shots when the waves are high after a storm. But the shots, though spread out over several months, will represent on the screen perhaps only a day or an hour. Thus the director utilises the (natural) repetition of a chance happening for the required filmic representation.

ON FILM TECHNIQUE

The recording of the animals that so often appear in films affords a further instance of the use of special methods in organising the adventitious. It is said that an American director spent sixty working hours and the corresponding amount of celluloid in order to get on the screen the exact spring that he needed of a kitten on a mouse. In another film a sea-lion had to be recorded.[39] The timorous animal swam rapidly and irregularly around its pond. Of course, the simple method would have been to take in the whole pond, setting up the camera the required distance away, and enabling the spectator to follow the movements of the sea-lion just as a given observer standing on the bank would have followed them. The camera could not, and had not, to watch thus ; it had before it a number of separate problems. The camera had to observe how the beast glided swiftly and dexterously over the surface of the water, and it had to observe it from the best viewpoint. The sea-lion had also to be seen from closer, making close-ups necessary. The editing-plan, that preceded the taking of the shots, was as follows :

1. The sea-lion swims in the pond towards the bank—taken slightly from above, the better to follow the movements of the beast in the water.

2. The sea-lion springs out on to the bank, and then plunges back into the water.

3. It swims back to its den.

Three times had the viewpoint of the camera to be altered. Once the photographing had to be from above, then the camera had to be placed so that the beast, springing on to the bank, would happen to be very near it, and the third time the sea-lion had to be taken swimming away from the camera, so as to show the speed of its movement. At the same time, the whole material had to be shown in connected form, so that, on the screen, in the apprehension of the spectator, the three separate shots of sea-lion should blend to the impression of one continuous movement of the animal, despite the fact that they were taken from different points. One cannot command a beast to swim in a desired direction or to approach a camera ; but at the same time its movement was exactly prescribed in the editing-plan, with which the construction of the whole picture was bound up. When the sea-lion was being taken from above, it swam—tempted by the throwing of a fish—several times across the pond until it came by chance into the view-field of the camera in the way the director required. For the close-up, the bait was thrown again and again until the sea-lion leaped on to the right place on the bank and made the necessary turn. Out of thirty takes made, three were chosen, and these gave on the screen the desired image of continuous movement. This movement was not organised by direct prescription of the work required, but attained by approximate control of adventitious elements and subsequent strict selection of the material gathered. The *chance* is synonymous of real, unfalsified, unacted life. In fifty per cent of his work the director encounters it. *Organisation and exact arrangement—* this is the basic slogan of film work, and it is chiefly accomplished by the editing. The editing-plan can exist before the moment of shooting, and then the will of the director transforms and subdues reality in order to assemble the work out of it. The editing-plan can appear during the process of shooting, if the director, come upon unforeseen material, use it simultaneously orientating his work according to that feasible future form that will compose, from the pieces shot, a united filmic image.

So, for example, in *The Battleship " Potemkin "* the brilliant shots taken in the mist by the cameraman Tissé are cut beautifully into the film with striking effect and organically weld themselves to its whole, though nobody had foreseen the mist. Indeed, it was the more impossible to foresee the mist because mists had hitherto been regarded as a hindrance in film-work.

But, in either case, the shooting must be related organically to the editing-plan, and consequently the paramount requirement of an exact spacial and temporal calculation of the content of each piece remains in force.

FILMIC FORM

When, instead of making a simple fixation of some action that takes place in reality, we wish to render it in its filmic form—that is to say, exchange its actual, uninterrupted flow for an integration of creatively selected elements—then we must bear invariably in mind those laws that relate the spectator to the director who edits the shots. When we discussed a haphazard, chaotic ordination of shots, we laid it down that this would appear as a meaningless disorder to the spectator. To impress the spectator is correctly to discover the order and rhythm of the combination.

How does one hit upon such an ordination? Certainly, generally speaking, this, like any other creative artistic process, must be left ultimately to the artist's intuition. None the less, at least the paths that approximately determine the direction of this work should be indicated. We have already made comparison above between the lens and the eye of an observer. This comparison can be carried very far. The director, as he determines the position of the camera in shooting and prescribes the length of each separate shot, can, in fact, be compared to an observer who turns his glance from one element of the action to another, so long as this observer is not apathetic in respect to his emotional state. The more deeply he is excited by the scene before him, the more rapidly and suddenly (staccato) his attention springs from one point to another. (The example of the motor-car accident.) The more disinterestedly and phlegmatically he observes the action, the calmer and slower will be the changes of his points of attention, and consequently the changes of set-up of the camera. The emotion can unquestionably be communicated by the specific rhythm of the editing. Griffith, the American, richly uses this method in the greater part of his films. Here belongs also that characteristic directorial method of forcing the spectator to insinuate himself into the skin of the actor, and letting him see with the latter's eyes. Very often after the face of the hero looking at something, the object looked at is shown from his viewpoint. The greater part of the methods of editing a film yet known to us can be linked to this regarding of the camera as observer. The considerations that determine changes of glance coincide almost exactly with those that govern correct editing construction.

But it cannot be claimed that this comparison is exhaustive. The construction of filmic form in editing can be carried out in several ways. For, finally, it is the editing itself that contains the culmination of the creative work of the film director. Indeed, it is in the direct discovery of methods for use in the editing of the material filmed that the film will gain for itself a worthy place among the other great arts. Film-art is yet in its period of birth. Such methods as approximation, comparison, pattern, and so forth, that have already been long an organic preparatory part of the existing arts, are only now being tested fumblingly in the film. I cannot here refrain from the opportunity of instancing a brilliant example of an unquestionably new editing method that Eisenstein used in *The Battleship " Potemkin."*

The fourth reel ends with the firing of a gun, on board the rebel battleship, at the Odessa Theatre. This seemingly simple incident is handled in an extraordinarily interesting way by Eisenstein. The editing is as follows :

1. Title :

" *And the rebel battleship answered the brutality of the tyrant with a shell upon the town.*"

2. A slowly and deliberately turning gun-turret is shown.

3. Title :

" *Objective—the Odessa Theatre.*"

4. Marble group at the top of the theatre building.

5. Title :

" *On the General's Headquarters.*"

6. Shot from the gun.

7. In two very short shots the marble figure of Cupid is shown above the gates of a building.

8. A mighty explosion ; the gates totter.

9. Three short shots, a stone lion sleeping, a stone lion with open eyes, and a rampant stone lion.

10. A new explosion, shattering the gates.

This is an editing construction that is reproduced in words only with difficulty, but that is almost shatteringly effective on the screen. The director has here employed a daring form of editing. In his film a stone lion rises to its feet and roars. This image has hitherto been thinkable only in literature, and its appearance on the screen is an undoubted and thoroughly promising innovation. It is interesting to observe that in this short length of film all the characteristic elements peculiar and specific to filmic representation are united. The battleship was taken in Odessa, the various stone lions in the Crimea,[40] and the gates, I believe, in Moscow. The elements are picked out and welded into one united filmic space. From different, immovable stone lions has arisen in the film the non-existent movement of a filmic lion springing to its feet. Simultaneously with this movement has appeared a time non-existent in reality, inseparably bound up with each movement. The rebel battleship is concentrated to a single gun-muzzle, and the General's headquarters stare at the spectator in the shape of a single marble group on the summit of their roof. The struggle between the enemies not only loses nothing thereby, but gains in clearness and sharpness. Naturally this example of the lions instanced here cannot be brought into relation with the use of the camera as observer. It is an exceptional example, offering undoubted possibilities in the future for the creative work of the film director. Here the film passes from naturalism, which in a certain degree was proper to it, to free, symbolic representation, independent of the requirements of elementary probability.

THE TECHNIQUE OF DIRECTORIAL WORK

We have already laid down, as the characteristic property of filmic representation, the striving of the camera to penetrate as deeply as possible into the details of the event being represented, to approach as nearly as possible to the object under observation, and to pick out only that which can be seen with a glance, intensified to eliminate the general and superficial. Equally characteristic is its externally exhaustive embrace of the events it handles. One might say that the film, as it were, strives to force the spectator to transcend the limits of normal human apprehension. On the one hand, it allows this apprehension to be sharpened by incredible attentiveness of observation, in concentrating entirely on the smallest details. At the same time, it allows events in Moscow and nearly related events in America to be embraced in a nearly simultaneous comprehension. Concentration on details and wide embrace of the whole include an extraordinary mass of material. Thus the director is faced with the task of organising and carefully working out a great number of separate tasks, according to a definite plan previously devised by him. As instance : in every, even in an average, film the number of persons in the action is seldom less than several dozen, and each of these persons —even those shown only shortly—is organically related to the film as a whole : the performance of each of these persons must be carefully ordered and thought out, exactly as carefully as any shot from the part of a principal. A film is only really significant when every one of its elements is firmly welded to a whole. And this will only be the case when every element of the task is carefully mastered. When one calculates that in a film of about 4,000 feet there are about five hundred pieces, then one perceives that there are five hundred separate but interlocked groups of problems to be solved, carefully and attentively, by the director. When one considers yet again that work on a film is always and inevitably limited by a given maximal time duration, then one sees that the director is so overloaded with work that successful carrying through of the film with direction from one man alone is almost impossible. It is therefore quite easily comprehensible that all notable directors seek to have their work carried out in a departmentalised manner. The whole work of producing a film disintegrates into a series of separate and, at the same time, firmly interrelated sections. Even if one only enumerates the basic stages superficially, one gets, none the less, a very impressive list. As follows :

1. The scenario, and its contained treatment.

2. The preparation of the shooting-script, determination of the editing construction.

3. The selection of actors.

4. The building of sets and the selection of exteriors.

5. The direction and taking of the separate elements into which incidents are divided for editing, the shooting-script script-scenes.

6. Laboratory work on the material shot.

7. The editing (the cutting).

The director, as the single organising control that guides the assembling of the film from beginning to end, must naturally make his influence felt in each of these separate sections. If a hiatus, a mishap, creep into the work of but one of the stages listed, the whole film—the result of the director's collective creation—will inevitably suffer, equally whether it be a matter of a badly chosen actor, of an uneven piece of continuity in the treatment, or of a badly developed piece of negative. Thus it is obvious that the director must be the central organiser of a group of colleagues whose efforts are directed upon the goal mapped out by him.

Collective work on a film is not just a concession to current practice, but a necessity that follows from the characteristic basic peculiarities of films. The American director is surrounded during his directorial work by a whole staff of colleagues, each of whom fulfils a sharply defined and delimited function. A series of assistants, each provided by the director with a task in which the latter's idea is clearly defined, works simultaneously on the many incidents and parts of incidents. After having been checked and confirmed by the director, these incidents are shot and added to the mass of material being prepared for the assembling of the film. The resolution of certain problems—such, for instance, as the organised shooting of crowd-scenes including sometimes as many as a thousand persons—shows quite clearly that the director's work cannot attain a proper result unless he has a sufficiently extensive staff of colleagues at his disposal. In fine, a director working with a thousand extras exactly resembles a commander-in-chief. He gives battle to the indifference of the spectator ; it is his task to conquer it by means of an expressive construction of the movement of the masses he guides ; and, like a commander-in-chief, he must have a sufficient number of officers at his disposal to be able to sway the crowd according to his will. We have said already that, in order to attain a unified creation, a complete film, the director must lead constant through all the numerous stages of the work a unifying, organising line created by him. We shall now examine these stages one by one, in order to be able to represent to ourselves yet more clearly the nature of the work of film direction.

Part II

THE DIRECTOR AND THE SCENARIO

THE DIRECTOR AND THE SCENARIST

IN production, affairs usually take the following course : a scenario is received, handed over to the director, and he submits it to a so-called directorial treatment—that is to say, he works over the entire material submitted him by the scenarist according to his own individuality ; he expresses the thoughts offered him in his own filmic speech —in the language of separate images, separate elements, shots, that follow one another in a certain sequence he establishes.

In short, if a film be compared with the scenario lying basic to it, it is possible to distinguish the theme, the subject treatment of the theme, and, finally, that imaginary filmic formation of the treatment that is worked out by the director in the process of production. Needless to say, these three stages of work must be directly and organically interdependent. None the less, it is evident that the work of the scenarist extends only up to a certain point, after which the share of the director begins. There is no art-form in which a sharp division between two stages of work is thinkable. One cannot continue a work from some point in its course, and not have been linked with it from its beginning. Therefore, as a result of the necessity for unification of two stages, the preliminary work of the scenarist and the subsequent directorial work, the following is inevitable : either the director must be directly associated with the work of the scenarist from the beginning, or, if this be impossible for some reason or other, he must inevitably go through the scenario, removing anything foreign to him, maybe altering separate parts and sequences, maybe the entire subject-construction. The director is ever faced with the task of creating the film from a series of plastically expressive images. In the ability to find such plastic images, in the faculty of creating from separate shots, by editing, clear, expressive " phrases," and connecting these phrases into vividly impressive periods, and from these periods constructing a film—in this consists the art of the director. Not always can the scenarist, especially when he has not a clearly filmically thinking brain and is thus in some degree himself a director, provide in ready form the plastic material required by the director. Usually it is otherwise, the scenarist gives the director the idea, as such—the detached content of the image, and not its *concrete form*. But in a collaboration of this kind the welding together of the two colleagues, the scenarist and the director, is certainly of tremendous importance. It is easy to put forward ideas that will wake no echo in the director and must remain a pure abstraction without concrete form. Even the theme itself of the scenario—in other words, its basis —must inevitably be selected and established in contact with the director. The theme conditions the action, colours it, and thus, of course, inevitably colours that plastic content the expression of which is the chief substance of the director's task. Only if the theme be organically comprehended by the director will he be able to subdue it to the unifying outline of the form he is creating.

Pursuing further, we come to the action. The action outlines a number of situations for the characters, their relations to one another, and, not least, their encounters. It prescribes in its development a whole number of events that already have, in some sort, feelable form. The action cannot be thought of without already some plastically expressive form. In most cases it is difficult for a scenarist, having graduated from the literary field, to steer his course by the conditions of externally expressive form. Already in planning the action the basic incidents that are to determine its shape must infallibly be mapped out. Here comes yet more clearly to light the inevitable dependence on the later directorial work. Even such a thing as the characteristics of a person of the action will be meaningless if not shown in a series of plastically effective movements or situations.

THE ENVIRONMENT OF THE FILM

To continue. All the action of any scenario is immersed in some environment that provides, as it were, the general colour of the film. This environment may, for example, be a special mode of life. By more detailed examination, one may even regard as the environment some separate peculiarity, some special essential trait of the given mode of life selected. This environment, this colour, cannot, and must not, be rendered by one explanatory scene or a title ; it must constantly pervade the whole film, or its appropriate part, from beginning to end. As I have said, the action must be immersed in this background. A whole series of the best films of recent times has shown that this emphasis by means of an environment in which the action is immersed is quite easily effected in cinematography. The film *Tol'able David* shows us this vividly. It is also interesting that the effecting of the unity of this colour of a film is based upon the scarcely communicable ability to saturate the film with numerous fine and correctly observed details. Naturally it is not possible to require of the scenarist that he shall discover all these details and fix them in writing. The best that he can do is to find their necessary abstract formulation, and it is the affair of the director to absorb this formulation and give it the necessary plastic shape. Remarks by the scenarist such as, perhaps, " There was an insufferable smell in the room " or " Many factory-sirens vibrated and sang through the heavy, oil-permeated atmosphere " are not in any sense forbidden. They indicate correctly the relation between the ideas of the scenarist and the future plastic shaping by the director. It may already now be said with a fair degree of certainty that the most immediate task next awaiting the director is that very solution by filmic methods of the descriptive problems mentioned. The first experiments were carried out by the Americans in showing a landscape of symbolic character at the beginning of a film. *Tol'able David* began with the picture of a village taken through a cherry-tree in flower. The foaming, tempestuous sea symbolised the *leit-motif* of the film *The Remnants of a Wreck*.

A wonderful example, affording unquestionably an achievement of this kind, are the pictures of the misty dawn rising over the corpse of the murdered sailor in *The Battleship " Potemkin."* The solution of these problems—the depiction of the environment— is an undoubted and important part of the work on the scenario. And this work naturally cannot be carried out without direct participation by the director. Even a simple landscape—a piece of nature so often encountered in films—must, by some inner guiding line, be bound up with the developing action.

I repeat that the film is exceptionally economical and precise in its work. There is, and must be, in it no superfluous element. There is no such thing as a neutral background, and every factor must be collected and directed upon the single aim of solving the given problems. For every action, in so far as it takes place in the real world, is always involved in general conditions—that is, the nature of the environment.

The action of the scenes may take place by day or by night. Film directors have long been familiar with this point, and the effort to render night effects is to this day an interesting problem for film directors. One can go further. The American, Griffith, succeeded in the film *America* in obtaining, with marvellous tenderness and justness, graduations of twilight and morning. The director has a mass of material at his disposal for this kind of work. The film is interesting, as said before, not only in that it is able to concentrate on details, but also in its ability to weld to a unity numerous materials, deriving from widely embraced sources.

As example, this same morning light : To gain this effect, the director can use not only the growing light of sunrise, but also numerous correctly selected, characteristic processes that infallibly relate themselves with approaching dawn in the apprehension of the spectator. The light of lamp-posts growing paler against the lightening sky, the silhouettes of scarcely visible buildings, the tops of trees tenderly touched with the light of the not yet ascended sun, awakening birds, crowing cocks, the early morning mist, the dew—all this can be employed by the director, shot, and in editing built to a harmonious whole.

In one film an interesting method was used of representing the filmic image of a dawn. In order to embrace in the editing construction the feeling of growing and ever wider expanding light, the separate shots follow one another in such wise that at the beginning, when it is still dark, only details can be seen upon the screen. The camera took only close-ups, as if, like the eye of man in the surrounding dark, it saw only what was near to it. With the increase of the light the camera became ever more and more distant from the object shot. Simultaneously with the broadening of the light, broader and broader became the view-field embraced by the lens. From the close-ups in darkness the director changed to ever more distant long-shots, as if he sought directly to render the increasing light, pervading everything widely and more widely. It is notable that here is employed a pure technical possibility, peculiar only to the film, of communicating a very subtle feeling.

It is clear that work on the solution of problems of this kind is bound up so closely with the knowledge of film technique, so organically with the pure directorial work of analysis, selection of the material, and its unification in creative editing, that such problems cannot, independently of the director, be resolved for him by the scenarist alone. At the same time, it is, as already mentioned, absolutely essential to give the expression of this environment in which the action of every film is immersed, and accordingly, in the creation of the scenario, it is indispensable for the director to collaborate in the work.

THE CHARACTERS IN THE ENVIRONMENT

I should like to note that in the work of one of the strongest directors of the present day, David Griffith, in almost every one of his films, and indeed especially in those in which he has reached the maximum expression and power, it is almost invariably the case that the action of the scenario develops among characters blended directly with that which takes place in the surrounding world.

The stormy finale of the Griffith film is so constructed as to strengthen for the spectator the conflict and the struggle of the heroes to an unimagined degree, thanks to the fact that the director introduces into the action, gale, storm, breaking ice, rivers in spate, a gigantic roaring waterfall. When Lilian Gish, in *Way Down East*, runs broken from the house, her happiness in ruins, and the faithful Barthelmess rushes after her to bring her back to life, the whole pursuit of love behind despair, developing in the furious tempo of the action, takes place in a fearful snowstorm ; and at the final climax, Griffith forces the spectator himself to feel despair, when a rotating block of ice, on it cowering the figure of a woman, approaches the precipice of a gigantic waterfall, itself conveying the, impression of inescapable and hopeless ruin.

First the snowstorm, then the foaming, swirling river in thaw, packed with ice-blocks that rage yet wilder than the storm, and finally the mighty waterfall, conveying the impression of death itself. In this sequence of events is repeated, on large scale as it were, the same line of that increasing despair—despair striving to make an end, for death, that has irresistibly gripped the chief character. This harmony—the storm in the human heart and the storm in the frenzy of nature—is one of the most powerful achievements of the American genius.[41] This example shows particularly clearly how far-reaching and deep must be that connection, between the content of the scenario and the director's general treatment, that adds strength and unity to his work. The director not only transfers the separate scenes suggested by the scenarist each into movement and form, he has also to absorb the scenario in its entirety, from the theme to the final form of the action, and perceive and feel each scene as an irremovable, component part of the unified structure. And this can only be the case if he be organically involved in the work on the scenario from beginning to end.

When the work on the general construction has been finished, the theme moulded to a subject, the separate scenes in which the action is realised laid down, then only do we come to the period of the hardest work on the treatment of the scenario, that stage of work when, already concrete and perceptible, that filmic form of the picture that will result can be foreseen ; do we come to the period of the planning out of the editing scheme for the shots, of the discovery of those component parts from which the separate images will later be assembled.

To bring a waterfall into the action does not necessarily mean to create it on the screen. Let us remember what we said regarding the creation of a filmic image that becomes vivid and effective only when the necessary details are correctly found. We come to the stage of utilising the pieces of real space and real time for the future creation of filmic space and filmic time. If it may be said at the beginning of the process that the scenarist guides the work— and that the director has only to pay attention so as properly to apprehend it organically, and so as, not only to keep contact with it at every given moment, but to be constantly welded to it—now comes a change. The guide of the work is now the director, equipped with that knowledge of technique and that specific talent that enables him to find the correct and vivid images expressing the quintessential element of each given idea. The director organises each separate incident, analysing it, disintegrating it into elements, and simultaneously thinking of the connection of these elements in editing. It is here of special interest to note that the scenarist at this later stage, just as the director in the early stages, must not be divorced from the work. His task it is to supervise the resolution to editable shape of every separate problem, thinking at every instant of the basic theme—sometimes completely abstract, yet current in every separate problem.

Only by means of a close collaboration can a correct and valuable result be attained. Naturally one might postulate as the ideal arrangement the incarnation of scenarist and director in one person. But I have already spoken of the unusual scope and complexity of film creation, that prevents any possibility of its mastery by one person. Collectivism is indispensable in the film, but the collaborators must be blended with one another to an exceptionally close degree.

THE ESTABLISHMENT OF THE RHYTHM OF THE FILM

The editing treatment of the scenario consists not only in the determination of the separate incidents, scenes, objects that are to be shot, but also in the arrangement of the sequence in which they are to be shown. I have already said that in the determination of this sequence one must not only have in mind the plastic content, but also the length of each separate piece of celluloid—that is to say, the rhythm with which the pieces are to be joined must be considered. This rhythm is the means of emotionally influencing the spectator. By this rhythm the director is equally in the position to excite or to calm the spectator. An error of rhythm can reduce the impression of the whole scene shown to zero, but equally can rhythm, fortunately found, raise the impression of a scene to an infinite degree, though it may contain in its separate, imagined, visual material nothing especial. [42] The rhythmic treatment of the film-scenario is not limited to the treatment of the separate incidents, to the finding of the necessary images comprising them. One must remember that the film is divided into separate shots, that these are joined together to form incidents, the incidents to sequences, these last to reels, and the reels together form the whole film. Wherever there is division, wherever there is an element of succession of pieces, be they separate pieces of celluloid or separate parts of the action—there everywhere the rhythmic element must be considered, not indeed because " rhythm " is a modern catchword, but because rhythm, guided by the will of the director, can and must be a powerful and secure instrument of effect. Remember, for instance, how exhausting, and how extinguishing in its effect, was the badly created, constantly confused rhythm of that big film, *The Ray of Death* ; and, on the other hand, how clever was the distribution of material in *Tol'able David*, in which the alternation of quiet and tense sections kept the spectator fresh and enabled him to appreciate the violent finale. The editable preparation of the scenario—in which not only the exact plastic content of each separate little piece is taken into consideration, but also the position in rhythmic sequence of its length when the pieces are joined to incidents, the incidents to sequences and so forth—the establishment of this position, which is already completely decisive for the final form that the film projected on the screen will take, is the last stage of the work of the director on the scenario. Now is the moment come at which new members of the collective team enter the work of creating the film—in fact, those who are concerned with real men and objects, with the movements and backgrounds in which they are locked. The director now has to prepare the material in order to record it on the film.

PART III

THE DIRECTOR AND THE ACTOR

TWO KINDS OF PRODUCTION

IN accordance with their acting, films can roughly be divided into two kinds. In the first group are included such productions as are based on one particular actor—the " star," as he is called in America. The scenario is written especially for the actor. The entire work of the director resolves itself to the presentation to the spectator, once again in new surroundings and with a new supporting cast, of some well-known and favourite figure. Thus are produced the films of Chaplin, Fairbanks, Pickford, and Lloyd. To the second group belong those films that are underlain by some definite idea or thought. These scenarios are not written for an actor, but actors must be found for their realisation when written. Thus works David Griffith. It is not, therefore, remarkable that in several of his pictures Griffith rejects such brilliant names as Pickford, Mae Marsh, and others, a whole series of heroes and heroines whom, having used them for one or two films, he gives up to other hands. To that extent to which a film is basically inspired by some thought, by some definite idea—and not merely by the display of clever technique or a pretty face—the relationship between the actor and the material of the film receives a special and specific character, proper only to the film.

THE FILM ACTOR AND THE FILM TYPE

In order to create a required appearance, the stage actor tries to find and create the necessary make-up, altering his face. If he has to take the part of a strong man in the play, he binds muscles of wadding on his arms. Suppose, for example, it were proposed to him to play Samson, he would not be ashamed of erecting pasteboard pillars on the set, to overthrow them later with one push of his shoulder. Such deceit in properties, equally with make-up drawn upon the face, is unthinkable in films. A made-up, property human being in a real environment, among real trees, near real stones and real water, under a real sky, is as incongruous and inacceptable as a living horse on a stage filled with pasteboard.[43] The conditionality of the film is not a property conditionality : it changes not matter, but only time and space. For this reason one cannot build up a required type artificially for the screen ;

one must discover him. That is why even in those productions the pivot of which is the inevitable and necessary " star," none the less the supporting actors for the second and third parts are always sought by the director from among many. The work of finding the necessary actors, the selection of persons with vividly expressive externalities conforming to the requirements made by the scenario is one of the hardest tasks of the director. It must be remembered that, as I have already said, one cannot " play a part " on the film ; one must possess a sum of real qualities, externally clearly expressed, in order to attain a given effect on the spectator. It is therefore easy to understand why, in film production, a man, passing by chance on the street, who has never had any idea of being an actor, is often brought in, only because he happens to be a vividly externally expressive type, and, moreover, the one desired by the director. In order to make concretely clear this inevitable necessity to use, as acting material, persons possessing in reality the properties of the image required, I shall instance at random the following example.

Let us suppose that we require for a production an old man. In the Theatre the problem would be perfectly simple. A comparatively young actor could paint wrinkles on his face, and so make on the spectator, from the stage, the external impression of an old man. In the film this is unthinkable. Why ? Just because a real, living wrinkle is a deepening, a groove in the face. And when an old man with a real wrinkle turns his head, light plays on this wrinkle. A real wrinkle is not only a dark stripe, it is a shadow from the groove, and a different position of the face in relation to light will always give a different pattern of light and shade. The living wrinkle lives by means of movement in light. But if we paint a black stripe on a smooth skin, then on the screen the face in movement will never show the living groove played on by the light, but only a stripe painted in black paint. It will be especially incongruous in cases of close approximation of the lens—that is, in close-ups.

In the Theatre, make-up of this kind is possible because the light on the stage is conditionally constant and throws no shadows.

By this example it may in some wise be judged to what degree the actor we seek must resemble his prescribed appearance in the scenario. It may be said, in fine, that in most cases the film actor plays himself, and the work of the director consists not in compelling him to create something that is not in him, but in showing, as expressively and vividly as possible, what is in him, by using his real characteristics.

PLANNING THE ACTING OF THE FILM-TYPE

Where the acting material is assembled in this way, the possibility of using a stock company, as in the Theatre, is naturally almost excluded.[44] In almost every film the director is compelled to work with ever new human material, often entirely untrained. But at the same time the work of the person being photographed must be strictly subjected to a whole series of conditions dictated by the film. I have already said that each piece shot must be exactly organised in space and time. The work of the actor being shot, as much as everything being shot, must be exactly considered. Remember that we have discussed the process of taking editable shots, whereby the same movements have to be repeated several times with great exactitude, in order to make it possible for the director to form into a single whole the incidents later composed by the junction of separate pieces. In order to work exactly one must know how, one must learn how, or at least be able to remember by heart. For the work of the film actor, or, if you prefer it, his acting, is deprived of that unbroken quality proper to the work of his colleague on the stage. The film image of the actor is composed from dozens and hundreds of separate, disintegrated pieces in such a way that sometimes he works at the beginning on something that will later form a part of the end. The film actor is deprived of a consciousness of the uninterrupted development of the action, in his work. The organic connection between the consecutive parts of his work, as result of which the distinct whole image is created, is not for him. The whole image of the actor is only to be conceived as a future appearance on the screen, subsequent to the editing of the director ; that which the actor performs in front of the lens in each given piece is only raw material, and it is necessary to be endowed with special, specific, filmic powers in order to imagine to oneself the whole edited image, meticulously composed of separate pieces picked sometimes from the beginning, sometimes from the middle. It is therefore understandable why it was first in films that there appeared exact directorial construction of the actor's work.[45] In most cases only the director knows the shooting-script so thoroughly and so well as to be able clearly to imagine it to himself in that shape in which it will later be transposed upon the screen, and therefore only he can imagine to himself each given part, each given image in its editing construction. If an actor, even a very talented one, allow himself to be inspired by a given separate scene, he will never be able, of himself, so to limit his work as to be able to give a part of his acting of exactly that length and that content later required by the editing. This will only be possible when the actor has entered as deeply and organically into the work of building the film creation as the director producing it. There are schools that maintain that the play of the actor must be ordered by the director down to its least details ; down to the finest movements of the fingers, of the eyebrows, of the eyelashes, everything must be exactly calculated by the director, instructed by him, and recorded on the film. This school represents an undoubted exaggeration that results in unnecessary mechanicalisation ; it is, none the less, not to be gainsaid that the free performance of the actor must be enclosed in a

ON FILM TECHNIQUE

frame-work of the severest directorial control. It is interesting that even such a director as Griffith—who is distinguished by a special " psychologicality " that should, strictly speaking, preclude the possibility of hard and fast construction—none the less does undoubtedly plastically " create " his actor. Griffith has a peculiar feminine type of his own, pathetically helpless and heroic at the same time. It is interesting to follow how, in various of his films, various women express the same emotional states by the same external means. Remember how Mae Marsh weeps in the trial in *Intolerance*, how the heroine in *America* sobs over her dying brother, and how Lilian Gish sobs in the *Orphans of the Storm* as she tells of her sister. There is the same heart-rending face, the same streaming tears, and the helpless, trembling attempt to show a smile behind tears. The similarity of method of many American actors who have worked under control of one and the same director shows markedly how far-reaching is the directorial construction of the actor's work.

THE " ENSEMBLE "

In the Theatre there exists a concept *"ensemble,"* the concept implying that general composition which embraces the work of all the actors collaborating in the play. The *ensemble* undoubtedly exists also in the film, and the same may be said about it as has been said about the edited image of the actor. The fact is that the film actor is deprived of the possibility of himself directly appreciating this *ensemble*. Very often an actor, from beginning to end of his part in front of the camera, does not once see the performance of the actor opposite him in the film, and is shot separately. None the less, however, when the film is subsequently joined, the scenes of this actor will appear directly connected with those of the other, whom he has never seen. The consciousness of the *ensemble*, the relationship between the work of the separate characters, consequently becomes once again a task of the director. Only he, imagining to himself the film in its edited form, already projected upon the screen, already joined from its separately shot pieces—only he can appreciate this *ensemble*, and direct and construct the actor's work in conformity with its requirements. The question of the bounds of the influence the director should exert on the work of the actors is a question that is still open. Exact mechanical obedience to a plan provided by the director has undoubtedly no future. But also a wavering free improvisation by the actor according to general suggestions from the director—a method hitherto a characteristic of most Soviet directors—is definitely inadmissible. Only one thing is still undoubted, that the whole image of the actor will only result when the separately shot pictures are united one to the other in editing, and the work of the actor in each separate shot has been firmly and organically linked to the clear understanding of the future whole. If such an understanding is present to the actor he can work freely, but, if not, then only the exact instructions of the director, the future creator of the editing, can correctly construct the acting work.

Special difficulties are encountered by the director with casually collected human material, but this casual material is, as we have said, nearly inevitable in every film ; and, on the other hand, this material is of exceptional interest. An average film lasts an hour and a half. In this hour and a half there pass before the spectator sometimes dozens of faces that he may remember, surrounding the heroes of the film, and these faces must be especially carefully selected and shown. Often the entire expression and value of an incident, though it may centre round the hero, depends from these characters of second rank who surround him. These characters may be shown to the spectator for no more than six or seven seconds. Therefore they must impress him clearly and vividly. Remember the example of the gang of blackguards in *Tol'able David*, or of the two old men in *The Isle of Lost Ships*. Each face impresses as firmly and vividly as would a separate, clever characterisation by a talented writer. To find a person such that the spectator, after seeing him for six seconds, shall say of him, " That man is a rogue, or good-natured, or a fool "—this is the task that presents itself to the director in the selection of his human material.

EXPRESSIVE MOVEMENT

When the persons are selected, when the director begins to shoot their work, they provide him with a new problem : the actor must move in front of the camera, and his movements must be expressive. The concept " an expressive movement " is not so simple as it appears at first sight. First of all, it is not identical with that everyday movement, that customary behaviour proper to an average man in his real surroundings. A man not only has gestures, but words also are at his disposal. Sometimes the word accompanies the gesture and sometimes, reversed, the gesture aids the word. In the Theatre both are feasible. That is why an actor with deeply ingrained theatrical training conforms with difficulty to the standards of the screen. In *The Postmaster*, Moskvin—an actor of undoubted exceptionally big filmic possibilities—none the less tires one unpleasantly with his ever-moving mouth and with petty movements beating time to the rhythm of the unspoken words. Gesture-movement accompanying speech is unthinkable on the film. Losing its correspondence with the sounds that the spectator does not hear, it degenerates to a senseless plastic muttering. The director in work with an actor must so construct the performance of the latter that the significant point shall lie always in the movement, and the word accompany it only when required. In a pathetic scene, when he learns from the godmother that the hussar officer has eloped with Dunia, Moskvin speaks a great deal and obviously, while at the same time, automatically and quite naturally, like a man accustomed to spoken business, he accompanies every word with one and the same repeated movement of the hand. During the shooting, when the words were audible, the scene was effective, and even very effective ; but on the screen it resulted as a painful and often ridiculous shuffling about on one spot. The idea that the film actor should express in gesture that which the ordinary man says in words is basically false. In creating the picture the director and actor use only those moments when the word is superfluous, when the substance of the action develops in silence, when the word may accompany the gesture, but does not give birth to it.[46]

EXPRESSIVE OBJECTS

That is why the inanimate *object* has such enormous importance on the films. An object is already an expressive thing in itself, in so far as the spectator always associates with it a number of images. A revolver is a silent threat, a flying racing-car is a pledge of rescue or of help arriving in time. The performance of an actor linked with an object and built upon it will always be one of the most powerful methods of filmic construction. It is, as it were, a filmic monologue without words. An object, linked to an actor, can bring shades of his state of emotion to external expression so subtly and deeply as no gesture or mimicry could ever express them conditionally. In *The Battleship "Potemkin"* the battleship itself is an image so powerfully and clearly shown that the men on board are resolved into it, organically blended *with* it.

The shooting down of the crowd is answered not by the sailors standing to the guns, but by the steel battleship itself, breathing from a hundred mouths. When, at the finale, the battleship rushes under full steam to meet the fleet, then, in some sort, the steadfastly labouring, steel driving-rods of the engine incarnate in themselves the hearts of its crew, furiously beating in tenseness of expectation.

THE DIRECTOR AS CREATOR OF THE " ENSEMBLE "

For the film director the concept of *ensemble* is extraordinarily wide. Material objects enter organically into it as well as characters, and it is necessary once more to recall that, in the final editing of the picture, the performance of the actor will stand next to, will have to be welded to, a whole series of other pieces, which he cannot see, and of which he can know only indirectly. Only the director knows and gauges them completely. Therefore the actor is considered by the director, before anything else, as material requiring his " treatment." Let us, in fine, also remember that even each actor separately who is, in real conditions, apprehended as something whole, as the figure of a human being whose movements are perceived as the simultaneous connected work of all the members of his body—such a man often does not exist on the screen. In editing, the director builds sometimes not only scenes, but also a separate human being. Let us remember how often in films we see and remember a character despite the fact that we saw only his head and, separately, his hand.

In his experimental films Lev Kuleshov tried to record a woman in movement by photographing the hands, feet, eyes, and head of different women. As consequence of editing resulted the impression of the movements of *one* single person. Naturally this example does not suggest a special means of practical creation of a man not available in reality, but it emphasises especially vividly the statement that, even in the limits of his short individual work unconnected with other actors, the image of the actor derives not from a separate stage of work, the shooting of a separate piece, but only from that editing construction that welds such pieces to a filmic whole. Take this as one more confirmation of the absolute necessity for exactness in working, and one more confirmation of the axiomatic supremacy of its imagined edited image over each separate element of the actual work in front of the lens. Also, quite obviously of course, the axiomatic supremacy of the director, bearer of the image of the general construction of the film, over the actor who provides material for this construction.

PART IV

THE ACTOR IN THE FRAME

THE ACTOR AND THE FILMIC IMAGE

I HAVE already spoken above of the necessity constantly to bear in mind the rectangular space of the screen that always encloses every movement shot. The movement of the actor in real three-dimensional space once again serves the director only as material for the selection of the elements required for construction of the future appearance, flat and inserted exactly into the space of the frame. The director never sees the actor as a real human being ; he imagines and sees the future filmic appearance, and carefully selects the material for it by making the actor move in various ways and altering the position of the camera relative to him. The same disintegration as with everything in film. Not for one moment is the director presented with live men. Before him he has always only a series of component parts of the future filmic construction. This does not necessitate a sort of killing and mechanicalisation of the actor. He can be as spontaneous as he likes, and need not in any way disturb the natural continuity of his movements, but the director, controlling the camera, will, owing to the nature of cinematographic representation, himself pick out from the entire work of the living man the pieces he requires. When Griffith shot the hands of Mae Marsh in the trial scene, the actress was probably crying when she pinched the skin of her hands ; she lived a full and real experience and was completely in the grip of the necessary emotion as a whole, but the director, for the film, picked out only her hands.

THE ACTOR AND LIGHT

There is one more element characteristic for the work of the director with the actor—that is light, that light without which neither object nor human being nor anything else has existence on the film. The director, determining the lighting in the studio, literally creates the future form upon the screen. For light is the only element that has effect on the sensitive strips of celluloid, only of light of varying strengths is woven the image we behold upon the screen. And this light serves not only to develop the forms—to make them visible. An actor unlit is—nothing. An actor lit only so as to be visible is a simple, undifferentiated, indefinite object. This same light can be altered and constructed in such a way as to make it enter as an organic component into the actor's work. The composition of the light can eliminate much, emphasise much, and bring out with such strength the expressive work of the actor, that it becomes apparent that light is not simply a condition for the fixation of expressive work by the actor, but in itself represents a part of this expressive work. Remember the face of the priest in *The Battleship "Potemkin"* lit from underneath.[47]

147

Thus the work of the film actor in creation of his filmic image is bounded by a technically complex frame of conditions specifically proper to the film. The exact awareness of these conditions lies only with the director, and the actor can only enter creatively, sufficiently widely and deeply, into the work of creating the film when he is a sufficiently tightly and organically welded member of the team —that is, if his work be sufficiently deeply embraced in the sphere of the preparatory work of the director and scenarist. Thus we have arrived, at the end of this chapter, once more at a conclusion of the necessity for an organic team.

PART V

THE DIRECTOR AND THE CAMERAMAN

THE CAMERAMAN AND THE CAMERA

WHEN the actors have been chosen, and the scenes exactly and editably prepared—then begins the shooting. Into the work enters a new member of the team—a man armed with a camera, who does the actual shooting—the camera-man. And now the director has a new problem to overcome : between the collected and prepared material and the future finished work stands the camera, and the man working it. Everything that has been said about the composition of movement in the space of the picture, about light bringing out the picture, about expressive light, must in actuality be brought into conformity with the technical possibilities of shooting. The camera, which appears for the first time in shooting, introduces a real conditionality into film-work. First and foremost : the angle of its vision. Normal human vision can embrace a little less than 180 degrees of surrounding space—that is to say, man can perceive almost the half of his horizon. The field of the lens is considerably less. Its view-angle is equal roughly to 45 degrees and, here already the director begins to leave behind the normal apprehension of real space. Already, owing to this peculiarity, the guided lens of the camera does not embrace the entirety of optical space, but picks out from it only a part, an element, the so-called picture. With the help of a number of camera accessories a yet greater narrowing of this view-field can be attained ; the frame itself surrounding the image can be altered, by means of a so-called " mask."

Not only does the small view-angle set bounds to the space in which the action develops both in height and in width, but by a technical property of the lens the depth of the space picked out is also limited. An actor shot from very close has not only to fit his movements into the narrow frame of the picture in order not to overstep its bounds, he must remember also that he must not recede in depth or approach, for he would then go out of focus and his image would be unclear. At the same time, the camera, over and above those limitations that condition the movements of the material shot, has also a number of accessories which, far from limiting, on the contrary broaden, the work of the director. Remember, for example, in the pictures of Griffith, those lyrically tender moments that appear as if taken through a slight haze. Here we have a method that unquestionably strengthens the impressions of the scene shot, and it is carried out solely by the cameraman taking his shot through a light, transparent gauze or with a specially constructed lens.[48]

Remember the extraordinarily impressive shot in *The Battleship "Potemkin,"* when the stone steps appear suddenly to rush up to meet the falling wounded. This effect could not have been attained without a special apparatus that enabled the camera to be tilted quickly from up downwards during the shot.

In the hands of the cameraman are those actual technical possibilities with the help of which he can transform the abstract ideas of the director to concrete. And these possibilities are innumerable.

THE CAMERA AND ITS VIEWPOINT

When the camera stands ready in position, the director does not now only orientate himself on the future screen image, as he did when working on the scenario or selecting and preparing the actor. He does not now only imagine or visualize it. Looking through the view-finder (a special appliance attached to the camera), the director sees on smaller scale the future picture that will later be projected on the screen. The scenario has been written, its special tasks exactly formulated. The prescription of the shooting of each scene, determining its plastic and rhythmic content, is ready, the cast is selected and ready for work, all preparation completed, and now the material thus prepared has to be fixed upon the celluloid. The camera when prepared for shooting embodies the viewpoint from which the future spectator will apprehend the appearance on the screen. This viewpoint may be various. Each object can be seen, and therefore shot, from a thousand different points, and the selection of any given point cannot, and must not, be by chance. This selection is always related to the entire content of the task that the director keeps in mind in aiming, in one way or another, to affect the spectator.

Let us begin, for argument's sake, with the simple showing of a shape. Suppose we wish to shoot a cigarette lying on the edge of a table. One can so set up the camera that the opening of the cardboard cartouche of the cigarette exactly faces the lens ; and as a result of the shot no cigarette will appear upon the screen—the spectator will see only the stripe of the edge of the table, and on it a small round black circle, the opening of the cartouche circled by its round white frame of cardboard. It follows that in order to enable the spectator to see the cigarette, it is necessary for the lens of the camera also to be able to " see " it. It is necessary, in shooting, to find such a position for the lens in relation to the object as will enable the whole shape of the latter to be seen with maximum clarity and sharpness.

If a torn cigarette is to be shot, the cameraman must so position the camera that the lens, and with it the eye of the future spectator, shall clearly see the tear of the paper, and the tobacco sticking through it.

The example with the cigarette is very elementary —it but roughly proves the substantial importance of the selection of a definite set-up of the camera in relation to the object shot. The problems solved by this selection, in actual practice, are many sided and provide one of the most important aspects of the joint work of director and cameraman.

Let us turn to the more complex. The task of the director may involve not only a simple representation of the shape of the given object, but of its relative position in this or that part of space. Let us suppose we have not only to shoot a wall-clock, but also to show that it hangs very high. Here the task of selecting the picture is complicated by a new requirement, and the cameraman, in choosing the set-up for the camera, either goes to a good distance, trying to get a part of the floor in the picture and thus show the height, or he shoots the clock from near but from below, bringing out its position by a sharp fore-shortening in perspective. If we take into consideration the fact that the material employed by the film director may be exceptionally complex in its form, it becomes clear how enormous a part is played by the selection of the camera-set-up.

To shoot a railway-engine well implies to be able to select that viewpoint from which its complicated form will be most exhaustively and vividly apparent. A correctly discovered set-up determines the expressiveness of the future image.

Everything said so far has related especially to the shooting of motionless objects that do not change their position in relation to the camera.

THE SHOOTING OF MOVEMENT

The work becomes yet more complicated when movement is introduced. An object not only has shape, this shape in the image alters itself functionally with its movement, and, moreover, its movement itself has a shape and serves as object of shooting.

The previous desideratum remains in force. The camera must be so directed that every happening in front of it shall be visible in its clearest and most distinct form. Why does a shot of an army parade taken from above produce so vivid an impression? Because it is just from above that, with the fullest sharpness and clearness, the energetic, rhythmic movement of troops can best be observed. Why is the impression of a rushing train or a racing car so effective when the object is shot so that, having appeared in the distance, it charges straight at the camera, and dashes past near it? Because it is in the perspective increase of the approaching machine that the speed of the movement is most distinctly represented. If we are to shoot a car and a chauffeur sleeping in it, the cameraman will place the camera on the ground near the car. But if we are to shoot the same car winding through the traffic of the street, the cameraman will shoot the scene from the third floor in order the better to pick out the movement in its form and essence. The selection of the camera set-up can intensify the expression of the image shot in many directions. The shooting of a railway-engine charging straight at the lens communicates to an exceptional degree the power of the gigantic machine.

In *The Battleship " Potemkin "* the muzzles of the guns, looking straight at the spectator, are exceptionally threatening. In *The Virgin of Stamboul* the galloping horses are shot by the cameraman from a road-ditch looking up, so that the hoofs dash by soaring, as it were, over the heads of the spectator, and the impression of a mad gallop is increased to a maximum. Here the work of the cameraman ceases to be a simple fixation of an incident independently of the director working on it. The quality of the future film depends not only on *what* is to be shot, but also on *how* it is to be shot. This *how* must be planned by the director and carried out by the cameraman.

THE CAMERA COMPELS THE SPECTATOR TO SEE AS THE DIRECTOR WISHES

By selection of the camera set-up, director and cameraman lead the spectator after them. The viewpoint of the camera is scarcely ever the exact viewpoint of an ordinary spectator. The power of the film director lies in the fact that he can force the spectator to see an object *not* as it is easiest to see it. The camera, changing its position, as it were, " behaves " in a given mode and manner. It is, as it were, charged with a conditioned relation to the object shot : now, urged by heightened interest, it delves into details ; now it contemplates the general whole of the picture. Often it places itself in the position of the hero and records what he sees ; sometimes it even " feels " with the hero. Thus, in *The Leather Pushers*, the camera sees with the eyes of a beaten boxer rendered dizzy by a blow, and shows the revolving, swimming picture of the amphitheatre.

The camera can " feel " also with the spectator. Here we encounter a very interesting method of film-work. It can be said with completest safety that man apprehends the world around him in varying ways, depending on his emotional condition. A number of attempts on the part of the film director has been directed towards the creation, by means of special methods of shooting, of a given emotional condition in the spectator, and thus the strengthening of the impression of the scene. Griffith was the first to shoot tragic situations as if through a light mist, explaining it by his desire to force the spectator to see, as it were, through tears.

In the film *Strike* there is an interesting sequence : workers out for a walk outside the town. In front of the strollers is an accordion-player. After the close-up in which the accordion is seen opening and shutting follows a series of pieces in which the men strolling are shot from various, often very distant, viewpoints. But the playing accordion remains held through all the shots, become barely visible, transparent. The landscapes and the groups walking afar off are visible through it. Here has been solved a peculiar problem. The director wished, in representing the picture of the stroll, laying it in the wide background of the landscape, to preserve simultaneously the characteristic rhythm of music heard sounding from far away. In this he succeeded. He succeeded thanks to the fact that the cameraman was able to find a concrete method for the realisation of the director's idea. To take this scene the accordion had to be swathed in black velvet, and it was necessary to calculate exactly the relative exposures of the shot with the landscape and of the separate shot of the accordion. A number of calculations had to be made, requiring a special knowledge of the craft of the cameraman and a technical inventive faculty. Here a complete blending of the work of director and cameraman was indispensable, and it conditioned the success of the achievement. The ideas of the director, in his work in making expressive the film image, only receive concrete embodiment when technical knowledge and the creative inventive faculty of the cameraman go hand in hand, or, in other words, when the cameraman is an organic member of the team and takes part in the creation of the film from beginning to end.

ON FILM TECHNIQUE

The selection of the camera set-up is but a special case of the work of selecting location. In working on location (and, on the average, fifty per cent of every production is made on location) [49] the first task of the cameraman and director is to select that part of space in which the scene is to develop. Such selection—like everything in film work—must not be by chance. Nature in the picture must never serve as background to the scene being taken, but must enter organically into its whole and become a part of its content. Every background *qua* background runs counter to the basic laws of films. If the director require in a scene only the actor and his performance, then every background, with the exception of a flat surface inconspicuous to the attention, will steal a part of the spectator's attention, and thus substantially nullify the basic method of film effect. [50] If something be brought into the picture besides the actor, this something must be linked to the general purpose of the scene. When, in *Way down East*, Griffith shows the lad Barthelmess knee-deep in thick grass, surrounded by trembling white daisies, bowing in the wind, in this picture nature does not serve as a chance background ; it is true that it is done in a rather sentimental way, but it vividly supplements and strengthens the image shown. The work on the formation of the " essence " of the picture, the necessity for an organic dependence between the developing action

157

and the surrounding, is so indispensable and important, that the finding and determination of the locations desired for exterior shots is one of the most complex stages in the preparatory work of the cameraman and director.

One of the first requirements set in the production work of the film director is exactitude. If, having thought out the filmic image of a scene, in taking it he desire to get that material out of which he can create what he has planned, he must inevitably think of each piece he is taking as an element of the future editing construction ; and the more exact is his work on the components of each element being taken, the more perfectly and clearly he will reach the possibility of realising his thought. From this derives the peculiar relation of the film director to the actor, to the objects, to all the real matter with which he works in the course of his production. Each separate piece of celluloid used by the director in taking a required shot must be used in such a way that its length shall exactly conform to the requirements of that general task which forms the basis of the filmic treatment of any given scene. In every given piece a movement begins and proceeds to an exact required point, and the time required for this movement must be exactly determined by the director. If the movement be accelerated or slowed down, the piece obtained will either over- or under-step the necessary length. Such an element of an incident, in departing from the length prescribed for it, will, in the process of editing, destroy the harmony of the filmic image planned. Everything chance, unorganised, everything unsubdued to the editing construction planned by the director in representing to himself the filmic image of each given incident—all this will lead inevitably to lack of clarity, to confusion in the final editing formation of the incident. An incident will awaken an impression from the screen only if it be well edited. Good editing will be achieved when for it is found the correct rhythm, and this rhythm is dependent on the relative lengths of the pieces, while the lengths of the pieces are in organic dependence on the content of each separate one. Therefore the director must enclose every shot he takes into a harsh, severely limited, temporal frame.

Let us, for example, suppose that we are editably taking an incident with an actor. The incident is as follows : The actor sits in an armchair tensely awaiting his possible arrest. He hears that some one has approached the door ; he watches intensely, sees the handle of the door beginning to move. The actor slowly takes out his revolver that he had hidden between the back and the seat of the chair ; the door begins to open. He quickly aims the revolver, but, there enters unexpectedly, instead of the policemen, a boy carrying some puppies (from the film *Beyond the Law*).

The editing is written as follows :

1. The actor sitting in the armchair alters his position, as if he had heard a knock.

2. His tense, watching face.

3. Taken by itself : the moving door-handle.

4. Close-up—the hand of the actor, slowly and fumblingly drawing the revolver.

5. The slightly opening door.

6. The actor aims the revolver.

7. Through the door steps the boy with the puppies.

The elements of the incident, by means of which the attention of the spectator is turned now to the man, now to the door, now concentrates upon the moving handle, now upon the hand of the actor or the revolver, must, finally, blend upon the screen to the single image of an unbrokenly developing incident. Undoubtedly the director must, for the creation of a sharp break between the slowly increasing tension and the unexpectedly rapid *dénouement*, establish a definite, creatively discovered rhythm of editing. Every element of the incident has to be taken separately. And everything that the actor performs in the shooting of each piece must be exactly temporally limited. But it is not sufficient to set temporal boundaries ; within these boundaries the actor must carry out the given series of movements, must saturate every piece with the given clear and expressive plastic content. If room for chance were left in the actor's work, then not only a pause, a slowing down, but a superfluous movement on the part of the actor would already shatter those temporal limits that must infallibly be set by the director. This shattering, as we have already said, would alter the length of the piece, and thereby destroy the effect of the whole construction of the incident. We thus perceive that not only must temporal boundaries be exactly established, but also the movement form they enclose ; the plastic content of the acting work in each separate scene must be performed exactly, if the director wish to attain a definite result in the creation of that filmic image of the scene that is to effect an impression on the spectator from the screen, not now in its real, but in its filmic form. The exactitude of work in space and in time is an indispensable condition, by fulfilment of which the film technician can attain a clearly and vividly impressive filmic representation.

The same striving for exactitude must govern the director and cameraman not only in scene-construction, but also in selection of the parts of location from which the space on the screen is to be constructed. It may appear to suffice that if a river or a wood be required for a shot, a " pretty " river or wood be found and then the shooting begun. In reality, however, the director never seeks a river or a wood, he seeks the required " pictures." These required pictures, corresponding exactly to the problems of each scene, may be strewn over dozens of different rivers ; they will, however, be blended to a whole in the film. The director does not shoot nature ; he uses it for his future composition in editing. The problem set by this composition may be strict to such a degree that director and camera-man often forcibly alter and reconstruct a part of nature in trying to obtain the form required. The breaking away of interfering boughs, the felling of a superfluous tree, its transplantation whithersoever may be necessary, the damming of a river, the filling of it with blocks of ice—all this is characteristic for the film technician, always and by all means making use of natural material for the construction of the filmic image required. The employment of nature as material reaches its extremest expression in the construction of natural scenes in the studio, when from real earth, real stones, sand, live trees, and water, are exactly created in the studio just those forms required by the director.

The selection of the shooting location and the determination of the camera set-up, as a whole technically termed " selection of the picture," are always complicated by yet another condition. This condition is light. We have already spoken of the powerful influence of light. Light it is that finally creates that form which is transferred to the screen. Only when the object is lit in the required manner and to the required intensity is it ready for shooting. The appearance on the celluloid projected upon the screen is only a combination of light and dark specks. On the screen there is nothing but light, and it is quite obvious, therefore, that in controlling the light at the taking we are actually performing the work of making the future image. Feeling for the quality and intensity of light is inseparably bound up with the knowledge of that relation between the object and its later appearance upon the celluloid which belongs exclusively to the technique of the cameraman.

THE LABORATORY

Everything that has been said already about the necessity for the close relation of all those collaborating in the production of the film relates also in full to the cameraman. Through the director, the work of whom on the various processes and happenings of reality he transforms to filmic material, the cameraman is bound to the other members of the team, the actor and the scenarist. He, in his turn, serves as the connecting link between the director and the technicians of the laboratory, the work of which is the next stage of working out the film material, directly following the shooting.

Only after the development of the negative and the printing of the positive does the director at last receive in pure form the film material from which he can assemble his work. Just as every other stage of film production, the work of the laboratory also involves more than the simple execution to pattern of standardised processes (chemical treatments of the exposed film). Its tasks are very often the continuation of the ideas originated by the scenarist and pursued by the director and cameraman. The Griffithian twilight in *America* could not have been obtained without a developer of the necessary synthetic properties and power. Only now, when before us appear all the pieces necessary for the creation of the film, at last in the shape of images printed on positive stock, only now ends the organic liaison between all the workers on the film production, that liaison which is an indispensable condition of the creation of a " real," significant, finished work.

The director now begins to join his detached pieces to a whole. We now leave him engaged on that basic creative process of which we spoke at the beginning of this essay.[51]

COLLECTIVISM : THE BASIS OF FILM-WORK

This essay on the film director has covered all the collaborators in the production of a film. It could not have been otherwise. The work of film-making has all the properties of an industrial undertaking. The technical manager can achieve nothing without foremen and workmen, and their collective effort will lead to no good result if every collaborator limit himself only to a mechanical performance of his narrow function. Team-work is that which makes every, even the most insignificant, task a part of the living work and organically connects it to the general task. It is a property of film-work that the smaller the number of persons directly taking part in it, the more disjointed is their activity and the worse is the finished product of their work—that is, the film.

(First published as Number Five of a series of popular scientific film handbooks by Kinopetchat, Moscow and Leningrad, 1926.)

III

TYPES INSTEAD OF ACTORS[52]

(ADDRESS DELIVERED TO THE FILM SOCIETY)

FIRST of all allow me, in the name of Russian film-workers, to greet in your person that organisation [the Film Society] which was the first to undertake the task of acquainting the English public with our films.

.   .   .   .   .

I ask you to forgive my bad English. Unfortunately my knowledge of it is so limited that I cannot speak, but must read my notes, and even then not very well. I shall endeavour to acquaint you in this short speech with some of the principles which form the basis of our work. When I say " our " I mean, in fact, the directors of the so-called left wing.

I began my work in the films quite accidentally. Up to 1920 I was a chemical engineer, and, to tell you the truth, looked at films with contempt, though I was very fond of art in other forms. I, like many others, could not agree that films were an art. I looked upon them as an inferior substitute for the stage, that is all.

Such an attitude is not to be wondered at,

considering how rubbishy the films shown at the time were. There are many such films even now ; in Germany nowadays they are called *Kitsch*. Primitive subjects calculated to appeal to the average bad taste—a cheap showman's booth entertainment that at first gives a good return to the owner, but in the long run demoralises the public.

The methods applied to the preparation of such films have nothing in common with art. The producers of such films have only one thing in mind, and that is to photograph as many lovely girls' faces from as many angles as possible, and to provide the hero with as many victories in fights as possible, and to wind up with an effective kiss as finale. There was nothing extraordinary in the fact that such films could not attract any serious attention.

.   .   .   .   .

But a chance meeting with a young painter and theoretician of the film—Kuleshov—gave an opportunity to learn his ideas, making me change my views completely. It was from him that I first learned of the meaning of the word " *montage*," a word which played such an important part in the development of our film-art.

From our contemporary point of view, Kuleshov's ideas were extremely simple. All he said was this : " In every art there must be firstly a material, and secondly a method of composing this material specially adapted to this art." The musician has sounds as material and composes them in time.

ON FILM TECHNIQUE

The painter's materials are colour, and he combines them in space on the surface of the canvas. What then, is the material which the film director possesses, and what are the methods of composition of his material?

Kuleshov maintained that the material in film-work consists of pieces of film, and that the composition method is their joining together in a particular, creatively discovered order. He maintained that film-art does not begin when the artists act and the various scenes are shot—this is only the preparation of the material. Film-art begins from the moment when the director begins to combine and join together the various pieces of film. By joining them in various combinations, in different orders, he obtains differing results.

.　　　.　　　.　　　.　　　.

Suppose, for example, we have three such pieces : on one is somebody's smiling face, on another is a frightened face, and on the third is a revolver pointing at somebody.

Let us combine these pieces in two different orders. Let us suppose that in the first instance we show, first the smiling face, then the revolver, then the frightened face ; and that the second time we show the frightened face first, then the revolver, then the smiling face. In the first instance the impression we get is that the owner of the face is a coward ; in the second that he is brave. This is certainly a crude example, but from contemporary films we can see more subtly that it is only by an able and inspired combination of pieces of the shot film that the strongest impression can be effected in the audience.

Kuleshov and I made an interesting experiment. We took from some film or other several close-ups of the well-known Russian actor Mosjukhin. We chose close-ups which were static and which did not express any feeling at all—quiet close-ups. We joined these close-ups, which were all similar, with other bits of film in three different combinations. In the first combination the close-up of Mosjukhin was immediately followed by a shot of a plate of soup standing on a table. It was obvious and certain that Mosjukhin was looking at this soup. In the second combination the face of Mosjukhin was joined to shots showing a coffin in which lay a dead woman. In the third the close-up was followed by a shot of a little girl playing with a funny toy bear. When we showed the three combinations to an audience which had not been let into the secret the result was terrific. The public raved about the acting of the artist. They pointed out the heavy pensiveness of his mood over the forgotten soup, were touched and moved by the deep sorrow with which he looked on the dead woman, and admired the light, happy smile with which he surveyed the girl at play. But we knew that in all three cases the face was exactly the same.

But the combination of various pieces in one or another order is not sufficient. It is necessary to be able to control and manipulate the length of these pieces, because the combination of pieces of varying length is effective in the same way as the combination of sounds of various length in music, by creating the rhythm of the film and by means of their varying effect on the audience. Quick, short pieces rouse excitement, while long pieces have a soothing effect.

.   .   .   .   .

To be able to find the requisite order of shots or pieces, and the rhythm necessary for their combination—that is the chief task of the director's art. This art we call *montage*—or constructive editing. It is only with the help of *montage* that I am able to solve problems of such complexity as the work on the artists' acting.

The thing is, that I consider that the main danger for an actor who is working on the films is so-called " stagey acting." I want to work only with real material—this is my principle. I maintain that to show, alongside real water and real trees and grass, a property beard pasted on the actor's face, wrinkles traced by means of paint, or stagey acting is impossible. It is opposed to the most elementary ideas of style.

But what should one do? It is very difficult to work with stage actors. People so exceptionally talented that they can live, and not act, are very seldom met with, while if you ask an ordinary actor merely to sit quietly and not to act, he will act for your benefit the type of a non-acting actor.

PUDOVKIN

I have tried to work with people who had never seen either a play or a film, and I succeeded, with the help of *montage*, in achieving some result. It is true that in this method one must be very cunning ; it is necessary to invent thousands of tricks to create the mood required in the person and to catch the right moment to photograph him.

For example, in the film *The Heir to Jenghiz Khan*, I wanted to have a crowd of Mongols looking with rapture on a precious fox-fur. I engaged a Chinese conjuror and photographed the faces of the Mongols watching him. When I joined this piece to a piece of the shot of fur held in the hands of the seller I got the result required. Once I spent endless time and effort trying to obtain from an actor a good-natured smile—it did not succeed because the actor kept on " acting." When I did catch a moment, and photographed his face smiling at a joke I made, he had been firmly convinced that the shooting was over.

. . . . .

I am continuously working on the perfection of this method, and I believe in its future. Of course, one can photograph in this way only short bits of separate actors, and it is the art of the director, with the help of *montage*, to make out of the short bits a whole, a living figure.

Not for a moment do I regret that I took this line. I more and more often work with casual actors, and I am satisfied by the results. In my last film I met the Mongols, absolutely uncultured people who did not even understand my language, and, despite this, the Mongols in that film can easily compete, as far as acting honours are concerned, with the best actors.

.   .   .   .   .

In conclusion I would like to tell you of my views on a very tricky question which I have met recently. I mean sound films.

I think that their future is enormous, but when I use the expression " sound film " I do not in any way mean dialogue films, in which the speech and various sound effects are perfectly synchronised with their corresponding visual images on the screen. Such films are nothing but a photographic variety of stage plays. They are, of course, new and interesting, and will undoubtedly at first attract the curiosity of the public, but not for long.

The real future belongs to sound films of another kind. I visualise a film in which sounds and human speech are wedded to the visual images on the screen in the same way as that in which two or more melodies can be combined by an orchestra. The sound will correspond to the film in the same way as the orchestra corresponds to the film to-day.

The only difference from the method of to-day is that the director will have the control of the sound in his own hands, and not in the hands of the conductor of the orchestra, and that the wealth of those sounds will be overwhelming. All the sounds of the whole world, beginning with the whisper of a man or the cry of a child and rising to the roar of an explosion. The expressionism of a film can reach unthought-of heights.

It can combine the fury of a man with the roar of a lion. The language of the cinema will achieve the power of the language of literature.

.   .   .   .   .

But one must never show on the screen a man and reproduce his word exactly synchronised with the movements of his lips. This is cheap imitation, an ingenious trick that is useless to anyone.

One of the Berlin Pressmen asked me : " Do you not think that it would be good to hear, for instance, in the film *Mother*, the weeping mother when she watches over the body of her dead husband ? " I answered : " If this were possible I would do it thus : The mother is sitting near the body and the audience hears clearly the sound of the water dripping in the wash-basin ; then comes the shot of the silent head of the dead man with the burning candle ; and here one hears a subdued weeping."

That is how I imagine to myself a film that sounds, and I must point out that such a film will remain international. Words and sounds heard, but not seen on the screen, could be rendered in any language, and changed with the film for every country.

ON FILM TECHNIQUE

Allow me to conclude this note by thanking you for the patience and attention with which you have listened through my address.

(Delivered, in the present translation by I. M. and S. S. N., to the Film Society, in Stewart's Café, Regent Street, February 3, 1929. Published, slightly amended, by the *Cinema*, February 6, 1929.)

IV

CLOSE-UPS IN TIME [53]

(ADDRESS FOR THE WORKERS' FILM FEDERATION)

DURING the summer of the year 1930 I attended a meeting in the Palace of Labour at Moscow. Work was ended. Outside in the street it was raining hard, and we had to wait for it to stop. The globules of water rebounded slightly from the sill ; now they were large, now smaller until they vanished in the air. They moved, rising and falling in curves of various form, in a complex yet definite rhythm. Sometimes several streams, probably influenced by the wind, united into one. The water would strike upon the stone, scattering into a transparent, shivering fan, then fall, and anew the round and glistening globules would leap over the edge, mingling with the tiny raindrops descending through the air.

What a rain ! I was but watching it, yet I felt to the full its freshness, its moisture, its generous plenty. I felt drenched in it. It poured down on my head and over my shoulders. Most certainly the earth, soaked brimful, must long have ceased to drink it up. The shower, as commonly occurs in summer, ended almost abruptly, scattering its last drops beneath the already brightening sun.

I left the building and, passing through the garden,

paused to watch a man working with a scythe. He was bared to the waist. The muscles of his back contracted and expanded with the even sweep of the scythe. Its damp blade, flying upwards, caught the sunlight and burst for a moment into a sharp, blinding flame. I stepped near. The scythe buried itself in the wet, rank grass, which, as it was cut away beneath, slowly gave down on to the ground in a supple movement impossible to describe. Gleaming in the slanting sunrays, the raindrops trembled on the tips of the pointed, drooping grass-blades, tumbled, and fell. The man mowed ; I stood and gazed. And once more I found myself gripped by an unaccustomed feeling of excitement at the grandeur of the spectacle. Never had I seen wet grass like this ! Never had I seen how the rain-drops tumble down the grooves of its narrow blades ! For the first time I was seeing how its stalks fall as they yield to the sweep of the scythe !

And, as always, according to my invariable custom (doubtless one familiar to all film directors), I tried to imagine to myself all this represented on the screen. I recalled the reaping scenes recorded and included scores of times in an abundance of pictures, and felt sharply the poverty of these lifeless photographs in comparison with the marvellous and pregnant richness I had seen. One has only to picture to oneself the flat, grey manikin waving a long pole, invariably in slightly speeded tempo, to picture the grass shot from above and looking like dry, tangled matting, for it to be clear in what measure all this is poor and primitive. I recall even Eisenstein's technically magnificent *General Line*, where, worked out in a complex editing construction, is shown a reaping competition. Nothing of it remains in my memory, save men rapidly waving poorly distinguishable scythes. The question was how to capture, how to reproduce to others this full and profound sensation of the actual processes that twice this day had made me marvel. I tortured myself on my homeward way, flinging myself in my thoughts from side to side, seizing and rejecting, testing and being disappointed. And suddenly, at last, I had it !

When the director shoots a scene, he changes the position of the camera, now approaching it to the actor, now taking it farther away from him, according to the subject of his concentration of the spectator's attention—either some general movement or else some particularity, perhaps the features of an individual. This is the way he controls the spacial construction of the scene. Why should he not do precisely the same with the temporal ? Why should not a given detail be momentarily emphasised by retarding it on the screen, and rendering it by this means particularly outstanding and unprecedently clear ? Was not the rain beating on the stone of the window-sill, the grass falling to the ground, retarded, in relation to me, by my sharpened attention ? Was it not thanks to this sharpened attention that I perceived ever so much more than I had ever seen before ?

ON FILM TECHNIQUE

I tried in my mind's eye to shoot and construct the mowing of the grass approximately as follows :

1. A man stands bared to the waist. In his hands is a scythe. Pause. He swings the scythe. (The whole movement goes in normal speed, i.e., has been recorded at normal speed.)

2. The sweep of the scythe continues. The man's back and shoulders. Slowly the muscles play and grow tense. (Recorded very fast with a " slow-motion " apparatus, so that the movement on the screen comes out unusually slow.)

3. The blade of the scythe slowly turning at the culmination of its sweep. A gleam of the sun flares up and dies out. (Shot in " slow motion.")

4. The blade flies downward. (Normal speed.)

5. The whole figure of the man brings back the scythe over the grass at normal speed. A sweep —back. A sweep—back. A sweep. . . . And at the moment when the blade of the scythe touches the grass—

6. —slowly (in " slow motion ") the cut grass sways, topples, bending and scattering glittering drops.

7. Slowly the muscles of the back relax and the shoulders withdraw.

8. Again the grass slowly topples, lies flat.

9. The scythe-blade swiftly lifting from the earth.

10. Similarly swift, the man sweeping with the scythe. He mows, he sweeps.

11. At normal speed, a number of men mowing, sweeping their scythes in unison.

12. Slowly raising his scythe a man moves off through the dusk.

This is a very approximate sketch. After the actual shooting, I edited it differently—more complexly, using shots taken at very various speeds. Within each separate set-up were new, more finely graduated speeds. When I saw the result upon the screen I realised that the idea was sound. The new rhythm, independent of the real, deriving from the combination of shots at a variety of speeds, yielded a deepened, one might say remarkably enriched, sense of the process portrayed upon the screen.

The chance spectators, who were ignorant of the nature of the method employed, confessed to having experienced an almost physical sense of moisture, weight, and force. I tried to shoot and edit the rain in the same way. I took long shots and close-ups at different speeds, using " slow motion." The slow striking of the first heavy drops against dry dust. They fall, scattering into separate dark globules. The falling of rain on a surface of water : the swift impact, a transparent column leaps up, slowly subsides, and passes away in equally slow circles. An increase of speed proceeds parallel with the strengthening of the rain and the widening of the set-up. The huge, wide expanse of a steadily pouring network of heavy rain, and then, suddenly, the sharp introduction of a close-up of a single stream smashing against a stone balustrade. As the glittering drops leap up—their movements are exceptionally slow— can be seen all the complex, wondrous play of their intersecting paths through the air. Once more the movement speeds, but already the rain is lessening. Closing, come shots of wet grass beneath the sun. The wind waves it, it slowly sways, the raindrops slide away, and fall. This movement, taken with the highest speed of the " slow-motion " camera, showed me for the first time that it is possible to record and reproduce the movement of grass before the wind. In earlier pictures I had seen nothing but a dry, hysterically trembling tangle. I am deeply convinced both of the need for and the sense of practicability achieved by this new method.

It is of the highest importance to appreciate, in all its profundity, the essence of this work in " slow-motion," and to exploit it not as a trick, but as a means of consciously, at required points, retarding or accelerating movement *to a precise degree*. It is necessary to be able to exploit every possible speed of the camera, from the very highest, yielding on the screen exceptional slowness of movement, to the very least, resulting on the screen in an incredible swiftness. Sometimes a very slight retardation just of the plain and simple walk of a human being endows it with a weight and significance that could never be rendered by acting. I tried to render a shell explosion by an editing construction of shots at various speeds : Slow at the beginning ; then very rapid flight ; slightly retarded development ;

the ground slowly sinks away, and then suddenly fragments of earth start flying very rapidly straight at the spectator ; for a fraction of a second an instantaneous change and they are flying slowly, crushingly and terribly, then an equally sudden change and once more they are flying fast. It came out excellently !

Cinematography with the " slow-motion " camera has long been practised. The disconcerting strangeness of retarded movement on the screen, the possibility of perceiving forms that ordinarily are imperceptible and invisible, yet none the less existent in actuality, exerts so powerful an impression on the spectator that it is already no uncommon thing for directors to insert shots taken in " slow-motion " into their pictures. (It is to the point here to note that the charm of a cleverly " captured " movement in a drawing often depends on the same " slow-motion " effect, only here the role of the " slow-motion " camera is played by the artist's eye.)

But all the directors who have exploited retardation of movement have failed to do the one thing that, in my view, is the most important. They have failed to incorporate the retarded movement in the editing construction as a whole—in the general rhythmical flow of the film. Suppose they have been using " slow-motion " to shoot a horse jumping, then they have shot it as a whole, and as a whole inserted it in the picture, almost as a separate " dragged in " sequence. I have heard that Jean Epstein shot a whole film in " slow-motion " (I think it was *The Fall of the House of Usher*, from E. A. Poe's story), using the effect of retarded motion to give a mystical tinge to every scene.

This is not at all what I mean. I refer to the incorporation of various degrees of retarded speed of movement integrally in the construction of a given editing phrase. A short-length shot in " slow-motion " can be placed between two longer normal-speeded shots, concentrating the attention of the spectator at the desired point for a moment. " Slow-motion " in editing is not a *distortion* of an actual process. It is a portrayal more profound and precise, a *conscious guidance* of the attention of the spectator.

This is the eternal characteristic of cinematography. I tried to construct the blow of a fist on a table as follows : The fist rushes swiftly down on to the table, and the moment it touches it the subsequent shots show a glass, stood nearby, slowly jumping, rocking, and falling. By this conjunction of rapid and slow shots was produced an almost audible, exceptionally sharply sensed impression of a violent blow. The full processes shown upon the screen by the editing together of shots recorded at various speeds seem endowed with a rhythm peculiar to themselves, a sort of breath of life of their own. They are alive, for they have received the vital spark of an appraising, selecting, and all-comprehending concept. They do not slip by like landscape past the window of a railway carriage beneath the indifferent glance of a passenger familiar with the route. They unfold and grow, like the narrative of

PUDOVKIN

a gifted observer, who has perceived the thing or process more clearly than anyone else has ever done before.

I am convinced that this method can be extended to work in shooting a man—his expression, his gestures. I already know by experience what precious material is afforded by a man's smile shot in " slow-motion." I have extracted from such shots some remarkable pauses, wherein the eyes alone are engaged in a smile that the lips have not yet begun to share. A tremendous future stretches before the " close-up of time." Particularly in sound film, where the rhythm is given point and complexity by its conjunction with sound, particularly here is it important.

(Written but not delivered as an address for the Workers' Film Federation Summer School, 1931, and published, in the present translation by I. M. and H. C. Stevens, in *The Observer*, Jan. 31, 1932, by courtesy of whose editor it is now reprinted.)

V

ASYNCHRONISM AS A PRINCIPLE OF SOUND FILM

THE technical invention of sound has long been accomplished, and brilliant experiments have been made in the field of recording. This technical side of sound-film making may be regarded as already relatively perfected, at least in America. But there is a great difference between the technical development of sound and its development as a means of *expression*. The expressive achievements of sound still lie far behind its technical possibilities. I assert that many theoretical questions whose answers are clear to us are still provided in practice only with the most primitive solutions. Theoretically, we in the Soviet Union are in advance of Western Europe and U.S.A.

Our first question is : What new content can be brought into the cinema by the use of Sound ? It would be entirely false to consider sound merely as a mechanical device enabling us to enhance the naturalness of the image. Examples of such most primitive sound effects : in the silent cinema we were able to show a car, now in sound film we can add to its image a record of its natural sound ; or again, in silent film a speaking man was associated with a title, now we hear his voice. The role which sound is to play in film is much more significant than a slavish imitation of naturalism on these lines ; the first function of sound is to *augment the potential expressiveness of the film's content.*

If we compare the sound to the silent film, we find that it is possible to explain the content more deeply to the spectator with relatively the same expenditure of time. It is clear that this deeper insight into the content of the film cannot be given to the spectator simply by adding an accompaniment of naturalistic sound ; we must do something more. This something more is the development of the image and the sound strip each along a separate rhythmic course. They must not be tied to one another by naturalistic imitation but connected as the result of the interplay of action. Only by this method can we find a new and richer form than that available in the silent film. Unity of sound and image is realised by an interplay of meanings which results, as we shall presently show, in a more exact rendering of nature than its superficial copying. In silent film, by our editing of a variety of images, we began to attain the unity and freedom that is realised in nature only in its abstraction by the human mind. Now in sound film we can, within the same strip of celluloid, not only edit different points in space, but can cut into association with the image selected sounds that reveal and heighten the character of each—wherever in silent film we had a conflict of but two opposing elements, now we can have four.

A primitive example of the use of sound to reveal an inner content can be cited in the expression of the stranding of a town-bred man in the midst of the desert. In silent film we should have had to cut in a shot of the town ; now in sound film we can carry town-associated sounds into the desert and edit them there in place of the natural desert sounds. Uses of this kind are already familiar to film directors in Western Europe, but it is not generally recognised that the principal elements in sound film are the asynchronous and not the synchronous ; moreover, that the synchronous use is, in actual fact, only exceptionally correspondent to natural perception. This is not, as may first appear, a theoretical figment, but a conclusion from observation.

For example, in actual life you, the reader, may suddenly hear a cry for help ; you see only the window ; you then look out and at first see nothing but the moving traffic. But *you do not hear the sound natural to these cars and buses* ; instead you hear still only the cry that first startled you. At last you find with your eyes the point from which the sound came ; there is a crowd, and someone is lifting the injured man, *who is now quiet*. But, now watching the man, you become aware of the din of traffic passing, and in the midst of its noise there gradually grows the piercing signal of the ambulance. At this your attention is caught by the clothes of the injured man : his suit is like that of your brother, who, you now recall, was due to visit you at two o'clock. In the tremendous tension that follows, the anxiety and uncertainty whether this possibly dying man may not indeed be your brother himself, *all sound ceases*

and there exists for your perceptions total silence.
Can it be two o'clock? You look at the clock and
at the same time you hear its ticking. *This is the
first synchronised moment* of an image and its caused
sound since first you heard the cry.

Always there exist two rhythms, the rhythmic
course of the objective world and the tempo and
rhythm with which man observes this world. The
world is a whole rhythm, while man receives
only partial impressions of this world through his
eyes and ears and to a lesser extent through his
very skin. The tempo of his impressions varies with
the rousing and calming of his emotions, while the
rhythm of the objective world he perceives continues
in unchanged tempo.

The course of man's perceptions is like editing,
the arrangement of which can make corresponding
variations in speed, with sound just as with image.
It is possible therefore for sound film to be made
correspondent to the objective world and man's
perception of it together. The image may retain
the tempo of the world, while the sound strip follows
the changing rhythm of the course of man's perceptions, or vice versa. This is a simple and obvious
form for counterpoint of sound and image.

Consider now the question of straightforward
Dialogue in sound film. In all the films I have seen,
persons speaking have been represented in one of
two ways. Either the director was thinking entirely
in terms of theatre, shooting his whole speaking
group through in one shot with a moving camera.

ON FILM TECHNIQUE

Using thus the screen only as a primitive means of recording a natural phenomenon, exactly as it was used in early silent films before the discovery of the technical possibilities of the cinema had made it an art-form. Or else, on the other hand, the director had tried to use the experience of silent film, the art of montage in fact, composing the dialogue from separate shots that he was free to edit. But in this latter case the effect he gained was just as limited as that of the single shots taken with a moving camera, because he simply gave a series of close-ups of a man speaking, allowed him to finish the given phrase on his image, and then followed that shot with one of the man answering. In doing so the director made of montage and editing no more than a cold verbatim report, and switched the spectator's attention from one speaker to another without any adequate emotional or intellectual justification.

Now, by means of editing, a scene in which three or more persons speak can be treated in a number of different ways. For example, the spectator's interest may be held by the speech of the first, and—with the spectator's attention—we hold the close-up of the first person lingering with him when his speech is finished and *hearing* the voice of the commenced answer of the next speaker before passing on to the latter's image. We see the image of the second speaker only *after* becoming acquainted with his voice. Here sound has preceded image.

Or, alternatively, we can arrange the dialogue so that when a question occurs at the end of the given speech, and the spectator is interested in the answer, he can immediately be shown the person addressed, only presently hearing the answer. Here the sound follows the image.

Or, yet again, the spectator having grasped the import of a speech may be interested in its *effect*. Accordingly, while the speech is still in progress, he can be shown a given listener, or indeed given a review of all those present and mark their reactions towards it.

These examples show clearly how the director, by means of editing, can move his audience emotionally or intellectually, so that it experiences a special rhythm in respect to the sequence presented on the screen.

But such a relationship between the director in his cutting-room and his future audience can be established only if he has a psychological insight into the nature of his audience and its consequent relationship to the content of the given material.

For instance, if the first speaker in a dialogue grips the attention of the audience, the second speaker will have to utter a number of words before they will so affect the consciousness of the audience that it will adjust its full attention to him. And, contrariwise, if the intervention of the second speaker is more vital to the scene at the moment than the impression made by the first speaker, then the audience's full attention will at once be riveted on him. I am sure, even, that it is possible to build up a dramatic incident with the recorded sound of a speech and the image of the unspeaking listener where the latter's reaction is the most urgent emotion in the scene. Would a director of any imagination handle a scene in a court of justice where a sentence of death is being passed by filming the judge pronouncing sentence in preference to recording visually the immediate reactions of the condemned ?

In the final scenes of my first sound film *Deserter* my hero tells an audience of the forces that brought him to the Soviet Union. During the whole of the film his worse nature has been trying to stifle his desire to escape these forces ; therefore this moment, when he at last succeeds in escaping them and himself desires to recount his cowardice to his fellow-workers is the high-spot of his emotional life. Being unable to speak Russian, his speech has to be translated.

At the beginning of this scene we see and hear shots longish in duration, first of the speaking hero, then of his translator. In the process of development of the episode the images of the translator become shorter and the majority of his words accompany the images of the hero, according as the interest of the audience automatically fixes on the latter's psychological position. We can consider the composition of sound in this example as similar to the objective rhythm and dependent on the actual time relationships existing between the speakers. Longer or shorter pauses between the voices are conditioned solely by the readiness or hesitation of the next speaker in what he wishes to say. But the image introduces to the screen a new element, the

subjective emotion of the spectator and its length
of duration ; in the image longer or shorter does
not depend upon the identity of the speaking man,
but upon the desire of the spectator to look for a
longer or shorter period. Here the sound has an
objective character, while the image is conditioned
by subjective appreciation ; equally we may have
the contrary—a subjective sound and an objective
image. As illustration of this latter combination I
cite a demonstration in the second part of *Deserter* ;
here my sound is purely musical. Music, I maintain,
must in sound film *never be the accompaniment*. It must
retain its own line.

In the second part of *Deserter* the image shows at
first the broad streets of a Western capital ; suave
police direct the progress of luxurious cars ; everything is decorous, the ebb and flow of an established
life. The characteristic of this opening is quietness,
until the calm surface is broken by the approach of
a workers' demonstration bearing aloft their flag.
The streets clear rapidly before the approaching
demonstration, its ranks swell with every moment.
The spirit of the demonstrators is firm, and their
hopes rise as they advance. Our attention is turned
to the preparations of the police ; their horses and
motor-vehicles gather as their intervention grows
imminent ; now their champing horses charge the
demonstrators to break their ranks with flying hoofs,
the demonstrators resist with all their might and
the struggle rages fiercest round the workers' flag.
It is a battle in which all the physical strength is

marshalled on the side of the police, sometimes it prevails and the spirit of the demonstrators seems about to be quelled, then the tide turns and the demonstrators rise again on the crest of the wave ; at last their flag is flung down into the dust of the streets and trampled to a rag beneath the horses' hoofs. The police are arresting the workers ; their whole cause seems lost, suppressed never to re-arise —the welter of the fighting dies down—against the background of the defeated despair of the workers we return to the cool decorum of the opening of the scene. There is no fight left in the workers. Suddenly, unexpectedly, before the eyes of the police inspector, the workers' flag appears hoisted anew and the crowd is re-formed at the end of the street.

The course of the image twists and curves, as the emotion within the action rises and falls. Now, if we used music as an *accompaniment* to this image we should open with a quiet melody, appropriate to the soberly guided traffic ; at the appearance of the demonstration the music would alter to a march ; another change would come at the police preparations, menacing the workers—here the music would assume a threatening character ; and when the clash came between workers and police—a tragic moment for the demonstrators—the music would follow this visual mood, descending ever further into themes of despair. Only at the resurrection of the flag could the music turn hopeful. A development of this type would give only the superficial aspect of the scene, the undertones of meaning would be ignored :

accordingly I suggested to the composer (Shaporin) the creation of a music the dominating emotional theme of which should *throughout* be courage and the certainty of ultimate victory. From beginning to end the music must develop in a gradual growth of power. This direct, unbroken theme I connected with the complex curves of the image. The image succession gives us in its progress first the emotion of hope, its replacement by danger, then the rousing of the workers' spirit of resistance, at first successful, at last defeated, then finally the gathering and reassembly of their inherent power and the hoisting of their flag. The image's progress curves like a sick man's temperature chart ; while the music in direct contrast is firm and steady. When the scene opens peacefully the music is militant ; when the demonstration appears the music carries the spectators right into its ranks. With its batoning by the police, the audience feels the rousing of the workers, wrapped in their emotions the audience is itself emotionally receptive to the kicks and blows of the police. As the workers lose ground to the police, the insistent victory of the music grows ; yet again, when the workers are defeated and disbanded, the music becomes yet more powerful still in its spirit of victorious exaltation ; and when the workers hoist the flag at the end the music at last reaches its climax, and only now, at its conclusion, does its spirit coincide with that of the image.

What role does the music play here ? Just as the image is an objective perception of events, so the music expresses the subjective appreciation of this objectivity. The sound reminds the audience that with every defeat the fighting spirit only receives new impetus to the struggle for final victory in the future.

It will be appreciated that this instance, where the sound plays the subjective part in the film, and the image the objective, is only one of many diverse ways in which the medium of sound film allows us to build a counterpoint, and I maintain that only by such counterpoint can primitive naturalism be surpassed and the rich deeps of meaning potential in sound film creatively handled be discovered and plumbed.

(Written for this edition and translated by Marie Seton and I.M.)

VI

RHYTHMIC PROBLEMS IN MY FIRST SOUND FILM

IT is sad to find that, since the introduction of sound and the predominance of talking films, directors both in the West and in the Soviet Union have suddenly lost the sense of dynamic rhythm that they had built up during the last years of the silent cinema. It is almost impossible to-day to find a film with the sharp dramatic rhythm of, for instance, the Odessa Steps sequence in *Potemkin*, or of certain episodes in the early picture *Intolerance*, which belongs to the first period when the hitherto mechanical film record became a creative medium. Most of the latest sound films are characterised by exceedingly slow development of subject and dialogue full of interminable pauses. Many directors are developing a talkie style that involves the use of explanatory words for matters that should be conceived visually ; this kind of style introduces elements from the Theatre into a medium where they are out of place. Theatre has its own technique, depending on the power of the spoken word since it is incapable of presenting visual changes in rapid sequence, while Cinema is based on the possibility of presenting a variety of visual impressions in a time and space differing from that obtaining in the natural material recorded.

ON FILM TECHNIQUE

I do not believe that this change of method is indicative of any audience change of taste. I think that the real situation is that directors hesitate to make experiments with sound, and particularly hesitate to apply montage to the sound strip.

Many hold the view that, with the introduction of sound into film, the cutting methods established during the development of silent films must all go by the board. The development of constructive editing of frequent changes of shot made possible in silent film the achievement of great richness of visual form. The human eye is capable of perceiving, easily and immediately, the content of a succession of visual shots, whereas, as they point out, the ear cannot with the same immediacy detect the significance of alterations in sound. Accordingly, they maintain, the rhythm of changing sound must be much slower than need be that of changing image. They are right, in so far as concerns the combination with a succession of short images of a series of equally short sound effects matched with them in a purely naturalistic relation. Certainly it would be impossible to compose the short shots of Eisenstein's Odessa Steps sequence in *Potemkin*—the soldiers shooting, the woman screaming, the children weeping—with sound cut in a parallel manner. Consequently, it is held, we must make each image longer, thus diminishing the richness of the visual form , the rapid montage of the silent film must give place to more leisurely scenes recorded from a more set distance and with a relatively fixed camera position, the construction being linked by the spoken word and not by the sequence of dynamically edited images. This policy, I maintain, is the line of least resistance, and instead of helping film to progress, holds it back, forcing it once again into its primitive position of mere photographic record of material actually suited to the Theatre. There is no necessity, in my view, to begin a sound when its corresponding image first appears and to cut it when its image has passed. Every strip of sound, speech, or music may develop unmodified while the images come and go in a sequence of short shots, or, alternatively, during images of longer duration the sound strip may change independently in a rhythm of its own. I believe that it is only along these lines that the Cinema can keep free from theatrical imitation, and advance beyond the bounds of Theatre, for ever limited by the supremacy of the spoken word, the fixture to one significant position throughout of decor and properties, the dependence of both action and audience's attention entirely upon the actor, and reduction of the world's wide globe to a single room less its fourth wall.

One of the most important problems in my *Deserter* was posed by the mass scenes—meetings, demonstrations, etc. First, it is necessary to understand that the mass never has been and never will be mere quantity ; it is a differentiated quality. It is a collection of individuals and quite different from their sum ; each mass consists of groups, each group of persons. These may be united by one emotion and one thought, and in that case their mass is the greatest force in the world. The conflicting processes at work within the groups to produce this result afford immediately obvious dramatic material, and accent upon the characteristics of individuals is an integral part of the creation of a living mass. What real method can there be of creating this qualitatively altered mass of individuals save by the editing of close-ups ? I have seen a German film in which Danton is shown speaking to the citizens of Paris ; he was placed at a window, and all we were allowed to know of his audience was their mass voice, like the traditional " voices off." Such a scene in a film is nothing else than a photograph of bad Theatre.

In the first reel of *Deserter* I have a meeting addressed by three persons one after the other, each producing a complexity of reactions in their audience. Each one is against the other two ; sometimes a member of the crowd interrupts a speaker, sometimes two or three of the crowd have a moment's discussion among themselves. The whole of the scene must move with the crowd's swaying mood, the clash of opposing wills must be shown, to achieve these ends I cut the sound exactly as freely as I cut the image. I used three distinct elements. First, the speeches ; second, sound close-ups of the interruptions—words, snatches of phrases, from members of the crowd ; and third, the general noise of the crowd varying in volume and recorded independently of any image.

I sought to compose these elements by the system

of montage. I took sound strips and cut, for example, for a word of a speaker broken in half by an interruption, for the interrupter in turn overswept by the tide of noise coming from the crowd, for the speaker audible again, and so on. Every sound was individually cut and the images associated are sometimes much shorter than the associated sound piece, sometimes as long as two sound pieces—those of speaker and interrupter, for example—while I show a number of individual reactions in the audience. Sometimes I have cut the general crowd noise into the phrases with scissors, and I have found that with an arrangement of the various sounds by cutting in this way it is possible to create a clear and definite, almost musical, rhythm : a rhythm that develops and increases short piece by short piece, till it reaches a climax of emotional effect that swells like the waves on a sea.

I maintain that directors lose all reason to be afraid of cutting the sound strip if they accept the principle of arranging it in a distinct composition. Provided that they are linked by a clear idea of the course to be pursued, various sounds can, exactly like images, be set side by side in montage. Remember the early days of the cinema, when directors were afraid to cut up the visual movement on the screen, and how Griffith's introduction of the close-up was misunderstood and by many labelled an unnatural and consequently an inadmissible method. Audiences in those days even cried : " Where are their legs ! "

ON FILM TECHNIQUE

Cutting was the development that first transformed the cinema from a mechanical process to a creative one. The slogan *Cut* remains equally imperative now that sound film has arrived. I believe that sound film will approach nearer to true musical rhythm than silent film ever did, and this rhythm must derive not merely from the movement of artist and objects on the screen, but also—and this is the consideration most important for us to-day—from exact cutting of the sound and arrangement of the sound pieces into a clear counterpoint with the image.

I worked out in fine rhythm, suitable to sound film, a special kind of musical composition for the May Day demonstration in *Deserter*. A hundred thousand men throng the streets, the air is filled with the echoing strains of massed bands, lifting the masses to exuberance. Into the patchwork of sound breaks singing, and the strains of accordions, the hooting of motor-cars, snatches of radio noises, shouts and huzzas, the powerful buzzing of aeroplanes. Certainly it would have been stupid to have attempted to create such a sound scene in the studio with orchestras and supers.

In order to give my future audience a true impression of this gigantic perspective of mass sound, its echoes and its multitudinous complexities, I recorded real material. I used two Moscow demonstrations, those in May and November of one year, to assemble the variety of sounds necessary for my future montage. I recorded pieces of various music and sound, varying in their volume, transitions from bands to crowd noises, and from hurrahs to the whirling propellers of aeroplanes, slogans from the radio and snatches of our songs. Just like long-shots and close-ups in silent film. Then followed the task of editing the thousand metres of sound to create the hundred metres of rhythmical composition. I tried to use the pieces like the separate instruments that combine to form an orchestra. I recorded two marching bands, and as passage of transition from one to the other cut between them some dominating sound like a mass hurrah or a whirling propeller. I endeavoured to bring the pieces already possessing a musical rhythm of their own into a new montage over-rhythm.

The images that go with this sound are edited with similar exactness, smiling workers, merry marching youths, a handsome sailor and the girls that flirt with him. But this sequence of images is but one of the rhythmical lines that make up the whole composition ; the music is never an accompaniment but a separate element of counterpoint ; both sound and image preserve their own line.

Perhaps a purer example of establishing rhythm in sound film occurs in another part of *Deserter*—the docks section. Here again I used natural sounds, heavy hammers, pneumatic drills working at different levels, the smaller noise of fixing a rivet, voices of sirens and the crashing crescendo of a falling chain. All these sounds I shot on the dock-side, and I composed them on the editing table, using various lengths, they served to me as notes of music. As finale of the docks scene I made a half-symbolic growth of the ship in images at an accelerated pace, while the sound in a complicated syncopation mounts to an ever greater and grandiose climax. Here I had a real musical task, and was obliged to " feel " the length of each strip in the same spirit as a musician " feels " the accent necessary for each note.

I have used only real sound because I hold the view that sound, like visual material, must be rich in its association, a thing impossible for reconstructed sound to be. I maintain that it is impossible artificially to establish perspective in sound ; it is impossible, for instance, to secure a real effect of a distant siren call in a closed studio and relatively near the microphone. A " distant " call achieved by a weak tone in the studio can never create the same reality of effect as a loud blast recorded half a mile away in the open air.

For the symphony of siren calls with which *Deserter* opens I had six steamers playing in a space of a mile and a half in the Port of Leningrad. They sounded their calls to a prescribed plan and we worked at night in order that we should have quiet.

Now that I have finished *Deserter* I am sure that sound film is potentially the art of the future. It is not an orchestral creation centring round music, nor yet a theatrical dominated by the factor of the actor, nor even is it akin to opera, it is a synthesis of each and every element—the oral, the visual, the

PUDOVKIN

philosophical ; it is our opportunity to translate the world in all its lines and shadows into a new art form that has succeeded and will supersede all the older arts, for it is the supreme medium in which we can express to-day and to-morrow.

(Written for this edition and translated by Marie Seton and I.M.)

NOTES AND APPENDICES

A.—GLOSSARIAL NOTES

IN the discussion of any technical subject it is necessary to employ technical terms. Technical cinematographic terms afford wide opportunities for ambiguity and obscurity in two ways. In the first place, they are usually not invented words, but words in common use extended to embrace technical meanings, to the confusion of the layman. In the second place, they vary slightly owing to differing practices in differing countries, or even in different studios, to the confusion of the expert. It is therefore desirable to establish, by definition, the sense in which technical terms have been employed in the preceding essays.

The word *Producer* in the film world is properly applied only to the business man, financial organiser, managing director of a producing concern; the driving-force rather than the technical guidance behind any given production. Producer in the stage sense has become *Director* in the films. This terminology is American in origin, but is now universal in England also.

The word *Scenario* is loosely applied to almost any written matter relating to the story preparation of a film in any of its stages. The course of development is roughly as follows*: The *Synopsis* is an

* *Theme* is a term of sense almost exactly congruous to its non-specialist meaning. It never represents a written document, except possibly in the case where the film's genesis is represented by the producer commanding, " Make me a war-film, a film of mother-love, or so forth."

outline of three or four typewritten pages containing the barest summary of character and action. It is made for the convenience of the producer or scenario-chooser, who may be too busy or unwilling to study potential subjects at length. In the adaptation of a book or a play, the synopsis represents the first stage. In the case of an original film-story it may rather be a précis of the next stage following.

This is the *Treatment*. A treatment is more extensive, usually from twenty to fifty pages. Here, although still written throughout in purely narrative form, we have, already indicated by means of a certain degree of detail in pictorial description, the actual visual potentialities of the suggested action. The use of the word scenario for either of these documents is more common with the layman than with the technician. Credit for a treatment is given, on a title or in a technical publication, more often by the words " Story by " than by association with the scenario. The words " Scenario by " imply work on a yet later stage—the shooting-script.

The *Shooting-script* is the scenario in its final cinematograph form, with all its incidents and appearances broken up in numbered sequence into the separate images from which they will be later represented. These separate images are called *Script-scenes*, listed, in the typewritten abbreviation of a usual shooting-script, simply as *Scenes*—e.g. Scene 1, Scene 2, etc. The words appearing upon the screen are also listed, as *Main-title* (the name of the film, and credit-titles), *Sub-titles* (never " captions "—this is a layman's term), *Inserts*, writings that are part of a scene, and *Superimposed titles*, a term carrying its own meaning.

It is evident from Pudovkin's essay on the scenario that an intermediate stage, quite unusual in England or America, intervenes in U.S.S.R. between the purely narrative *treatment* and its complete cinematographic analysis, the *shooting-script*. In this stage the titles stand already numbered, so do the separate tiny incidents, but there is no indication yet of the images to be selected to compose them. Such an incident Pudovkin terms a " scene," using the word almost in the sense in which it is used in a classical French play, to indicate not merely a change of place, but even a change of circumstance such as the entrance or exit of a player. To avoid confusion, the word scene has been avoided in this text, being rendered by " incident," except in the example given of this stage of treatment.*

The *Sequence* is a convenient division, into a series of which the action naturally falls. The sequences are already feelable even in the purely narrative treatment, and may each contain numbers of incidents, or scenes (in the Pudovkin sense). *The sequence of the stealing of the Princess* embraces all the business of running away with her, possibly involving interactions at several different geographical points. *The* " *scene* " (Pudovkin's sense) *of the Princess being stolen* probably covers only the actual carrying her out of her bedroom ; dragging her down the stairs would be another " scene " (incident, in the phraseology

* Those interested to study further the Soviet method of writing scenarios are referred to two published examples : that of Eisenstein and Alexandrov's " *The General Line*," published as a booklet in German, and extracts from Eisenstein, Alexandrov and Montagu's " An American Tragedy," published by the late H. A. Potamkin in " Close-Up."

I have employed). The separate parts that compose such a " scene," the as yet further indivisible atoms of the film-structure,* are termed variously according to their function considered at the moment. In their philosophic function we term them separate *images*; materially, separate *pieces of celluloid*; functionally, in the shooting-script, *script-scenes* (abb. *scenes*); as separate tasks upon the floor of the studio, or as separate parts of a finished, edited film, *Shots*; while in the cutting-room we find that each is represented by several subsimilar pieces, varying in number according to the number of times its action was respectively shot, spoken of as the several *Takes* of one shot.

On the floor of the studio we *Shoot* or *Take* the shots. The latter expression is perhaps the more common in speaking of a script-scene in single aspect (" How many times did we take that scene ? "), the former as a general term (" We shot ten scenes before lunch " ; " We could not shoot to-day, because of fog "). The word *Turn*, a transliteration of which is used in several European languages instead of *shoot*, is used in English only of the special activity of a cameraman (" Who turned for you on that picture ? "). Note that in our last example *Picture* is used to mean *whole film*. This sense is slang rather than technical. The *picture* should properly imply the composition space of an image†—i.e., *Picture-shape*, meaning screen-shape. The camera *Set-up*

---

* The actual subdivisibility of the atom is in film paralleled only by those instances (double exposure and the like) in which a single shot is blended from the effects of more than one separate camera-action.

† The composition space termed *picture* on the floor is termed a *frame* in the cutting-room, though its height, as a unit of the length of

refers to its position in relation to the shot object, not only its distance from the object, but also its angle to it. If we alter the one or the other we alter the set-up. The *Camera-angle*, in this sense, is the relation between the vertical and horizontal axes of the object shot on the one hand, and the plane of the film at the moment of shooting on the other. The *distances* of the camera from the shot object are technically designated as *Long-Shot, Mid-Shot,* and *Close-Up*, with their manifold supplementaries. No two studios, directors, or scenarists will agree absolutely about the measure of these shots, which have constancy only in their relation to one another. One technician will describe a distance showing the figure from crown to knee as a mid-shot, another as a medium long-shot. The full tally is something like *distance-shot, long-shot, medium long-shot, mid-shot, semi-close-up, close-up, big close-up* (or, in the appropriate special case, *big head*).

It is important to gain a clear conception of the activities embraced here by the word *Editing*. The word used by Pudovkin, the German and French word, is *montage*. Its only possible English equivalent is *editing*. But in England, in the trade, the editor is too often conceived of as a humble person, called in after the damage, or good, has been done upon the floor, to accomplish a relatively mechanical task upon material the effect of which has been already settled. The word *editing*, as used here in its correct sense, has a far wider, constructive application. It

the picture, has then become more significant than its general shape. The *frame*, three-quarters of an inch high on the actual piece of standard size celluloid, is the concrete unit, repetition of which gives, in projection of a shot, the illusion of movement.

covers manifold activities, not only those which compose in the cutting-room an appearance from single images, but those which, in the work on the script, predetermine and select those images and their sequence which will be necessary to form the later appearance proposed. In its later uses by the Russians—and here we often retain *montage*—it implies mounting or amounting of all the affective impulses of sound or vision that in one way or another amountedly affect the spectator. The degree to which the verb *monter*, to *build* or *edit*, is still comprehended in England as implying little beyond the relatively mechanical concept to *cut*, indicates the degree to which an understanding of the creative process implied by its wider sense may be fruitful for the future advancement of the industry.

B.—SPECIAL NOTES

(i) NOTES TO " THE FILM SCENARIO AND ITS THEORY "

1. It is interesting to note that at least three major films turned out so long that they were issued in two parts intended to be booked at successive weeks : Fritz Lang's *Nibelungs* (*Siegfried*, called *Nibelungs* in England, and *Kriemhild's Revenge*, called in England *The She-Devil*) ; the same director's *Dr. Mabuse* and Gustav Molander's *Jerusalem* from the Selma Lagerlof story. American super-productions of unusual length concede an interval at half-way on their premier showing, and are shortened subsequently for general release. The over-long Stroheim pictures

ON FILM TECHNIQUE

Greed for Universal and *Wedding March* for Paramount were ruthlessly cut down and the wholes have never been seen. On the Continent, where single-feature programmes are the rule, a film usually attains 9,000 feet—$1\frac{3}{4}$ hours. In England and U.S.A., with the habit of double programmes, only exceptional films attain 90 minutes and the usual length is 70.

2. Neglect of this rule, to establish clearly the theme first of all and select all incident only to express it, was almost certainly the root cause of the failure of Pudovkin's penultimate film, *A Simple Case*. Not all its later devised ingenious embellishments could save it, the fault was in its genesis.

3. This example may be obscure to the reader not grounded in reformist or revolutionary politics. To a Russian an anarchist is a definite type—shock-headed, piercing eyes, spouting, impractical—in vivid contrast to the communist ideal of an athletic, disciplined, handy-man, that the hero finally becomes. The replacement in the scenario of a vaguely turbulent character by an anarchist is thus, to a Russian, a gain in *definiteness*. It is as if a character, vague and intangible, were described in an English scenario as being " in the army." By tightening in revision the character is made a sergeant-major. Everyone in England knows what a sergeant-major is like ; the other persons in the story can be readily characterised by their reactions to him. The gain in definiteness is obvious.

4. How far and under what conditions are " spoken phrases " admissible in sound films ? The author gives his view on this question in essays VII and VIII.

5. Here in the original follows a sentence : " But it is necessary to know them, and the reader's attention is recommended to the short bibliography at the end of this sketch." A fruitless recommendation, for, alas, the printer omitted the bibliography.

6. The classic example of the creation by extraneous methods of a tension not implicit for most audiences in the given dramatic material is the Separator Sequence in *The General Line.*

7. Scenes and script-scenes. Refer to Glossarial Notes.

8. Here a wide textual alteration has been made. In the original the author gives guidance for sensing the amount of material required in each reel (rather than in the scenario as a whole), for " it must be borne in mind that each reel must, to a certain extent, represent a self-contained part of the picture. In order that the short interval necessary for changing the reel in exhibition shall not break up the unity of impression, effort must be made to distribute the material in such a way that the intervals occur at the place of junction of one just completed part of action to the beginning of the next. In a technically well-constructed scenario the conclusion of a reel is used as a special method completing the action, analogous to the dropping of the curtain at the end of an act in the Theatre."

These remarks were conditioned by the fact that, at the time of the sketch, and even now, most places of film exhibition in Russia are equipped with only one projector. The conception of the reel as a self-contained dramatic part has no value for the producer in Western Europe and America, where two-projector exhibition is universal, unless perhaps

ON FILM TECHNIQUE

for the amateur. It should be noted, indeed, that in
production for two-projector exhibition the reverse
requirement obtains. The cutter should take care
not to divide his reels at the end of a sequence. A
short footage is almost always lost to view in each
change-over, owing to the precautions taken by the
operator to avoid at all costs the shattering appearance on the screen of the tag " End of Reel X " or
" Reel X + 1." For example, the penultimate and
last reels of *Two Days*. Here the Russian, relying on
his interval, shows at the end of the penultimate reel
a short shot of the father kneeling by his hanged son ;
slow fade-out. Interval for lacing up the next reel.
Fade-in, father rising to his feet. We are aware that
he has been long dazed with sorrow, and has at last
reached a critical impulse, to fire the house of his
son's executioners. On a Western apparatus the
change-over swallows all, or the best part of, the
fades. The father appears merely to indulge in a
more or less irrational kneeling-down and almost
immediate standing-up, and much of the " rightness " of the psychology of his impulse is lost. Care
should be taken, therefore, by the cutter to divide his
reels preferably at a place of cross-cut shots where
loss of perhaps the last foot of one and the first foot
of another will be insignificant.

9. Note that in a talking-film script, the dialogue
is set out bunched up on the right-hand side of the
page, as in a play, not between the scenes and level
with them, as the spoken sub-titles here.

10. Refer to Glossarial Notes.

11. A girl member of the Young Communist
League.

12. This paragraph remains equally true for

sound films in Pudovkin's view. So long as an image appears it should not be casual, but selected for its expression ; similarly speech should not be casual— the speech that might happen to be uttered—but rigidly selected and arranged for maximum expression. See his essays VII and VIII.

13. The principle has a useful application, by converse inference, for the editor (the cutter and titler, called in after the damage is done) as well as for the scenarist. Suppose he be confronted with this weak scene of Olga walking out on her husband, already made, he can slightly strengthen it by weakening the preceding title—that is, making it more indefinite. Thus : " Olga, unable to endure her hard-hearted husband, came to a crucial decision."

14. A long experience of titling enables me to be not contradictory, but perhaps more definite. Three considerations affect titles ; they are, in order of descending importance : (a) content, (b) style, (c) compression.

The absolutely clear significance of the content for the development of the action is paramount. That satisfied, the use of phraseology in spoken titles helping to characterise a speaker or his mood, or of style in continuity titles wedded to the momentary spirit of the film, may be exceedingly valuable. Compression, though to be considered only after the other two desiderata, is highly important ; though few spectators are analphabets, reading is, to many of them, an exercise, and, if the screen be full of type, an astonishing number make no effort to begin on it at all.

15. Methods of measuring title-length vary. That

given here, though used in several studios, is an excessively large approximation. A more exact allowance is one foot for each of the first five words, and one foot for each subsequent pair of words. This presupposes that a material part of the time taken in reading a card is taken up, firstly, in adjustment to the first appearance of the card, secondly, in adjustment to each new word ; length of words is regarded as temporally relatively unimportant, for most long words are recognised when only a part of their length has been spelt out. For this view there is experimental support.

16. To it belongs also the science of selection of fount (or script), tone, and background.

17. To avoid interruption of the flow of rapid action by length in a title, the Russians introduced the method of " split-titles," that is, distribution of the essential content to be rendered on to two or three separated cards ; each is thus shown short in footage and the tempo undisturbed. Still faster, in his penultimate film, Pudovkin cut alternate frames of a title and a picture in battle scenes. This gave an effect of almost machine-gun rapidity. Alternate frame effects can also be got, perhaps more easily, in what is called an " optical printer."

18. The text is here slightly amended. The author gives as his simple form the iris-in and iris-out, mentioning what is called the fade only as a variant. Irises were used far more in the past than to-day, the fade has now been found to be less distracting to the spectator. The mere reversal of their respective positions, with little phrase alteration, is effective in modernising the passage.

19. See Note 18.

20. These effects have lately come very much into fashion ; they are called " wipes," and are most usually effected not in the camera but on the printer.

21. The mix *need* not be effected at once in the camera ; it can be made subsequently in the printing, or by various trick processes. As a matter of fact, however—though there is no theoretical reason why it should be so—such processes and printing machines are, in practice, nearly always imperfect, and result in a loss of photographic quality.

22. Accomplished by means of a camera accessory, such a shot is termed a " pan." Accomplished by free-hand, it is usually termed a " swinging " shot.

23. There is strong difference on this point. A costly process, owing to the time taken for the complex preparation of such a shot, the prodigal Americans use it more and more frequently, for such purposes as the following of a character along passages, up flights of stairs, and so forth. Tracking (and panning) are in disfavour with the left-wing Russian school, for, naturalists, they hold such methods easily tend to remind the spectator of the presence of the camera.

24. The same effect is often obtained by gauzes or cigarette smoke in front of the lens.

25. Scenes and script-scenes. Refer to Glossarial Notes.

26. A further wide textual alteration. Discussion was given of the editing of the reel (" each reel is a more or less complete whole, corresponding, to a certain degree, to an act upon the stage ") and of

the scenario separately. In considering reels, the author repeated the desideratum that their material must be independent and self-contained, though now adding that, with two-projector exhibition, this is unnecessary. In considering the scenario as a whole, the author suggested the various size of reels as a means of sparing to the end the energy of the spectator. The early ones long, while he is fresh, the middle reels shorter, and the last reel, if necessary, longer again, so that the pure final action need not be interrupted by new lacing-up. These observations are significant in Western Europe and America for amateurs only. Refer to Note 8.

27. In the original, the author here repeated almost word for word, the account of these scenes already given.

(ii) NOTES TO " FILM DIRECTOR AND FILM MATERIAL "

28. The great significance here alluded to by Pudovkin is the economic consequence that cost of performance becomes a mere fraction of cost of production. Whereas in the theatre or concert hall, chief analogies in the entertainment industry, costs of repeat performance are relatively much nearer original production costs. This, not anything in their respective intrinsic possibilities of creative method, determines the paramountcy of theatre for esoteric groups, and puts the cinema as a mass art out on its own with limitless financial resources.

29. The original here speaks of the impossibility of approaching " scenes," using the word in the classical French sense. See Glossarial Notes.

30. The net is " cheated." Any movement or

PUDOVKIN

object outside the picture-frame or otherwise un-
remarked is said to be " cheated."

31. Communist mixed Boy and Girl Scouts.

32. By a curious error of mistranslation on the
part of the German renters of this film it has been
customary to refer to this warship as an armoured
cruiser (*Panzerkreuzer*). Both in actuality and in the
Russian name of the film the *Potemkin* is a pre-
dreadnought battleship, the full name of which is
Potemkin Tavritcheski (ex *Pantelimon*, ex *Kniaz Potemkin
Tavritcheski*). It was completed in 1900, and its
details are given as follows : Displacement, 12,480
metric tons ; complement, 741 ; guns, four 12",
sixteen 6", fourteen 11-pounders, six 3-pounders ;
5 torpedo-tubes, speed, about 16 knots. It closely
resembles those English classes of pre-dreadnought
—*Bulwark*, *Formidable*, *Majestic*, *Canopus*—of which so
many examples were lost during the war.

33. These are the marble steps leading from the
statue of the Duc de Richelieu on the boulevard to
the docks below.

34. In the German edition the translators here
inserted Ruttman's *Berlin* as a film of this kind. This
is absurd ; *Berlin* was most carefully scripted and
exactly executed, and the instance was repudiated
by Pudovkin when brought to his attention.

35. The counter to this rule is, of course, Dziga-
Vertov with his theory of the " Kino-eye." Dziga-
Vertov holds that the director should stage nothing,
simply going about quietly and unobservedly
accumulating material with the camera, his " Kino-
eye," and that only such a film as one in which the
director's " interference " with the natural course
of events is limited to choosing and eliminating

details can properly be called documentary. It is all a matter of degree. At the one pole there is the arbitrary, staged and acted event—*Chang* or the sandstorm in *Turksib*, at the other the lurking about the streets of Ruttmann in *Berlin* or Dziga-Vertov. But even Dziga-Vertov would doubtless repeat and " interfere " in the sense of the next text paragraph to secure certain material.

36. In England it is the whole work of one member of the producing team, the " continuity " or floor-secretary, to aid the director to keep watch on correspondences of this kind.

37. Recall that the director's field will alter with every lens. Modification of the amount of space to be embraced may often be effected not by change of set-up but by change of lens.

38. In " The Dynamic Square," Eistenstein eloquently pleads for all those male shapes utterly banned from proper screen expression by its at present accepted frame.

39. *The Mechanism of the Brain*, Reel One.

40. At the former Imperial summer residence in Livadea, near Yalta.

41. Pudovkin is himself a declared and practising disciple of the American Griffith in this matter. Compare the steady, inexorable flow of spring river ice and the marching, demonstrating workers in *Mother* ; compare the storm, existing for the story not in reality but only in emotion, that sweeps away the English at the finale of *Jenghiz Khan*. This last is his most daring and remarkable achievement. For the risk of introducing an emotional environmental effect is that it is much less likely than a real one to be apprehended unconsciously by the audience ;

it may become a symbol, requiring conscious effort for comprehension. and risk passing the audience by, e.g., the Regeneration Sequence in *Simple Case.*

42. Recall again the Separator Sequence, *General Line*, Reel Two.

43. Example : The grimacing and painted Krauss standing on a real hill, pretending to influence a real fox, real foxhounds and horses ; a preposterous scene in *The Student of Prague.*

44. It requires such an abundance of stock on the regular pay-roll as can only be afforded by the wealthiest film-company. The herding of extras into a film-city, in which all companies centralise their studios, has, however, something of the same effect.

45. Many historians of the Theatre would disagree.

46. For Pudovkin's views on the proper relation of speeches and movements in dialogue film see essays VII and VIII.

47. Remember also the face of the Mongol in the finale of *The Heir to Jenghiz Khan.*

48. Soft-focus, refer note 24.

49. This is a considerable over-estimate for the conditions of commercial film production in the West. Companies with big studio investments hate going on location ; they must keep their studios occupied to cover their overheads.

50. This, of course, the elimination of the supererogatory, is what makes the Close-up the keystone of the whole power and effectiveness of the cinema. A measure—the ultimate possible—of the unconsciousness of the West and its innocence of theory

was seen at that meeting of the Academy of Motion Picture Arts and Sciences, the would-be learned society of Hollywood, at which were delivered Eisenstein's remarks on "The Dynamic Square." This meeting was called to consider Wide Film. A prominent cameraman from Fox was recounting his experiences. Although one could not approach close enough to the subject to secure a close-up, he declared this was no drawback, for the image on the screen was so large that the characters' expressions could none the less be clearly discerned even in mid-shot ! Despite the presence of a multitude of directors and leading technicians from every studio, this astounding appraisal excited no remark. To this day, though their pragmatism has taught them to drop Wide Film after stinging losses, the big companies are probably quite mystified and unable to account for the public's indifference to it.

51. There is a growing tendency, alas, in England and America for *the director too* to leave, his picture at this point passing to an " editor." It derives from commercial envy of the " quickies," and must tend, with them, to standardisation and mechanicalisation of style.

52. In spite of this address it should be noted that Pudovkin does very often use actors. Inkishinov, Baranovskaia, Batalov, Baturin, are examples of more or less experienced actors in leading roles in his films. Other equally important parts are, it is true, played by complete novices and he certainly handles them all, experienced and otherwise, with the technique prescribed here for the handling of types. Dovzhenko uses types rather more, and only Eisenstein invariably.

53. Various means of obtaining " Close-ups in Time " have been used previously by directors other than the quoted Epstein. Turning the camera fast—though not in actual exaggerated slow-motion as in these experiments—is not at all uncommon for certain underlinings. Some of Fairbanks athletic feats were probably recorded in this way to emphasise their grace. Eisenstein, on the other hand, has always emphasised his moments by repetitive cutting. Recall the repetition in the enthroning in the tractor in the last reel of *General Line*, in the bridge scene of *October*, and as for the Odessa Steps scene in *Potemkin*—you will find that the soldiers march down this whole length two or three times if all the descent shots are added together. These are other technical means to the same end as the experiments in *A Simple Case* here described.

FILM ACTING

FILM ACTING

LIST OF ILLUSTRATIONS

LIST OF ILLUSTRATIONS

LIST OF ILLUSTRATIONS

FILM ACTING

CHAPTER I

THE THEATRE AND THE CINEMA

DISCUSSION of such questions as the interrelationship between film and stage, the necessity for the cinema to absorb and benefit from the traditions and discoveries of the theatre, the respective problems of film acting and stage acting, etc., is often along entirely wrong lines. The only profitable basis for such discussion, too often disregarded, is the consideration of the cinema in its aspect as a step in the *development* of the theatre.

To understand what we must discard, and what preserve or alter, in our stage heritage we must first appreciate those technical possibilities which distinguish the new nature of cinema from the nature of theatre.

I use with purpose the word *possibilities*, because not only theoreticians, but many practical film workers also, limit their achievement by regarding the cinema as little more than a photograph, mechanically recording what in essence basically remains a theatrical performance conditioned by the specific technical conditions of the theatre.

The intrinsic possibilities of the cinema are only

realised in full when its new technical means are exploited, not merely in a mechanical fixation of the forces already found and used by the stage, but also in the discovery of novel, often more profound and more expressive methods of communicating to the spectator the concept of the creative artist. We shall always be in a position to use a camera merely to photograph a theatrical performance, and this mere mechanical use of it can, in fact, be of definite service in educational work. But, I repeat, the mechanical transference to the screen of a stage show, with all the limitations conditioned by the latter's technical methods, is not the proper line of development of the cinema.

The fight against theatricality in the cinema in no way implies antagonism to the stage as such. It only puts before us as our task, simply and clearly, *the examination and analysis of the contradictions arising in the process of the development of the theatre, and their resolution in the cinema, not by slavish imitation of the theatre's solution, but by use of the cinema's own technical possibilities.* It means repudiation of a number of theatrical methods and discovery and acceptance of analogous specific filmic methods.

It is thus clear that, to discover the specific character of the work of the film actor, our first task is to analyse the contradictions in the work of the stage actor. And, equally essential, to appreciate sharply the distinction between the material-technical basis of theatre and the material-technical basis of cinema.

What prime basic contradiction of the theatre is

eliminated in the cinema ? Every several work of
art may be defined as an act of collective perception
and modification of reality. This is to say that every
work of art is to be regarded not as a process of two
factors—the creative artist and the work created—
but as a more complex process, consisting of three
factors: the creative artist, the work created, and the
spectator apprehending it.

The act of perception of a fragment of reality,
recorded and fixed by the artist in the work he
creates, resumes life and repeats itself in perception
by a multitude of spectators. In concert with the
artist, the spectator likewise perceives a part of reality, and, in his act of doing so, thereby transmutes
the work of art to a social-historical phenomenon,
i.e. from a paper, or canvas or celluloid symbol to an
actual process.

A stage show, exactly as any other work of art, has
real existence only in respect to its contact with the
spectator. The Soviet artist has for his spectator
the whole population of the Soviet Union ; ultimately, the population of the world. What does
any given stage show represent in terms of its embrace of the mass spectator ? The numerical embrace of one stage production performed in an
average-sized theatre throughout one year would be
approximately 100,000 spectators. The embrace of
a theatrical art work is widened by its production
in a number of other theatres. But, even granted a
high technical level of the theatrical network, the
productions staged in Moscow will differ qualita-

tively from those staged in Odessa, Kiev, and **Kazan**. They will inevitably vary with the coefficients of method and skill of the producers, with the casts, with the technical resources of the respective theatres. Even in the same town it is certain that there will be qualitative difference in production of the same play in different theatres. Suppose we go farther, and consider the ultimate embrace of the many-millioned spectator of the colkhoz,[1] we immediately encounter a qualitative difference of the highest degree. Contrast a production at the First Moscow Art Theatre, and at a colkhoz theatre, which not even the most perfect conceivable organisation of the on-tour system could contrive to service with acting forces of first strength.

Consequently, in the theatre, the widening of its network is in direct contradiction with the quality of its performance. The theatre has, however, one further technical means of expanding its spectator-embrace, and that is, increase in the size of its auditorium. Here too, however, there is a definite limit beyond which this contradiction implicit in the very nature of the stage show comes once again to the fore. The first desideratum for the actor is that he must be distinctly seen and heard. In order to be distinctly perceptible to a larger number of spectators the actor studies voice delivery, learns to make his gestures obvious and clear without losing their intrinsic character, he learns, in short, to move and

[1] Collective farm, each with its own cultural facilities, including theatre.—Tr.

speak in such a way that he can be seen and heard distinctly from the last row in the gallery.

But the broader an acting gesture, the less it can be shaded. The more intensified the actor's tones, the more difficult it is for him to transmit to the spectator the finer shades of his voice. Loudness of tone and widening of gesture lead to generalised form and stylisation, which tend as a technique inevitably to become dry and cold. The depth and realism of the image that the actor creates tend to vary inversely with the size of the audience that sees his performance. Increase in size of a theatrical building has thus a boundary beyond which the building itself dictates the actual form of the production, even its transmutation into specialised forms of mass spectacle; festivals, carnivals, parades, etc.

We perceive from these considerations that stage art, in the circumstances obtaining in practice, evinces a contradiction between numerical increase of its audience (along two possible lines) and qualitative improvement of performance.

How is this contradiction escaped in the cinema? The degree of quality in the work of art is fixed once and for all at the time of single production of the film. The quality attained can be conveyed unmodified to any audience by means of a cinema network capable of development to any dimension. The measure of spectator-embrace is solved simply by the specific technical character of the cinema. The spectator-embrace can be increased in number to include the entire population of the

233

world. The quality of the performance at any given point in the network, however remote from the centre, varies solely as the quality of the technical equipment of the given theatre at which it takes place, and this is merely a matter of standardisation. At some future date it may well be that every dwelling will have a projection equipment, operated by some improved form of radio-television, and giving the possibility of simultaneous and uniform presentation of a film in every conceivable corner of the globe.

Certainly the same means might be used for simultaneous and ubiquitous transmission of a theatrical performance. But the cinema's property of indefinitely repeating its performance at its fixed and optimal degree of quality will remain unique.

The second aspect of the contradiction in theatrical acting, also referred to above, quality varying inversely with the size of the auditorium, is equally solved in the cinema. The size of the cinema theatre is no handicap to performance, for the possibility of increase in size of the screen, or in number of the sound-reproducers, is unlimited. Thus, at the time of shooting, the actor can speak without straining his tones in the slightest, he is free to exercise the finest shading of voice and gesture. We shall later have to discuss the importance of this fact for the special character of film acting.

I now come to a new contradiction, arisen from the influence upon theatrical development of our contemporary life. The artist, drawing the specta-

tor into a joint perception and modification of
reality with him in the process of creating and
apprehending the work of art, has a general tendency to embrace his fragment of reality as widely
and deeply as he can. In an epoch such as ours,
wherein the tempestuous development of reality
continually outpaces the generalisation of it in
human thought, it is natural that this tendency
should express itself in an endeavour to deal realistically with the innumerable only newly discovered
facets of this reality.

The eager desire to discover, beyond each
generalisation, the living complexity of life, ever
new-faceted, inevitably gives rise to a desire to
embrace a maximum number of events in the work
of art and consequently to expand it over a maximum
embrace of time and space.

To contrive the increase in the work of art of the
space-time embrace of reality, each art form has its
own specific methods deriving from its own specific
material technique. In the theatre, for example,
the principal means of attaining this end is the
splitting-up of the performance into separate acts
and scenes. A one-act performance of two persons
engaged in dialogue and lasting without interval
for an hour embraces exactly that, an hour's conversation between two persons stationary in one
place—and no more. To embrace a bigger slice
of time we split the act into two scenes. The first
can be played as springtime in Berlin, the second as
summer in Moscow. Such a division of an act into

parts gives us the possibility of embracing not only bigger time, but also bigger space.

In his productions of classical plays, Meyerhold tries to imbue them with a contemporary content, and consequently is perpetually overflowing the limited framework which, in the classics, holds the action within a unity of time and space. In order to create in the audience, by means of the show, the necessary feeling of the dialectical complexity of the event, Meyerhold expands each act by technical stage devices that have the object of theatrically expressing the new content which the modern spectator, and the artist in concert with him, perceives in reality.

Thus in his productions Meyerhold splits the act not only into scenes but into many episodes within scenes. An interesting example is his production of Ostrovski's *The Forest*, in which, by means of this splitting, he literally guides his two actors throughout a whole province without them leaving the stage.

But development along this line, while remaining at the same time conditioned by the material limitations of stage technique, inevitably comes to a dead end fixed by an insoluble and purely material contradiction. It is impossible to conceive a stage performance cut up into one- and two-minute bits. Such a performance would presuppose entirely new engineering inventions enabling scenic changes at the speed of lightning, enabling the spectator to transfer his attention from one point of stage space to the other with the speed of the successive bits.

THE THEATRE AND THE CINEMA

In his production of *Razbeg*,[1] Okhlopkov makes an attempt to scatter separate tiny scenes throughout the whole space of the auditorium, so that to follow the change of episode, the spectator is obliged to turn his head right, left, up, sometimes even straight behind him. Of course, if a mechanically perfect seat could be devised that would save the spectator the unnecessary exhaustion (and the crick in his neck) caused by the movements imposed on him, the problem might be said to have been by this means resolved in his favour. But is it worth while inventing such seats, when the technical basis of the cinema solves precisely this problem with the utmost ease?

In the hoary days of cinema, when the style was more ultra-theatrical than ever since, and it had not yet occurred to anyone that the film could be anything but a simple photograph of a staged play, even then, the cinema used scenes each of which was no longer than 5 minutes long. In other words, the longest scenes of the film at its birth were equal to the shortest scenes of the stage at its most modern.

The possibility of lightning-like change of action, also, was inherent and realised in the most infantile days of cinema. The possibility of almost infinite wideness of embrace both in space and time was already appreciated and realised in the very first works by serious masters of film art.

The splitting-up of the stage performance into

[1] *Impetus*, a play from the novel of the same name on colkhoz life by V. Stavski, produced at the Krasnaya Presnya Theatre in Moscow.—*Note by V. I. P.*

pieces, a natural development of theatre accentuated in these days by the present eagerness to embrace wider space-time fragments of comprehensible reality, reaches, at a certain stage of its development, a point of standstill on the stage and, at the same time, a starting-point in the cinema. The 3-minute bit that is an unthinkable high limit of speed for a scene change in the theatre is, in the cinema, the last limit of slowness.

What is the new material-technical base which eliminates from the cinema this second contradiction, shown above to be an obstacle implicit in theatrical development ? In the main this new technique is enabled by two instruments. First, a movable photographing apparatus, that serves in some sort as a technically perfected spectator's eye. This eye can retreat from its object to any distance in order to embrace the widest possible spacial field of vision. It can approach the tiniest detail in order to concentrate upon it the whole attention. It can jump from one point in space to another, and the sum total of all these movements requires, to all intents and purposes, no physical exertion on the part of the spectator. Second, a microphone, almost as readily movable and representing an attentive ear, capable of apprehending every sound without strain, be it the barely audible whisper of man or the roar of powerful sirens made faint by distance.

The purpose of this study is to define the main respects in which this new material-technical basis affects the work of one of the most important members of the creative ensemble in cinema or in theatre—the actor.

It would, of course, be wrong to assume that the new technique affects the actor's work only by lightening it, in that it removes the necessity for him to overcome a whole series of specific theatrical contradictions (such as the intensification of voice-tone and exaggeration of gesture needed to overcome the space separating actor from spectator in a large building, as mentioned above).

The new material-technical basis of the cinema not only affects the actor's work by lightening it in certain respects, it also imports many difficulties not present in stage work, or present there in milder and more tractable form.

Before discussing the specific work of the film actor it will be best first to consider those aspects of the actor's work common to both film and stage, and therefore inescapable in either.

CHAPTER II

THE BASIC CONTRADICTION OF THE ACTOR'S WORK

THE fundamental of the actor's job, both in film and on the stage, is the creation of a whole and lifelike image. From the very start of his work the actor has to set out to grasp and ultimately embody this image, shaping himself in the course of stage rehearsal or, in the cinema, in the so-called 'preparatory work.'

Both in stage and screen work the actor has to embody the image in its deepest sense, ideologically and teleologically. But this task is not only conditioned objectively, it is also conditioned, of course, subjectively.

The image that has to be worked out is conditioned not only by the intention of the play as a whole, but also by the nature of the actor's self, it is related to himself as an individual personality. Any problem involving modification of his personality, however one may regard it, is obviously *per se* indissolubly linked with the continuous actual existence of the actor as a live individual, with all the elements of character and culture contributing to his formation. The relation between the proposed image and the actor as a live person is particularly strong at the beginning of his work. For this is the period at which emphasis lies on the element of his

emotional attitude to the image, his so-called
'feeling' of some aspect of the image that particularly excites him and thereby serves as the essential
point of departure of his work on it. Only later
does the actor proceed to the task of thoroughly
understanding and grasping the play as a whole,
appreciating its ideological content. Then his
work widens and becomes the solution of the most
generalised problems of the play.

The work of the actor on the image is thus
oriented two ways. The image the actor builds as
his work develops, on the one hand is constructed
out of himself as a person with given individual
characteristics, and on the other is conditioned by
the interaction of this personal element and the
intention in general of the play.

The final object of the actor and his performance
is to convey to the spectator a real person, or at
least a person who could conceivably exist in reality.
But at the same time, all the while he is creating this
image, the actor none the less remains a live,
organically whole self. When he walks on the stage,
nothing within him is destroyed. If he be a nice
man acting a villain, he still remains a nice man
acting a villain. Hence the creation of the image
must be effected not by mere mechanical portrayal
of qualities alien to him, but by the subjugation
and adaptation of the qualities innate in him.

An image of the necessary reality will only be
achieved when the given series of expressions, both
internal and external, required by the play is

expressed not by a set of words, gestures, and intonations dictated by formula or whimsy and mechanically repeated, but as result of the subjugation and
re-expression of the actor's own living individuality.
This manner of constructing a rôle will give it an
organic unity that it will never receive if it be
arbitrarily separated from the living organic unity
of the actor as a person.

The duality of the creative process in the actor's
creation of the image is only an aspect of the duality
or dialectic of every process of comprehension of
reality, indeed every practical getting-to-grips-with-it
by man with any phenomenon. In political work,
for example, which is creative in the sense in which
is the fulfilment of every task, there is the dialectic
of the conflict and unity of theory and practice.
Theory is checked by practice, practice generalised
by theory, and only as resolved resultant of these
conflicts does work proceed correctly. The emotional side and the logical side represent the duality
in an actor's work of creating an image. If his
construction is to have the organic unity of life,
logic of synthesis must be informed by personal
emotional excitement, and, correspondingly, emotional urgings must be based upon and checked in
the light of the logic of the play. This consideration
immediately exposes the limitations, both in theatre
and in cinema, of the often recommended naïf and
natural ' type.'

The idea that the alpha and omega of acting can
be expressed by a ' type ' is based upon the regarding

THE BASIC CONTRADICTION

of acting as a sort of mechanical process capable of being disintegrated into separate and quite unconnected bits. It ignores the fact that the actor does, in fact, exist as a live person, if a type, then a person unconscious of the inner meaning of his work, and thus, to say the least, unable to further the creation on stage or screen of the unification and wholeness necessary for living verisimilitude of image.

Here let us reaffirm our principal desideratum for acting both on stage and screen. *The aim and object of the technique of the actor is his struggle for unity, for an organic wholeness in the lifelike image he creates.*

But the technical conditions of work on the stage and for the screen impose a number of demands on the actor that perpetually tend to destroy his unity and continuity in the rôle.

The splitting-up of the performance on the stage into acts, scenes, episodes, the still more subdivided splitting-up of the actor's work in the shooting of a film, set up a corresponding series of obstacles through and over which the entire creative collective (actor-producer in the theatre, actor-director-cameraman-etc. in the film) must combine to carry the organic unity of line of the actor's image.

This unavoidable technical split-up of his work is immediately in direct contradiction with the actor's need to preserve himself in his acting whole and undivided. In both play and film, this contradiction always obtains. In actual performance, the actor plays in bits. Between two entries, between two performances, though not playing, his existence is continuous.

Bad actors and bad theoreticians get round this contradiction between the mechanical splitting dictated by the conditions of performance and the need for the actor to strive to live uninterruptedly in the image by maintaining that the gestures and words necessary for the part can simply be mechanically memorised, and thus suspended, as it were, over the intervals.

Where one regards the actor as a ' type ' who only mechanically repeats externally dictated gestures, the intervals between the separate bits of acting do, it is true, look like *vacua* that do not need to be filled with living material linking up the part as a whole on and off the stage, not only during a performance or shooting, but also during rehearsal.

This superficial attitude to the actor's work is especially prevalent in the cinema. But, actually, *the discontinuity of the actor's work must never be ignored, but always treated as a difficulty to be overcome.* Let it be admitted that splitting-up into bits is less serious on the stage than in the cinema. The technical conditions of stage work allow the bits of continued existence in the given image to be longer. And there is a whole series of methods in the work of the stage actor's study of the image designed to the end of bringing about a maximum of linkage of the separate bits of the rôle into one whole within the actor himself. First and foremost of theatrical methods for this purpose is rehearsal. During rehearsal the stage actor does not limit himself by the hard-and-fast conditions imposed by the text of the play. Stanislavski makes his actors in rehearsal act not only their parts as they stand in the play, but supplementary action not, in fact, in the text, but necessary to enable the actor completely to 'feel' himself into his part.

Rehearsal work of this kind enables the actor to feel himself an organic unity moving freely in all directions within the frame of the image planned. *Essentially, it is precisely this work that links the separate bits of his acting to the feeling, however discontinuous in fact, of a unified, continuous real image.*

Rehearsal work of this kind is precisely the opportunity for the actor to transform the abstract thought and general line of expression that he has hit on to express the image into concrete acts and manners of behaviour.

If the actor remain only at the 'thinking' stage of his creative work, even for a moment, then in respect to that moment he ceases to be an actor. If the actor decide that the person he is portraying might have killed a man between acts one and two, then he should not only include the murder as an abstract element of his treatment of the image in the second act, but he should, in fact, actually practise acting this murder non-existent in the play, so that he may inwardly feel not only the concept of the murder, but, as really as possible, all the potentialities of the murder and its influence on the character of the image.

This sort of rehearsal work, designed to connect the complexity of the objectively planned image with the live and actual individuality of the actor and all its wealth of individual character and culture, might be termed the process of being *absorbed into* or *embodying* the rôle.

Stanislavski in one of his essays speaks of the art of living an image and the art of presenting an image, distinguishing by these terms two kinds of acting, the first basing itself on inner impulse, the second on externalised theatrical forms.

Stanislavski says: "While the art of living an image strives to feel the spirit of the rôle every time and at each creation, the art of presenting an image strives only once to live the rôle, privately, to show it once and then to substitute an externalised form expressing its spiritual essence: the hack actor disregards the living of the rôle and endeavours to work out once and for all a ready-made form of expression of feeling, a stage interpretation for every possible rôle and possible tendency in art. In other words, for the art of living representation, living the rôle is indispensable. The hack manages without it and indulges in it only occasionally."

This is, in effect, what we have said, using for the word 'living' the term 'absorption' or 'embodiment,' since it is specifically that process of setting up a profound linkage between the subjective personal element of the actor and the objective element of the play. If the image be properly constructed, then this linkage has been set up. It is a linkage that, as Stanislavski says, is present in the work of every good actor, absent from that of the hack, whom Stanislavski rightly regards as better vanished from the stage.

One may agree or disagree with the necessity for living the rôle in the complex and meticulous sense of the Moscow Art Theatre school of actors, but in any circumstances the organic relation between the actor's individuality and every live element in the image he plays is indispensable.

This relation is a precondition for any verisimilitude in the image. Naturally, all that has been said of the organic continuity and unity of the rôle applies equally to the organic continuity and unity of the performance as a whole. Stanislavski's basic postulate of the necessity for an actor to discover ' intermediate action ' remains in force.

It should here be noted that the process of personal identification with an objectively planned image is necessary not only in film and stage work. I suggest that a concrete feeling of connection between the individuality and the image to be created is normal and essential for the creative process in every art.

There is a body of instructive evidence about their work from writers, who describe how, frequently, they mouth the words of the characters they are inventing in order to test by concrete, personal sensation the phrases, words, and intonations they are seeking.

We recall that Gogol declared all the characters

in *Dead Souls* to be, in fact, dark sides of his own nature that he wished, by expression, to annihilate in himself.

The system of rehearsal is the special means the theatre takes to aid the actor in his struggle to incarnate himself in his rôle.

CHAPTER III

DISCONTINUITY IN THE ACTOR'S WORK IN THE CINEMA

ALL that has been said hitherto of the paramount importance and necessity of the actor's striving for wholeness in his image in the theatre applies, of course, with equal force to the work of the film actor. It might, indeed, be said that realism, that is, by implication, the lifelike unity of the image, is a problem more pertinent and urgent to the film actor than even to the actor in the theatre. It is characteristic of the stage that effective performance is, as a matter of fact, possible upon it on a basis of exaggeration of theatrical convention, performance having an abstractly æsthetic character maximally removed from direct reflection of reality, but the cinema is characteristically the art that gives the *utmost possibility* of approach to realistic reproduction of reality.

I emphasise here as elsewhere the word 'possibility.' This is in order that the reader shall not think our analyses of possibilities, or our recommendations, the attempt to fix a static complex of methods as sole law of expression for cinema once and for all. Certainly the cinema too is capable of production in conventionalised style, style abstracted from direct representation of reality; certainly the cinema also is capable of generalisation, can develop it to any degree, even to the limit of the supreme antithesis black and white. But none the less, the cinema is par excellence the art form capable of maximum capture of living reality in direct representation.)

The question of the degree of generalisation to be employed in any given specific instance in an art form—this is always a question of the sense of proportion of the skilful creative artist, and the measure of its rightness is ultimately the reaction felt by the spectator when the work of art is complete: either acceptance by the experience of a real emotion— always the highest valuation for a work of art—or else cold negation.

But in discussing possibilities, I endeavour to determine the general tendency of development of the specific given art form, which, after all, the creative artist must take into account, however personal his own solution.

In the cinema, exactly as in the theatre, we immediately come right up against the problem posed by the discontinuity of the actor's work being in direct contradiction with his need for a continuous creative ' living-into ' and embodiment of the image played.

Owing to the special methods used in filming, which we shall discuss later, this contradiction becomes in practice even more acute than in the theatre. If we assemble some of the stories that stage actors have to tell about their experiences on occasional film work, we shall find a whole host of denunciations, protests, even indignant swear words, all inspired by the notorious and fantastically exaggerated discontinuity of the film actor's job.

Actors maintain that either they have to portray the image they play in extremely abstract manner, limited as they are in study to a superficial reading of the scenario, or, alternatively, they deliver themselves bound into the hands of the director and his assistants, becoming will-less automata, executing in obedience to a series of shouts and orders a mechanical task the purport of which is incomprehensible to them. Actors further hold that they lose every possibility of feeling the unity of the image, every possibility of preserving during the process of shooting a sense of live continuous individuality, owing to the fact that they act the end of their rôle to-day, the beginning to-morrow, and the middle the day after. The various bits are tangled, they are terribly short; from time to time somebody photographs a glance that relates to something the actor will be doing a month hence when somebody else has photographed a hand movement that has to do with the glance. The image created by the actor is split into minutest particles, only later to be gathered together, and, *horribile dictu*, this gathering is effected not by him but by the director, who, in the majority of cases, does not allow the actor to come anywhere near to or observe the process or even have the remotest connection with it. Such, on general lines, is the protest of the stage actor who has done work for the cinema.

But is it really true that the cinema, owing to its technical peculiarities, so inflexibly dictates an inevitable elimination of all possibility of the actor concretely feeling the wholeness of his rôle ? Is it really inevitably necessary to make the actor work in such conditions, which, as creative artist, he is unable to accept? Of course not. We must recognise that the system of work with the actor hitherto in vogue with the majority of considerable directors is not only not perfect, but plainly and simply wrong. And it is our task to discover lines along which, just as in theatre (and we have already seen that discontinuity exists also in stage acting, but to a lesser degree), the actor can be furnished with working conditions enabling him to effect the essential process of living-into his rôle.

Let us state here in set terms that, however the solution be found, it will not be by avoidance of splitting up the acting of the actor during the process of shooting itself; for from this we not only shall not escape, but, in fact, must not escape if we are properly to appreciate the essence of the path along which the cinema's main development lies. We must not avoid this splitting up, but simply seek and find corresponding technical methods to aid the actor in struggling against and overcoming it, thereby re-establishing for him the possibility of internally creating and preserving a feeling of the sum total of the separate fragments of acting as a single image, organically livened by himself. The theatre helps the actor by development and particularisation of the method of rehearsal. We in the cinema must find means of following the same path.

First for a moment let us understand whence derives this distorted degree of splitting up we have just admitted as characteristic for cinema. The discovery and establishment of the need to split up the actor's acting into *editing pieces* derives immediately from the methods, technical in the narrowest sense, found appropriate by directors and from the making of films as such. From the earliest moment of appearance of the cinema, those who most profoundly and seriously adopted it, whether consciously or otherwise, as an art form capable of development on independent lines were directors, and accordingly it is natural that the most important works first achieved in cinema were attained under the ægis of marked directorial control.

The directors sought, and indeed found, in cinema specific potentialities enabling them, by its means and its means alone, to exert an impression on the spectators not only powerful, but in certain instances more powerful than that which could have been achieved in any other medium.

It is the directors who discovered those special forms of composition for the at first wholly visual, subsequently compound (partly sound) images of film termed *montage* or constructive editing. Rhythmic composition of pieces of celluloid introduced the element of rhythmic composition indispensable for impression in any art. In providing the indispensable basis for making the cinema an art at all, it at the same time made it an especially notable one, for it enabled also a wealth of embrace of the actual world impossible to any other art save perhaps literature.

The perception and realisation of the camera-microphone combination as an observer ideally mobile in space and time not only gave straightway to the film an epic sweep, it not unnaturally tended to distract the director and scenarist associated with him from proper recollection of the importance of bearing constantly in mind that a living human individual is an individuality of at least a given profundity and complexity of its own. The possibility of swinging the focus of attention of the technical recording apparatus to a boundless number of different points of interest, their combination in the cutting process, the possibility of eliminating action from a film at given intervals, as though contracting or expanding time itself, all these possibilities led to results that placed the cinema pre-eminent among the arts in its capacity for breadth of comprehension of material of the real world. At the same time, however, the distracting process of exploring these possibilities led directors at a given stage in the development of film to a point at which they began to use the living man, the actor, merely as one component in the film, side by side with and equivalent to other components, material of equal and undifferentiated value, ready to take its turn and place and submit as inanimately to editorial composition in the closing stages of the creative work on the film.

The actor became, so to say, shuffled, sorted out, used, in effect, like an aeroplane, a motor-car, or a tree. ⌈Directors, in searching for the right methods of constructing a performance cinematographically, missed realising that to get fullest value in a performance, cinematographic or otherwise, by a living being, that living person must not only not be eliminated in the process, must not only be preserved, but must be brought out; and if this bringing out be not realistic, that is, not unified and alive, in the end the man in the film will be a great deal more lifeless than the aeroplane and the motor-car (which, it must be confessed, is precisely what has happened in the work of some of our directors). With the actor used as a machine, in a mechanical way, became associated a whole flood of theoretical outpourings based on a mechanical extension of the editorial methods of alternation in length of pieces in cutting into a methodology for the actor's work on the floor.⌉ These technical outpourings could, in fact, only unfairly be dignified with the name of theory, inasmuch as they were only justifications of an empiria based on experiments concerned with something quite different, the main problems of editorial composition in film.

Their trend, however, was roughly as follows. On the screen we have long-shots and close-ups. Therefore the actor must exactly adapt his behaviour in front of the camera to the requirements of these various camera-angles. On the screen there exists an undoubted interaction of effect between two adjacent pieces of film, an interaction which obtains though the content of the first piece be acting by an actor and that of the second any phenomenon the director or scenarist may require, taking place at any point of space whatever, however far removed from the actor in actual fact. Therefore the actor must be able to act his short piece without beginning or end and in absence of that which eventually will influence the content of his acting by interaction with it on the screen.

On the screen we can move the actor in the action with lightning speed from any one point in time or space to another, which we cannot do in the actual shooting on the floor. Therefore the actor must be able to act separate bits separated from one another by any time interval and trust their combination entirely and solely to the director, the only person guided by fore-perception of the film in its already completed state.

This is the way in which some have imagined the sum total of technical activity demanded of the actor. This mechanical understanding lacks all appreciation of the main fact, which is that the creative process of the actor is and must remain the fight for the feeling of the living substance of that image any component separate action in the make-up of which, however far removed from its fellow, will none the less be connected with it within the actor. And, further, that the technique of this

DISCONTINUITY

process can and must be no more and no less than the methods of this fight. No help has ever been afforded the actor in this direction, and consequently, truth to tell, the technique of acting in the cinema has remained at a low level.

I must emphasise yet again that, in speaking of the unity of the image and divining a technique to help the actor to achieve it, I in no way renounce or repudiate the indispensability of making separate, relatively short pieces in the process of shooting. There is a tendency afoot to help the actor by transforming his work to longer pieces and longer shots. This tendency is really nothing but a step along the line of least resistance, squeezing back into the cinema by contraband route the specialities and technique of the stage. This tendency is one that ignores, or deliberately turns its back upon, precisely those potentialities of the cinema that have set it in a place distinct and apart from the other arts, a place, as I have already said, earned directly by the multitude, and therefore shortness, of the pieces composing a film. This path is open to anyone. The film *Groza* [1] must, from this point of view, be considered as definitely reactionary. At the same time it undoubtedly has an important instructive lesson for us, as it is one of the first in our cinema that has given the actor a chance to feel himself a live human being in the process of his acting on the floor.

Of course, it is not this road leading to the mere

[1] *The Tempest*, directed by Petrov, from the play by Ostrovsky.—TR.

bounding of cinematograph performance by stage limits of time and space that is the right road for the cinema. We must give battle on that general front that includes the uttermost wealth of possibilities the cinema can give, and whereon, as is the natural course, we shall consequently encounter the maximum number of obstacles.

CHAPTER IV

THEORETICAL POSTULATES OF DISCONTINUITY

THE aim of the theatre, as of any other art form, is, let us repeat the definition, the collective comprehension and modification of reality by its reflection in the work of art. The only basic weapon in the arsenal of methods the theatre has at its disposal for carrying out this process is the actor's dialogue. That embrace of reality to the maximum degree which is the aim and purpose of the artist is, in the theatre, fundamentally possible only by means of the actor, the human being, by means of his gesture, his speech, and his linkage to other persons in dialogue.

It is true that, in the performance on the stage, apart from the human individual, the material shaping of the action also plays a part in the direct representation to the spectator of the reality outside the actor. But none the less, the theatre is of such a character that the primary basis conveying the content of the performance is the speaking human being, i.e. the actor linked to other actors by dialogue.

The representation of the reality outside the actor in the theatre is exceedingly limited by its technique. There are certain instances in which the material part of the performance, the background, is given prominence. But when the theatre chooses this line, it rapidly exhausts its possibilities of development. In general the portrayal of wide and varied events environmental to any given element of human activity is possible only by their description in the text; that is to say, once more and again by human speech spoken on the stage, that is, by the actor.

The direct portrayal of events organically connected in content with the action but separated from it in space or time can, in the long run, only be rendered on the stage by their narration. Messengers, or a compère, are typical theatrical devices often introduced for the purpose.

The world of reality, grasped by the artist in his creative act of comprehending it, in the main can penetrate the theatre only through the actor, his voice, his gesture, his movements, his behaviour. This is the characteristic of the theatre.

The cinema is different. That which on the stage can only be narrated, on the screen can be directly represented. The special technical basis of the cinema, already discussed above, is to a remarkable degree capable of direct portrayal, direct transmission to the spectator of any event occurring in reality.

It might be argued that direct portrayal is neither necessary nor even specially desirable. In the process of generalisation essentially typical of every creative act, especially in art, one might renounce the direct representation of separate events dispersed in time and space and gather them into a generalising whole that the artist might situate anywhere in any single spot. No one can dispute the necessity for generalisation in the creative process. But its realisation to the extent of an idealistic compromise with facile and old-fashioned forms and rejection of new possibilities never heretofore available must, in my view, be regarded as essentially wrong and reactionary.

I once had occasion to talk to a playwright who frankly admitted that, when planning a play on aviation, he realised without doubt that material of such a nature would fall more clearly, expressively, and effectively into the form of a film.

Here is a concrete example, a notable and significant phenomenon of our present-day reality, the world development of aviation, one which in considerable degree conditions a change and development in the psychology of mankind, and which in its full richness can be mastered and transmitted to the audience only by direct representation of events so far-reaching in scope and occurring in such dimensions that they cannot possibly be accommodated on the stage of a theatre.

On the stage the actor will tell of a flight, in literature the author will add to the tale a description of the circumstances exterior to the inward emotions of the person flying, but only the cinema can unite for the benefit of the spectator the direct and fullest sensation of both.

A direct portrayal, for reasons sufficiently obvious,

invariably exerts an especially strong and vivid impression. In strength of influence on the spectator, the theatre, owing to its directness of representation, even of its limited material, has hitherto held foremost place among the arts. If we take into consideration the capacity of the cinema directly to introduce material immeasurably richer than that which the theatre can ever hope to tackle, we perceive how, of its own nature, the cinema can approach or even transcend literature in its exceptional power of impression.

The cinema is in a sense a potential mirror, directly representing events in the wholeness of their dialectical complexity. In the wholeness of this reflection resides a profound force irresistibly dragging the spectator himself into participation in the creative process. The directness of representation of cinema material, even having regard to the element of generalisation inseparable from its composition, forces the spectator to take himself an active part in comprehending it at the moment of its portrayal.

It is noteworthy that Lenin, with that striking simplicity and clarity in understanding the essence of things invariably characteristic of him, immediately determined the cinema as first and foremost a powerful means of the widest embrace and understanding of reality and its transmission to the many-millioned masses—and this just on the basis of a chance report of purely technical character.

I refer to the well-known programme for the

cinema, in which Lenin emphasised the importance of the cinema's astonishing ability to portray the world, to acquaint broad peasant and working-class masses with the nature of other countries, and so forth.

Our cinema, at least in so far as the work of its best directors is concerned, has developed and is developing principally in the direction of incorporating in films the maximum possible wealth, in direct representation, of the variety of events of reality, sometimes indeed at the expense of the necessary degree of generalisation.

This characteristic cannot, in my view, be regarded as explicable simply as the outcome of the individual taste of the directors. We should, in my view, bear in mind the fact that the living reality around us is pushing forward under our noses with so manifold a growth that, more often than not, in grasping it and passing it on to the spectator, we have no time to pause and mould its complexity into the limits of a generalisation.

Realise the multitude of dogmas that has been exploded and destroyed during the revolution. The fight, still continuing, against dogma, against the remnants of capitalist consciousness, often expresses itself in the offer by the artist, instead of a formula, of its living content, as though directly appealing to the spectator to co-operate by himself performing, in his act of comprehension, the necessary generalisation of the complexity presented to him.

FILM ACTING

The point is illustrated by an example only indirectly related to our subject. That exceptionally gifted writer, Leo Tolstoy, who achieved a book, *War and Peace*, amazing in its vitality and in the endless wealth of real and live material it contains, wrote as he grew older *Resurrection*, a book in which page after page, chapter after chapter, is full of generalisations, dissertations, deductions, in which the persons move less and act less, in which the persons are themselves fewer and the space of action narrower.

And this same Tolstoy towards the close of his life constantly wrote philosophical treatises devoid both of life and live characters.

The above remarks on Tolstoy are not, of course, in any sense a valuation of the various stages of his art. I desired only to instance by this example the fact that whole and important works of art can be created in a creative tension deriving from a vigorous youthful perception of reality, without renouncing the widest direct portrayal of the innumerable separate elements of reality.

The advancement of generalisation is, of course, one path of development, but it is none the less liable to grow into dogma; that is to say, at a given stage to cause a change over into senile decay, to change from an art capable of moving people to cold and dry sermonising.

This is why, in pondering the various paths open to the cinema, I cannot but recall the achievement attained by Tolstoy's amazing genius in *War and Peace*, and reflect with alarm on the fate of that same genius of Tolstoy frozen stiff into the iceberg of idealist dogma.

We must not be frightened by the wealth of material in our films. I have often come across rabid protagonists of the famous Chaplin film *Woman of Paris*. This film is certainly an example of the highest directorial and acting skill, but the trouble is that its partisans not only praise the film as an example of skill, but desire to elevate its methods into a pattern for the basis of film art. The film is staged in a deeply intimate manner. The action hardly even leaves the limits of a couple of rooms. The one solitary exterior that occurs in the film portrays a section of roadway on which the dramatis personæ meet for the last time and separate on their respective ways.

The painstaking attention of its author-director is concentrated on the minutest details of the small drama that unrolls in the intimate circle of its four or five characters. This is all very excellent and possible in its way and in no wise to be rejected by us. The film *Groza* (*The Tempest*) is very similar in its cinematic treatment to the Chaplin film.

But it seems to me that this type of film is not merely unsuitable to many of our Soviet film writers, but in general is liable to distract the cinema from its specific, exceptional, and most effective possibilities.

For Chaplin all the wealth of events linked together in the complicated life of human society was not necessary, because these phenomena have long ago been transmuted by bourgeois thought into a corresponding number of dead dogmas. Chaplin, living in a bourgeois milieu, easily detaches his world of four persons from the ' rest,' because the ' rest ' for him and for the audience to which he appeals is just a world of ready-made ideas fixed and not especially exciting. The universally accepted ideas and norms of a bourgeois audience represent a wall with which it screens itself from the perils of a developing society, and it is the bourgeois artist's job to preserve this wall intact. Contact with the richness of the outer world must inevitably be alarming for the bourgeois artist. Whereas with our audience and our artists it is, of course, quite different.

The organic link between the tense-strung complexity of our epoch and the character of the work of art in cinema is certain. And a striving towards maximum mastery of reality in content, the realisation of the maximum possibility of direct representation of reality on the screen, just as certainly leads to the specific method characteristic of film art —*montage* or the editing together of numerous relatively short pieces.

We must, further, mention here an additional specific potentiality of cinema which also inevitably entails the splitting up of the actor's work in the process of being shot.

Imagine an actor delivering an emotional speech in a large auditorium. The listening crowd reacts to the words of the orator. It applauds, it interrupts with isolated calls and shouts. Suppose we desire to portray the crowd not as a thousand-headed faceless mass, but as a many-imaged unity, if we appreciate the fact that a mass is comprehended in its real content and significance only when are perceptible its component individual groups, and within these their component individuals. Then we shall be obliged to transfer the position of the camera rapidly from place to place, we shall be obliged, in the course of the oration, to change alternately from long shot embracing both orator and audience to separate closer shots, penetrating into the thick of the mass, and glimpsing a group or single listener reacting by shout or gesture. We shall inevitably have to split up the one speech of the orator into separate pieces, in order that they may be welded in the process of editing into a whole with the separate pieces of members of the audience reacting, and thereby derive unity from the multiplicity of many-imaged details.

It might be argued that, for the purpose of an editing construction of this type, it is unnecessary to break the whole speech of the orator into separate pieces in the shooting. It might suffice to shoot the speech as a whole and subsequently to chop it on the cutting bench into the necessary separate pieces interleaved with the given auditor pieces. But film directors who strive to exploit the cinema's possibilities to the full cannot follow this course. They use not only words out of the orator's speech. Realise what tremendous importance in the construction of the whole image of man in action have his gestures and his pantomime connected with his utterances. This pantomime, at times of the most fine and complex order, plays a part no less important than the intonation of the voice.

Now, the culmination of the impression effected by an uttered word or sentence depends upon a movement of the hand; again, the closing of the eyes may add an unexpected touch of pathos to another word or phrase. Only the cinema, by virtue of the mobility of the camera, can so direct the excited attention of the audience that, at any given moment of his acting, the actor can, as it were, turn to the audience his most poignant, most expressive, side.

And it is this method of shoving the play of the actor right up under the nose of the audience that inevitably necessitates the splitting of the single process of the speech into separate pieces in the actual shooting.

At one moment we see the face of the orator with eyes tight shut. At another his whole body straining with arms held high. For an instant we catch his glance directed straight at us. A nervous movement of his hand behind his back may also serve as a definite and colourful characterisation of some moment.

Such material can only be obtained by shooting bits of the speech separately, with change of position of camera and microphone. Simultaneous shooting by several cameras at once, placed at separate points, will not give us an unhamperedly sharp and vivid editing treatment on the screen, because a camera placed for a close-up would be bound to get in the way of a camera taking a long-shot at the same time. Separate, interrupted shooting is indispensable.

The question must be formulated simply in this way: should the immensely rich possibilities afforded by the cinema for the purpose of deepening the play of the actor be sacrificed to the natural desire of the actor to dwell in his acting image as wholly and uninterruptedly as possible, or should one search for means of helping him that none the less permit these possibilities to be maintained and exploited to maximum advantage ?

The difficulty of solving this problem is, basically, the long and the short of the difficulty confronting the cinema actor, and the methods and ways of solving it are, in sum, the conditioning methods of his technique.

We have already seen that this difficulty exists also in the theatre. The break between two stage entrances of an actor does not differ materially from the break between two shots in the cinema.

The whole content of a stage play could, after all, take the form of a single continuous speech that one actor-speaker could utter without leaving the boards. In general, however, the theatre variegates its content, introducing action shared in by numerous dramatic personæ, and portraying directly numerous deeds and events, not merely reporting them in speech. It splits the course of the play into acts, thereby eliminating chunks of time

FILM ACTING

The actor could, really, remain on the stage throughout the duration of a whole act without for a second being switched from the action, but the theatre as a rule insists on taking him off into the wings, because realistic enlargement of the action demands the introduction of new characters, and these new characters must not only push various old ones temporarily into the background, but even from time to time squeeze them from the orbit of the audience's attention altogether. Whereupon the first actor must stand in the wings waiting for the moment when the development of the play's action will once more drag him front stage.

I repeat that this 'split-life,' this discontinuous animation, of the stage actor, does not differ organically from the 'separate-shot-acting' of the film actor in the course of the shooting of a film.

The contradiction between the personality of the actor and his striving in the process of his acting to become a linked part of the whole circumstances environing the wide sweep of development of a realistic film, this contradiction, I repeat, exists not only in theatre and in cinema, but is analogous to the contradiction in creation general to all arts.

And, we must affirm once more, the solution of this contradiction will be achieved not by its elimination, but by proper understanding of the significance of the methods of acting technique, and consequently of the means legitimate to employ.

CHAPTER V

REHEARSAL WORK

WHAT are the basic methods the actor finds ? We have already seen that the theatre supports him in his fight for organic unity of the acting image by means of a detailed methodology of rehearsals.

In these rehearsals, obedient to the will of the actors and producer, the stern temporal conditions limiting the players are for a space removed and substituted by more unified and uninterrupted work aiding the actor to link, in whatsoever direction may be necessary, his live personality with the image he plays.

At rehearsals the actor, free from breaks in time or position, can link the separate pieces of his rôle into one whole, can concretely live into his image, checking it by a series of pieces of his rôle outside the play, but undoubtedly organically belonging to the image. In short, at rehearsals he can do all that work which will enable him later on to feel every separate piece of his rôle, however interrupted it may be mechanically in the course of the performance, as his own, belonging to him, and if not uninterrupted in the sense of his physical presence on the stage, at least inwardly uninterrupted in the unity of his feeling and understanding of the rôle.

FILM ACTING

What do we do in the cinema in the way of providing technical help to the actor in his difficult creative work? It must be admitted that this assistance, where it is even given at all, is in most producing collectives of an exceedingly perfunctory character. Sometimes there are attempts at just a preliminary working-through the script with the actor by the director. The rôle is discussed, the rôle is, in fact, talked all round and about, so-called actor and director ' rôle-conferences ' take place. Something on the lines of so-called ' round-table conferences ' in the theatre (work in the theatre preliminary to rehearsals) takes place in the cinema to a greater or lesser degree. But no practical preliminary work with the actor on the lines of linking the image found at the ' round-table conference ' with its outer expression, actually the basic starting-point of the work needed to transform an actor thinking about a rôle into an actor acting it, has ever been used as a normal course.

In his preliminary work on the image the actor has, quite ridiculously and unnecessarily, been mechanically separated from practice, from the concrete work on himself as a live, connectedly and unitedly moving and speaking human being. The actor has approached the work of being shot, a process already requiring technically fixed and defined methods of execution, quite unaided, and able only academically to image to himself the general meaning of his rôle, in no way having linked it to his concrete live individuality. Such has been the

position in the best cases; in the worst the actor
purely and simply has not known anything about his
rôle apart from the sum total of directorial instructions restricted to each piece being shot. Naturally,
each shot is proceeded by a sort of travesty of a
rehearsal, but this cannot be considered seriously,
for no antecedent work has ever been done upon it
to give it an inner link to the unity of the actor's
image.

It is this incorrect attitude to the tasks of acting
work that has given rise to the pseudo-theory of the
montage (edited) image (a theory for which no single
individual is responsible). This theory deduces,
from the fact that an impression of acting can be
composed mechanically by sticking pieces together,
the illegitimate assumption that separate pieces, not
connected inwardly within the actor, will necessarily give an optimum result.

The true significance of the edited image is quite
different; it has considerable importance for the
cinema actor, and we shall speak of it later.

Just as in the theatre, so in the cinema, the
methodology of rehearsals is all-important for the
actor.

In fact, as we have already observed, this methodology is even more important in the cinema than in
the theatre, since the hyper-discontinuity of acting
work in shooting desiderates a correspondingly
especially clear, definite, and detailed absorption by
the actor of the wholeness of his rôle.

Systematic rehearsal work in the cinema prior to

shooting has so far been conducted only by way of experiment.

I cannot speak of the work of the Experimental Film Collectives, as they have made no verbal or written record of their experiences in this field. I shall discuss the experiment of Kuleshov in his film: *The Great Consoler*.[1]

Kuleshov wrote a shooting script, that is, a script worked out in technical detail as it is to be shot on the floor and edited afterwards. All the shots in this script, numbered and with their numerical order preserved, were transferred to a miniature studio floor. In fact, prior to the shooting of the film, he staged a performance consisting of very short scenes each in length identical with the piece later to be edited. As far as possible Kuleshov played each scene through on the studio floor in such a way that subsequently, after most careful rehearsal, it could be transferred back to and shot without alteration on the actual floor used in shooting.

His rehearsal system attained three results. First, it achieved the preliminary work with the actor to the deepest possible degree. Second, it gave the executives the opportunity to ' see ' the film, as it were, before it was shot, and make in time any correction or alteration that might be required. And third, it reduced to a minimum the waste of time during the preliminaries to each shot, which, as is well known, in general run away with a great deal of money.

[1] A film blended of O. Henry's life and *Alias Jimmy Valentine*,

REHEARSAL WORK

The combination of these results gave Kuleshov's work a somewhat peculiar style. First and foremost, in striving at all costs to make the rehearsal performance an exact pattern of the future screen performance, Kuleshov undoubtedly not only rehearsed his actors, but also to some extent adapted his film to a form more convenient and simple for the carrying out of the rehearsal.

It is not a coincidence that Kuleshov's film contains few dramatis personæ. It is not a coincidence that Kuleshov has no crowd scenes. It is not a coincidence that the extremely sparse and limited exteriors take the shape either of empty country roads or of city streets on which one never meets a soul save those few dramatis personæ.

Kuleshov, of course, wrote his script in this way, set the action in these scenes, chose this subject and this number of characters precisely to give himself the chance to fit the film rapidly and easily into the framework of a stage performance, one, moreover, of necessity played on a stage rather especially primitively fitted out.

I do not think this work of Kuleshov should be treated as wrong in principle. The effort was undoubtedly a most interesting experiment. The experiment was not wrong, but any mechanical deduction that might be made from it along the line of converting the method into a dogmatic recipe to be used in the shooting of any and every film would most undoubtedly be wrong.

Our task remains, of course, the finding of such

ways, such forms, and such methods of adjusting a rehearsal period as will in no wise handicap the film in the field of its exploration of every possible wide and rich development.

We are still faced with the problem how to organise preparatory rehearsal work on a film which definitely and markedly strives to develop along cinematic lines, that is, including a series of scenes embracing a large spacial canvas, locations, and circumstances such as cannot be reproduced on a rehearsal floor.

We must not and cannot pander to a desire to play the future film through on a rehearsal floor to the extent of eliminating from it elements which, though they have no direct physical link with the actor in his acting, yet none the less contribute to the film the power and richness that make it a truly cinematic work of art.

In my view the discovery of the correct methods for the rehearsal period will only be attained by keeping clearly and exclusively to our main purpose. This purpose is, of course, the actor's work on his acting image. All the rest, the demonstration of the whole film to the executives, the learning by rote of set-ups in advance (which latter is, in fact, never completely possible unless the film limits the canvas it shoots to the space within the studio walls), must be subordinated to the maximum fostering of conditions aiding the actor to solve his main technical problem—embodiment in the image.

What, then, are the main postulates of the methodology of the rehearsal period? First let us consider the editing structure set out in the sheets of the shooting script. The sheets of the shooting script list a series of short pieces. Nearly every element of the actor's behaviour linked to the inner order of the action is interspersed with numerous pieces showing the audience either parallel action by other actors at quite a different location, or epically developed elements of events into which the actor is incorporated by developments of the general action, or both.

Suppose such a scene: a person in a room is talking to a man who excitedly awaits a meeting with his brother. The brother is expected by air. The excited wait is interrupted by the ring of a telephone bell. Information is given that the aeroplane is about to land. On the screen the action changes to an aerodrome where we see the plane landing and a sudden crash that causes the death of the brother arriving. The next piece to follow portrays the waiting brother receiving the terrible news.

Should one in the rehearsal period strive to work out separately the two pieces of the state of the waiting man, separated as they will be on the screen by the conventionalised plane crash?

For work with the actor this would not only be unnecessary, but wrong and harmful. The only correct course is to rehearse both pieces in conjunction, thus enabling the actor to stay in the acting image without interruption, and to replace the specifically cinematic element of the portrayal of the crash by a single telephone call announcing the disaster.

Suppose on the screen an actor, fleeing from pursuit, swim a river, and meet on the opposite bank a man whom he was seeking in order to deliver to him some message, it would, of course, be futile and stupid to waste time and energy by staging an actual swim across a river during the rehearsal period. What is important for the actor during rehearsal is the presence somewhere in his rôle of a serious obstacle requiring to be successfully negotiated, and the inclusion of this sensation of recent victory over the obstacle in his feeling during his conversation with the person met beyond the river. In rehearsal conditions, any physical obstacle could serve as equivalent for the river, a window, for example, through which he might have to climb, or a door he might break down, before entering the room.

I choose obvious examples of this kind in order to make clear the simple point that the separate shots (or editing pieces) of the shooting script, divided into its multitudinous incidents, an abundance of which cannot be reproduced on the stage, should properly be transmuted into some other form for the actor to facilitate his concentration in rehearsal on the absorption of the unity of the acting image.

This new form of script might be termed an ' actor's script.' (In an actor's script the separate pieces concerning him would be approximated to one another for the paramount purpose of preserving for him as far as possible a longer duration and less interruption in his acting. The whole material of the director's editing or shooting script would be preserved. Only it would be rearranged in a new sequence, enabling nearer approximation of the shots in the actor's rôle, thus giving him larger pieces of united inner movement.

Of course, such a linking up of the separate pieces in a rôle will in some cases entail the replacement of certain pieces by equivalents, as in the just instanced case of the telephone ring instead of the plane crash.

The actual task of translating a shooting script into actor's scripts is certainly one which requires considerable practical experience for its proper performance. But its purpose is clear and simple.

Stage practice, particularly the practice of the Stanislavski school in the matter of ' interval ' or ' hiatus ' pieces in rehearsal alluded to by us before, can be particularly fruitful for film rehearsals.

Kozintsev has stated that during rehearsal work with the actors on his latest film, *The Youth of Maxim*, he concentrated solely on those parts of the rôle outside the actual action of the film.

The point of his observation is, once again, the fact that the main problem of director and actor invariably boils down to the establishment in rehearsal of the inner unity of any given piece with the rôle as a whole.

So as not to confuse the actor with theatrical conventions alien to the cinema, the director must surround him at rehearsal with real equivalents practical within the limits of a stage or rehearsal room. So as not to force the actor to waste energy in imagining such things as rivers that he will meet in the actual story, the director and actors in rehearsal add equivalent pieces, enabling the inner content of the actor's behaviour to remain unchanged, the river he will have to swim being replaced by some analogous obstacle such as those I have already suggested.

Let me once again emphasise the extreme danger of introducing into cinema rehearsal work specifically theatrical conventions unconnected with actual problems of shooting.

Kuleshov's method of solving the rehearsal problem by having the whole future film played over on the floor involves such a danger.

I repeat once more, also with emphasis, that an ' actor's script ' such as I describe requires careful, meticulous, and profound modification to replace real-life conditions set out in the editing script with equivalent real conditions practicable for the rehearsal stage. And this process can no doubt best be effected in actual concert with the actor.

We should approach the problem wrongly if we excluded *a priori* from this process all possibility of creative work on the script by the actor himself.

The beginning and end of the old system was its orientation around the reduction of the actor's work to an almost mechanical performance of a ' task ' allotted him by the director. We shall never escape

REHEARSAL WORK

from the old system of treating the actor as a prop, as a type, if we do not set the question of creative inter-influence of actor and director right at the forefront of work on the film, already at the stage preceding shooting.

Hitherto the actor, encountering only the complexly constructed shooting script of the director, able to envisage his own future work only abstractly, has been deprived of the possibility of determining clearly and concretely any possible disagreement he might have with the directorial conception of the part. I suggest that an ' acting script ' and rehearsal work with it will provide that now missing concrete basis for a creative mutual influencing of actor and director.

The director's will and effort are devoted to maximal expression of the whole of the film, and his work on the editing or shooting script is oriented from this angle, exploiting in this script all the wealth of the specific methods provided him by the technique of the cinema. But subsequently he should compress the shots in this shooting script into an acting script. This new acting or rehearsal script would not merely represent the solution of the given shooting problems as set out in the shooting script, but also the concrete fulfilment of the requirements postulated by the actor's need for aid in maintaining unity and vividness in his image. From this script, in the process of rehearsal, new data would doubtless be forthcoming, justifying a second edition of the shooting script, inevitably, quite properly and to creative advantage replacing the first. And only in this last form would the script actually go forward for shooting.

This is a means, it seems to me, whereby might be achieved a real linking of the actor to the unity of the work of the whole shooting collective.

CHAPTER VI

THE EDITING IMAGE

WE now come to the shaping of the editing image. This concept, the subject of the most acrimonious controversy, is in fact the crux of the novel and different nature of the cinema, distinguishing it from the theatre.

When the stage actor works on his inward embodiment into the acting image, his work is bound inextricably with two tasks: firstly, the search for its external form of expression—voice, gesture, grimace —and secondly, the clear consideration of that general ideological tendency of his rôle that links his work with the performance as a whole and with each of its details separately.

Let us analyse the first task. In working on his external expressiveness, the stage actor naturally moulds the whole process of his acting into a rhythmic form. His speech receives in delivery intonational emphasis or weakening according to whether he wishes at any given movement to seize and hold the audience by the 'content' or the 'emotional' side of his speech. In his pattern of movements and gesture he also creates moments of rise and fall, of vividness and restraint, of strength and weakness. But an actor moving and speaking on the stage always remains at relatively the same constant distance from the spectators, in a position in space more or less constant in respect to them. For the spectators to see his hand, he must show it to them; for the spectators to see his face, he must turn it to them; for the spectators to hear his whisper, he must raise it to the level of loudness.

The cinema has to create its analogous rhythm of externally expressive form in a different manner. I have already described how the camera and microphone can move to approach or recede from the actor, how they can espy the finest movements of his body, eavesdrop the most delicate intonations of his voice. By this means the acting of the actor, treated in long shot and in close shot, angled from various set-ups, is rendered especially vivid and expressive.

If the stage actor, in the course of working out the maximum external expressiveness of his rôle, wish, at some given moment of the performance, to centre the whole attention of the audience on, let us suppose, his smile following the word 'No,' then he knows perfectly well that not only must his word be spoken well and his smile smiled well, but that the audience must listen to the word and watch the smile especially attentively.

For this purpose, the actor uses in support of the stage delivery of his rôle all the complex mechanism of theatre technique. He can use sets, or composition of the action in them, leading the attention of the audience away from his colleagues and fixing it, precisely at the crucial moment. on himself. He can use a pause immediately following, spotlights, concentrating their light on him alone.

In the cinema all this complicated system of methods can be reduced to a single close-up. The close-up in the cinema is an integral part of the rhythm of external expression of the actor.

The editing of separate camera angles in the cinema is the more vivid and expressive equivalent of the technique that obliges a stage actor who has inwardly absorbed his acting image to 'theatricalise' its outer form.

The film actor must clearly understand that the moving of the camera from place to place is not simply a means of realising purely directorial methods. The understanding and feel of the possibilities of the shooting of shots from various angles must be organically included in the process of the actor's own work on the external shaping of his rôle.

The film actor must feel the urge and the necessity for a given camera position for the shooting of any given piece of his rôle in precisely the same way as a stage actor feels the necessity, at a given point in the course of his rôle, for making an especially emphasised gesture, or for advancing to the footlights, or for ascending two steps of a scenery stairs.

The actor must appreciate that it is in this very movement of the camera that lies latent that essential sensitivity that removes work in the field of art from the sphere of shapeless naturalism.

However profoundly the stage actor embodies himself into his rôle in the course of his work on the image, he must not, and in fact does not, forget the need always to consider also the objective content and value of the final result—his behaviour in acting on the stage during the actual performance portrayed to the audience. The image, however deeply absorbed by the actor, does not exist in the performance as a separate entity. Linked by the course of the action, it is subject to the complex interplay and mutual influence of all the forces comprising the performance as a whole.

The supremely important social class significance of the actor's performance is determined by the performance as a whole. There is not an element in the performance, be it the acting of a colleague, or the material composition of a scene, but must be linked to the final form of the whole and therefore of the remaining parts. Even during the very first moments of work on the image, when the actor is mainly seeking and feeling for ways of embodying himself as a given individual in the image he intends to play, he is yet clearly conscious of and sets before himself as his aim the figure sketched out by the libretto of the play, which figure eventually will move and speak upon the boards. He appreciates what the future stage image is and how it is embedded in the entirety of the performance. But on the stage the actor who sought and shaped the rôle yet remains in the finally discovered and shaped performance a live person. The image he finally finds and fixes in himself and in the performance, he never separates from himself as from a living, feeling, and speaking person.

THE EDITING IMAGE

In the film it is quite otherwise. The culminating achievement of the actor's work—in the theatre the stage image—is in the cinema something of a quite different order. As final result appears the edited image—a screen image of the actor, recorded and fixed once and for all upon the film, a final and optimum version of his work's achievement, which, quite apart from any other distinction, has in the course of its expression been subjected to a technical finishing process quite impossible of application to a living being.

Just as in the unity of the stage show the image of the actor is ' produced ' in the fullness of its content by the complex interaction of all the forces comprised in the performance, so in the cinema the separate pieces of shot acting of the actor are moulded into a unified image the unity and orientation of which are determined not merely by the unity found by the actor within himself, but also by the exceedingly complex interaction of those many pieces containing alien phenomena, situated exterior to the actor.

The most comprehensive, the profoundest lines determining the content of the image, are discernible, of course, only when the whole composition of the film is available.

We have already noted that the wealth of events of the world of reality which the cinema can embrace is much wider than that accessible to the theatre. While the relationship between a given actor and the whole performance is on the stage determined principally in the conflict between the actor and his colleague, an actor using dialogue like himself, in the cinema the actor encounters not only man. In the completed film the acting actor is brought into relationship with the whole tremendous complexity of objective reality, and in this respect therefore is placed in a position nearer to that of a part of a literary work than to that of a *dramatis persona* in a play.

Thus the concept of the edited image by no means implies (as some have sought to declare) a negation of the necessity for unified work by the actor on his rôle. The concept of the edited image is by no means an affirmation of the doctrine that the film actor is merely a type actor providing piecemeal material for mechanical composition into a pseudo-whole in the process of editing.

On the contrary, this concept, analogous to that of the stage image, demands from the film actor firstly a knowledge of how consciously to exploit the possibilities of vari-angled shooting for the purposes of his work on the external shaping of his rôle, and, secondly, clear consideration of its creative place in the edited composition of the whole film, in order that he may understand and bring out the most comprehensive and profound bases of his acting.

In stage work there exists a clear and precise concept, the ensemble; in the creation of the ensemble participates not only the producer, but also each separate actor, building his work in direct connection with the whole of the performance. In the cinema the equivalent concept has reached in its

Non-professional as an old woman.
" SIMPLE CASE," *Pudovkin*.

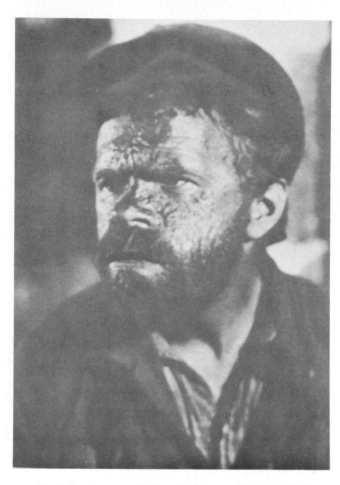

Savitsky, non-professional (former Siberian Red
Partisan), as a strike-breaker.

"MOTHER," *Pudovkin.*

Tchistiakov, then non-professional (book-keeper since become actor), as the father.

"MOTHER," *Pudovkin*.

Batalov, actor, as the son.
" MOTHER," *Pudovkin.*

Rogulina, then first-year student at the G.I.K. (State Institute of Cinematography, Moscow), as Masha, wife of the Red Army Commander.

"SIMPLE CASE," *Pudovkin.*

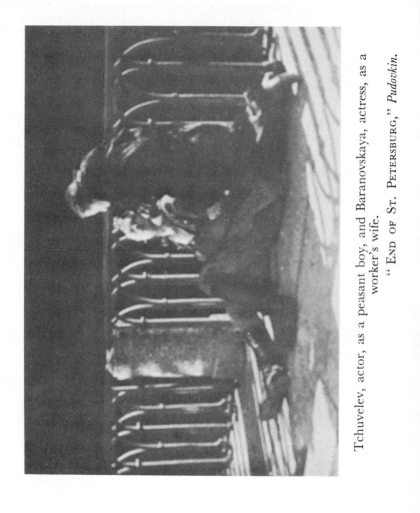

Tchuvelev, actor, as a peasant boy, and Baranovskaya, actress, as a worker's wife.

"END OF ST. PETERSBURG," *Pudovkin.*

Tchuvelev, actor, as a peasant boy.
" END OF ST. PETERSBURG," *Pudovkin*.

Pudovkin as a police officer, and Baranovskaya, actress, as the mother.
" MOTHER," *Pudovkin.*

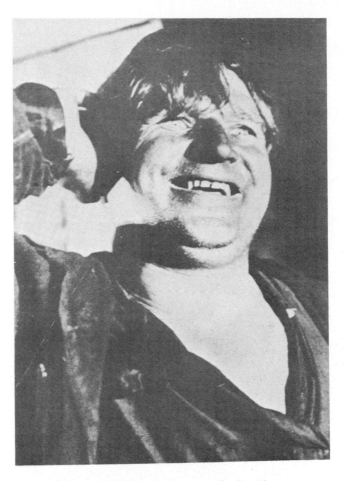

Sovrotchin, actor, as a strike-breaker.
" MOTHER," *Pudovkin.*

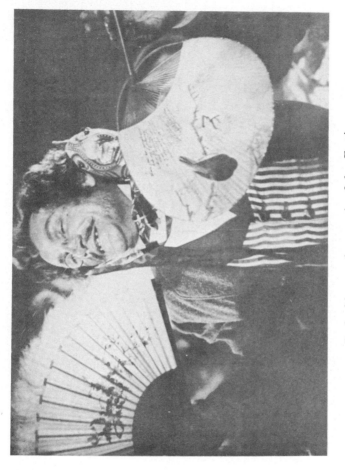

Pudovkin as a bourgeois of the *Empire*.
" NEW BABYLON," *Kozintsev and Trauberg.*

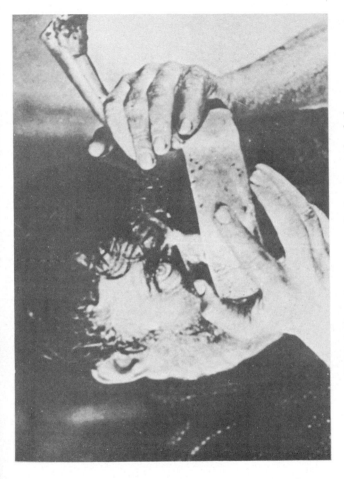

Tchistiakov, then non-professional, as the father.
" MOTHER," *Pudovkin*.

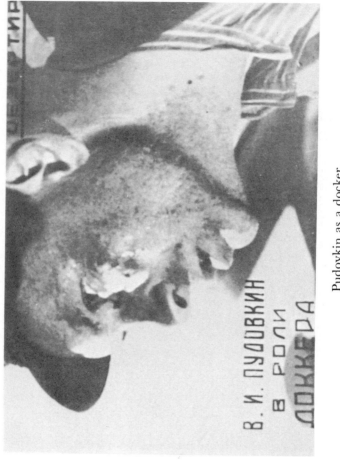

Pudovkin as a docker.
" DESERTER," *Pudovkin.*

Baranovskaya, actress, as the mother.
" MOTHER," *Pudovkin.*

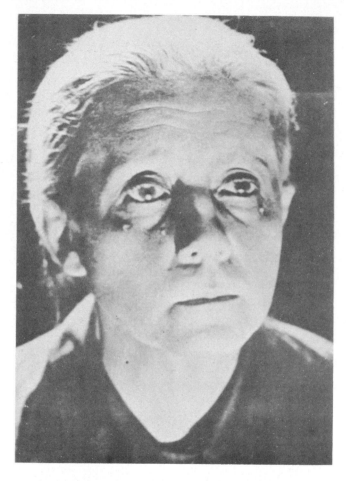

Baranovskaya, actress, as the mother.
" MOTHER," *Pudovkin.*

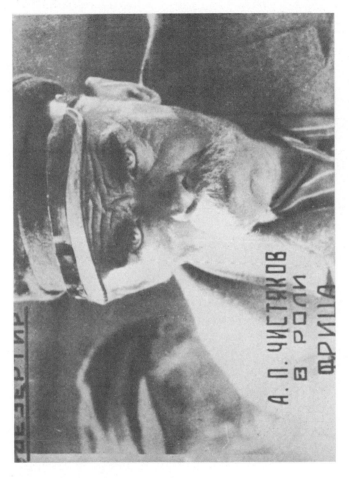

Tchistiakov, now actor, as Fritz, a German workers' leader. "DESERTER," *Pudovkin.*

Livanov, actor, as a German worker.
" DESERTER," *Pudovkin.*

shaping almost the limit of technical precision. A film, a work the material of which includes the acting of actors, can attain, in the exactitude and precision of its rhythmic construction, the exactitude of the rhythmic construction of a musical composition. Hence the especial strictness and rigidity of the requirements to which film actors must subordinate their work in the course of its external shaping, those film actors, that is, who value not only their own rôles, but the film as a whole.

The stage actor knows well that an unhappily chosen or badly played tune preceding his speech can not only damage but distort the rôle he is trying to create. The film actor must understand that a piece of a landscape or some other phenomenon, either preceding or following the piece with his acting in it, will indubitably enter as a component into the line of his image as it will be apprehended by the audience watching the screen.

The edited image is that final and definite form that enters into interaction with the third element comprising the work of art—the spectator. In distinction from the stage image, it is divorced from the living actor, and for this very reason, in order not to lose realistic unity, must be conceived by the actor and thought out carefully from the very first stages of his work on himself and his rôle.

While on the stage the actor can more exactly adjust his place in the whole during the actual course of the second performance to the audience, the film does not give him this opportunity. Further, the work of the actor in endeavouring to reach sharpest apprehension of the film as a whole is more complex and difficult. Therefore it must be regarded as particularly paradoxical that this side of his work, the study of his relation to the film as a whole, is far more deeply provided for in the theatre than in the cinema.

Here we should mention still another difficulty characteristic of the work of the film actor. In the theatre exists the so-called 'living link' between an actor and his emotionalised audience. It is a well-known fact that performances of a show differ, and that this difference depends on and is caused by differences of audience composition. There exists an abundance of stories concerning notable actors and how the living reaction of audiences has forced them at various times to find new business for their rôles, or to discard business they had previously found and used.

All stage actors declare that they derive the real high-pressure tension and inspiration necessary for full value in their acting only from the feeling of the audience being moved.

In the cinema we are in the presence of an entirely new phenomenon: never, not even during the most important moment of his acting, when the actor is face to face with the camera recording his final achievement, has he the chance to feel directly the reaction of a single spectator. He can imagine his spectator only as a future spectator.

In the 'living link' between actor and spectator

should be distinguished two elements, which we shall analyse separately in their relation to the cinema.

The two elements are these : first, the general excitement and inspiration felt by the stage actor aware of thousands of eyes centred upon him, conscious of a thousand-fold concentration of attention upon his acting, and second, the presence of the living reaction of the audience, as it were itself taking part in the creative process of the development of the rôle, and thereby helping the actor.

The first element, direct consciousness in the actor of the multiple spectator, is completely absent in the cinema. At the moment of shooting, the actor sees in front of him only the dumb mechanisms of the camera and sound-recording apparatus. The system used for lighting, which entails the surrounding of the actor with lamps, seems also as though deliberately engaged in isolating him into the space allotted for the taking of the scene, a space so small that sometimes the actor is even cut off from seeing the whole of the room in which the action takes place.

But does it follow that the feeling of an audience and the creative excitement and inspiration deriving from the audience are thereby necessarily excluded from the work of the film actor ? I hold that it does not. True, this feeling of the audience can come into existence only in a new and peculiar manner.

I remember a conversation with the now late V. V. Mayakovski.[1] He told me once about the feeling he experienced when, during the years of

[1] Committed suicide in 1932.—TR.

revolution, he declaimed his verses to an enormous crowd that had collected in front of the balcony of the building of the Moscow Soviet.

V. V. complained that nowadays he never felt that tremendous inspiration he did then. Only in one circumstance, he said, do I feel the same excitement, if not an even greater than in those days, and that is when I make a speech on the wireless.

I maintain that Mayakovski was completely and utterly sincere. It is interesting that to a man like him, who undoubtedly had organically lived and nourished his creative process on the reaction of the mass audience, the broadcasting studio did not feel like a solitary confinement cell isolating him from his listeners. That creative imagination which is part and parcel of every great artist, which makes him one with and related to all the world of reality, enabled him not only to appreciate intellectually, but to feel directly, that the words spoken into the microphone spread immediately over a gigantic area and became received by millions of attentive listeners.

Let us be clear that Mayakovski was not referring to an intellectual understanding of the importance of wireless, but to a direct excitement and inspiration caused in him by work before the microphone. Once more I repeat that Mayakovski likened this excitement to that which he had felt when directly before him he had seen listening a crowd thousands strong.

I consider that for a film actor who really and truly

lives in his art the possibility of such an excitement is not excluded. On the stage an actor plays before hundreds of persons, in the film actually before millions. Here is a dialectical instance of quantity increasing over the boundary into quality to give rise to a new kind of excitement, not less real and, of course, not less significant.

Let us turn to the second element. The collaboration in creation on the part of the spectator, his living reaction to the acting, his acceptance and applause of the right and felicitous, his cold repudiation of anything mistaken—none of this, also, can be present in the taking of a film.

Hence, I urge, upon the director, who is the one and only witness of the acting during the shooting of a film, reposes an especial responsibility, in no way corresponding to any equivalent in the theatre. The solitude of the actor during the taking of the scenes weighs upon him. The director, of course, if he desire to give the actor the maximum of help, if he wish to create for him the optimum conditions for free, easy, and sincere acting, can so react to the work of the actor as to become for him a fine, responsive, and friendly—if sole—spectator.

I put forward this point in all seriousness, the possibility for the director to make the actor believe in him not merely as a theoretician, as a thinker and mentor, but also as a directly affected, either admiring or disappointed, spectator.

The finding of this inner contact between director and actor, the establishment of a profound mutual trust and respect, is one of the most paramountly important of all the problems in the technique of the work of a film collective.

My own practice in working with actors, which I must confess myself quite unable up to date to codify into any coherent or unified form that might in any degree be called a system, is based entirely on this contention, that all the most important moments of an actor's work are based absolutely on this trust in me on the part of the actor.

I recall how, taking full advantage of the silence of the cinema in the old days, I used literally to be unable to restrain myself from uttering words of excited praise that reached and encouraged the actor in the middle of his acting by reason of their obvious and complete sincerity.

It is of interest to mention here that Baranovskaia in *Mother* categorically declared to me (we were then about half-way through the film) that she could not act unless I were in my accustomed place beside the camera. I cite this declaration as further confirmation of the fact that the presence of the director responsively reacting to the actor's acting is an organic necessity for the latter. I recall that I have invariably tried to establish the most intimate personal relationship possible with all the actors playing principal rôles in my films before the actual work of shooting began. I have always regarded it as important to win in advance the deep-seated trust of the acting ensemble, so that later the actors could fall back on this trust and not feel solitary.

THE EDITING IMAGE

Many speak of the inevitability of a duality in the actor during his acting, when with one side of himself he lives and plays in the acting image, and with the other as though controls this play objectively. In my view this second, controlling side, is not at all a kind of imaginary spectator dwelling within the actor. This second side must, inevitably, be rooted in the living spectator existing external to the actor; it takes into account and bases itself on the former's reaction, fulfilling its essential purpose in doing so, for otherwise the actor would be locking himself within his own subjective circle and becoming a coldly abstract phantom.

I believe that the coldness and externally mechanical formalisation of acting often encountered in the cinema can usually be explained by coldness and mechanical formalisation in the director's method of work with the actor in shooting.

I emphasise that the decisive importance of the work of the director on the actor in shooting is characteristic for the cinema, and no equivalent obtains with anything like equal sharpness in the theatre.

Let us note here, deriving from this, one more characteristic difference between stage and film technique in acting.

In the theatre the actor must not only find the image, absorb it, approximate himself to the external forms of its expression, sense the necessary rhythmic forms of its playing and its link with the show as a whole, but he must during the repeated rehearsals

FILM ACTING

fix all this and ' can ' it in a definite shape. Although
it is not disputed that at each subsequent performance the actor will continue in a degree to develop
his rôle, yet the element of learning by rote, fixing,
and ' canning ' his acting is inevitably present in the
theatre to a considerable degree. Thus the stage
producer at a given point cedes his place to the
spectator, and the show reaches its perfect form
without, already, his direct participation.

In the cinema the burden of the element of
' canning ' and memorising is removed from the
minds of actor and director by the mechanism of the
visual and sound cameras and by the laboratory,
which indefinitely multiplies copies from a single
negative. In fact, until the very last, the culminating moment of their joint creative work, the actor
and the director in the cinema march in the liveliest
and most direct contact.

CHAPTER VII

DIALOGUE

WE now proceed to the next element in the film actor's work which offers special difficulties. This is the absence, occurring in certain circumstances, of the opposite number in a duologue. We can scarcely imagine an instance of an actor in the theatre being obliged to talk to an opposite number in reality absent. In the cinema this happens time and again owing to technical complications resulting from the desire to exploit the method of editing in construction of dialogue.

The stage, of course, is familiar with what is termed monologue, where the actor's direct opposite number in dialogue is the audience. But the cinema has a host of very different examples.

To cite an obvious one, let us take the case of a scene in which an actor addresses a crowd of Mongols, responding to their reactions. Quite likely the actor's words would be recorded separately in Moscow and joined up with pieces of scenes taken in Siberia.

Certainly it is possible to counter this example with arguments, valid to some extent, denying the necessity, at least in the normal course, for breaches of this kind in the living linkage of the protagonists of the general action. But I hold that such breaches, perhaps usually less crude and of less degree, are inescapable in cinema. Let us take as another case a continuous close-up incorporating several separate dialogue bits, and for which the actor, instead of the connected development of the dialogue, receives only the short opening cue.

Granted that we remove all the technical difficulties deriving from faulty organisation of production, I think we must and shall be able to find means whereby, without losing a jot of the wealth of possible methods of editing treatment of dialogue, we shall yet be able to realise in practice a preservation of the live link between the actor and his opposite even in such work.

In the silent days it was easier. There one could build around an actor to be taken in close-up a background as complicated as might be wished and eliminate it in shooting by the angle from which the camera was trained upon the actor.

In the sound film matters are more difficult. The microphone cannot set exact limits to its sensitivity. The microphone picks up all the sounds occurring around it up to a given strength and distance away, consequently the actor can only be isolated in close-up by eliminating in actuality any and every sound not meant to be recorded in the given section of film. In the silent film one could remove everything superfluous for the finished film and needed only by the actor to help him in his playing, not only by means of the isolating frame of the lens in the given camera set-up, but also by use of the directorial scissors, which could snip off the introductory business needed by the actor to get into his stride for the given acting moment. At first glance it might seem that in sound cinema both these avenues are closed. Practice, however, has found ways round the difficulty.

As a rule, the sound film can be taken just as freely as the silent, relying upon possible future alteration on the cutting bench of the material obtained. The words of an opposite number, the exhortations of the director, any and all noise accretions required by the actor for living intercourse with the human beings surrounding him in the process of shooting, can be removed by the scissors, always supposing there has been exact and correct organisation of the material during the taking of the scene.

A piece which, edited on the screen, comprises only a short moment of the actor's acting can equally in sound film be shot as a longish piece of acting, only the culminating moment of which forms the piece used in editing construction. The beginning and end of the piece can be cut away by the scissors.

Working out methods for this is simply a question of developing the practical side. This practical side must simply develop, guided always by common sense, along the line of maximum assistance to the actor in enabling him to stay as long and connectedly as possible in the acting image. The sound record on the film is, in general, as pliable a material as the picture film on which the image is recorded. This record can be cut and edited, more—on occasion must be cut and edited.[1]

Let us consider, for example, the pauses that separate from one another separate significant moments in the speech of one or several actors. Not always can these pauses be recorded in reality. Consider an instance we have already discussed.

An orator is addressing a listening crowd. His words are interrupted by general hubbub, applause, individual shouts and yells. In taking such a scene, not even a director most set in stagy treatment of the cinema and most scornful of the paramountcy of editing would be content with only one long shot showing the scene as a whole, and not transfer the camera from the orator to various of the individual listeners reacting to his speech and back again. But with shooting in this way, in separate pieces, the pause that separates a completed sentence, or a part of a sentence left incomplete, on the part of the orator from the shout of listeners or the latter's applause would not be recorded. Inasmuch as the two pieces—orator and listener—have been shot separately, the length of the pause on the screen will depend not on its length in reality, but on the

[1] In most sound systems used in the West, a cut sound track results at its point of junction (in spite of sound-masking measures, such as the so-called *blupe* splice) in a definite if slight ' plop.' A great deal of elimination of surplus sound, or combination on a single track of sounds recorded separately, is effected therefore not by cutting, but by what is called ' re-recording.' In theory this does not affect Pudovkin's principle of possible pliability here enunciated, but in practice—owing to the fact that a new celluloid track is dearer than a scissors snip—it does affect the extent to which that pliability is in fact utilised.—TR.

amount of blank film the director inserts at the end
of the orator's phrase and before that of the shouting
listener.

From this example we see that in the process of
filmic construction arises constantly the necessity to
create in editing elements that enter integrally into
the tissue of the live actor's acting. Later we shall
see more clearly still how this very element, a pause,
an element the tremendous importance of which is
familiar to every stage actor, is inevitably dependent
on the directorial scissors, that is, on the skill and
instinct of the director. Here is a reason, one of
many, for finding a way of making possible a direct
participation by the actor even in the editing of
the film.

The work of editing, of cutting and joining together the pieces of acted film, demands subtle effort
of the utmost creative importance in the field of
sensing the rhythm of dialogue. Theoretically, it is
perfectly possible for the actor, in concert with the
director, to set the final polish on the former's acting
solely by manipulating his screen image and screen
voice recorded on pieces of film.

There is no reason why the work of the real actor
should terminate before the editing process. The
actor should take a direct creative part in it, he must
clearly feel editing as the process of finally polishing
the shape of things.

I am so stubborn in emphasising the necessity for
the actor thus to participate in the editing, because
hitherto it has been a course in practice scarcely ever

adopted, and in consequence has led to the preval-
ence of a most incorrect idea of creative editing as a
period during which the dictator-director mutilates
and damages the living work of the actor in the
interests of the ritual inventions of his directorial
mind.

The actor should be as close to the editing as the
director. He should feel that he can lean upon him
at every stage of the work. *Editing should be precious
to him, as shaping of his performance into the ensemble is
precious to the stage actor, and he should be similarly eager
and anxious for its success and the final linkage of every
element of his work into the whole.*

I wish to turn back for a moment to our discussion
of the living link between actor and theatre audience.

The reacting spectator will only correctly and profoundly apprehend the show when the producer and
actor, by means of the exhaustive use of all the resources of their technique (using the term in its
broadest sense), have succeeded in correctly guiding
his attention. If the spectator for some reason or
other at a given moment of the show look, not at the
hero when the action hangs on the words of the hero,
but at some secondary character walking about in
the corner of the stage, the smooth crescendo of the
action is bound to be broken. The spectator will
receive an impression other than that intended by
author, producer, and actor.

The technique of the stage has the effect of guiding
the awakened attention exclusively along a channel
creatively planned and discovered as the optimum

DIALOGUE

form for portrayal of the material of the show. And each individual actor knows that, in the execution of his rôle, his stage technique must help him at the suitable moment to concentrate attention only on himself, at times even only on some detail of his acting, or, alternatively, to efface himself and thereby transfer the spectator's attention to a colleague.

This process determines the rhythm of the show, that rhythm that is, in fact, the breath of life of any work of art, the rhythm that moves the audience and which, in actual fact, determines that excitation of the spectator without which no work of art can properly be regarded as such.

The induction of the spectator into the rhythm of the show and the inducing of him to follow it constitute one of the most difficult problems of the theatre. In the cinema the technique of editing is brought in to help solve it.

Let me recall here the principles on which I tried to build the screen dialogue in *Deserter*. Imagine four people sitting in a room. They are talking to each other. We know that when a spectator sees four characters seated spaced out on a stage, his attention, rendered intent by rhythm, moves from one character to another in obedience to definite laws. Now he looks at the speaker, now at the listeners, now at a particular one of them. This transference of his attention is, in fact, dictated to him by the line of the inner content of the scene. Each of the four actors has a definite significance in the development of the action. Their interlocking, the dependence of the possible actions of one on the words of the other, is what causes the spectator to throw his attention from one *dramatis persona* to another, and the temporal and spacial diagram of this transference is naturally in direct causal relationship to the importance the spectator grants at each given moment to the given *dramatis persona*.

We know that the cinema, with its camera capable of movement and its consequent close-up, has the possibility of selecting only that object necessary at a given moment as though concentrating the spectator's attention upon it. The non-stationary camera as though takes upon itself the responsible task of dictating to the spectator the precise rhythm and sequence of attention transference that has been planned in advance by author, director, and actor. The cinema does not leave the spectator the freedom allowed him by the stage.

The rhythmic construction of a scene editably shot and then presented upon the screen achieves, as we have said, a precision and exactitude only paralleled by that of music.

I shall take three various possible forms of edited dialogue (these by no means exhaust the possibilities).

First, let us imagine one of the four actors is speaking. We see on the screen only the speaker; we hear the question he asks of one of his companions. The spectator awaits the answer to the question. In the theatre he would have turned his head and looked at the person who was going to

DIALOGUE

answer, whereas in the cinema, the director, sensing
the inevitability of this impulse on the part of the
spectator, replaces with lightning speed the image
of the questioner with the image of the person ques-
tioned.   The spectator first sees this actor, then
hears the expected answer.   In the edited sound film
the image of the actor appears narrowly in advance
of his words.

Now case two.   A person is speaking; we see him
on the screen.   He finishes speaking, but our interest
is still centred on him for some reason—probably we
expect him to continue his speech.   At this moment,
however, one of the others join in; we hear his
words, but for the moment we do not see him, and
only when the impact of his words on our consciousness has aroused our interest, do we turn our head to
look at him.   The edited sound film is so constructed that a portion of the words of the second
actor is heard over the image of the first, and the
image of the second actor, a fraction delayed,
appears only after a given lapse of time.   Here the
sound precedes the image.

The third case.   A person speaks; we are interested in the reaction of the other actors to this speech.
We watch them as they listen to the continuing
speaker.   Our attention is transferred back and
forth from speaker to listeners and again to speaker.
In the sound film follow alternately images of the
speaking actor and the listening actors with the
words of the speaking actor constant over the images
of both.

If we analyse carefully these simplest examples of forms of edited dialogue, we see that we have here two complementary kinds of rhythm marching side by side. The first is a sound-dialogue rhythm in which words alternate with pauses, a question is succeeded by an answer. And these speeches and pauses alternate in the same way as they do in objective reality. The dialogue is here recorded, as it could be if played through on a theatre stage.

What, now, is the second kind of rhythm, that of the alternation of the images of the individual actors?

We have seen in these examples how the alternation of the images may not always coincide with the alternation of the voices of the given actors. The image is at times ahead of the appearance of a new voice, at times behind, or changes rhythmically during the continuous speech of one and the same voice. The alternation of images here fundamentally represents the emotional and intellectual attitude of the spectator towards the content of the dialogue, towards the content of each rôle, towards each of the persons taking part in the given scene.

In fact, when a director edits a scene, he estimates by how much the words should precede the image, or the image the words. It stands to reason, for example, that, if the importance at the given moment of the actor who has just finished speaking be considerable, then the spectator must be offered a considerable portion of the words of another speaker before he will tear his attention away from the first and transfer it to the second.

DIALOGUE

While if, conversely, the argument of the second be impatiently awaited by the eager spectator, being anticipated as vital and important in the course of the development of the action, then a single syllable may suffice to swing the attention of the spectator away from first to second.

Hence we perceive that the process of editing does not imply a purely mechanical function of separate images. The combination of the two complementary rhythms—objectively recorded speech and edited image—yields as result the entire revelation of the significance of the scene; it is the means whereby the director hints to the spectator the requisite attitude to the scene that will reveal its inner content, and indeed also the relationship of that content to the unity of the whole of the film.

Hence we repeat once more, the interrelationship of pieces determined in the editing treatment of a scene is no mere mechanical matter. It is a problem solution of which involves the profoundest generalisation of the content of the scene. In resolving it, there must be borne in mind the relative importance of every character, or, from another point of view, the logical course of interest of the eager spectator, for the rhythm here found will determine the actual course of his attention, and therefore, in the end, the unity and clarity of his reaction to the film.

CHAPTER VIII

DUAL RHYTHM OF SOUND AND IMAGE

ONE of the most important elements in the solution of the problems of sound cinema is the knowledge and ability to master the possibilities offered by the cinema in duality of sound and image rhythm. In attempting to realise these possibilities, the director in editing makes himself the first, as it were the fundamental spectator. For the purpose of getting the very best out of the actor, as we have seen, the actor himself can be included in this editing work. And if so, in this process is developed and utilised in its appropriate function that second side of the actor that in the theatre supervises and checks from the spectator's angle, as it were, by responding to audience reaction.

To realise his full value in the cinema, the actor can and should not only play his rôle, but be capable, as well as the director, of bringing to life in the editing process the editing treatment planned, thereby compelling the spectator to accept, in its creatively found due proportion and significance, the rôle he plays. By sharing in the discovery of the appropriate forms of rhythmic alternation of pieces of image and sound, the actor shares in the persuasion of the spectator to the desired inner valuation of his acting in any given scene in its relation to the whole.

What follows here does not bear directly on the acting of actors in film, but for information, since it is desirable that actors should fully understand all the possibilities of film and editing, I should like to cite one example of editing from *Deserter*, showing a combination of the two rhythmic lines of sound and image in accordance with a principle entirely different from that already described.

In the simple examples of the editing of dialogue elements already given, it has chanced that the sounds reproduced the line of reality objectively, whereas the image represented the subjective attitude to reality of the spectator.

The combination could, of course, equally easily be effected vice versa; that is, the image could be fixed objectively in the line of reality, the sound could render the subjective valuation of this reality in respect to the spectator.

The last part of *Deserter* portrays a workers' demonstration in Hamburg and its dispersal by the police. How is this done? First, I shall follow the line of the image.

The quiet streets of Hamburg; street traffic; the traffic policeman in control. Suddenly appears a symptom of disquiet. The policeman's eye catches sight of a distant banner. Panic on the streets. They empty. The demonstration approaches. Its step is sure and confident. The mass of workers grows, again and again new detachments pour to join the demonstration from the side-streets. Summoned by alarm signals, motor-cycles and motor-cars filled with police come tearing up. They meet. A clash. The demonstration stops. Mounted and foot police hurl themselves at the workers, a battle begins, centring around the scarlet banner carried at the head of the demonstration. The banner falls, but is raised again and again. The battle rages, its fortunes swaying, but becoming more and more intense—the police are gaining the upper hand. The demonstration is defeated. The banner crashes to the ground with the hero clinging to it and a policeman clinging to the hero. Those arrested are beaten up and led away. Then suddenly, at the very last moment, when the defeat of the workers has overwhelmed the spectator by its apparent inevitability, the banner, torn from the hands of the enemy, soars once again above the crowd and, passed from hand to hand, moves farther and farther away, establishing the moral if not the physical victory of the demonstration.

This is how the image goes. If it be plotted from the viewpoint of its emotional effect, it can be represented by a complex curve with a rise at the beginning, a relative drop in the middle, a vacillation, a deep drop near the end, and a final rise at the conclusion.

Now, there is a sound line in association with this image. I decided to render this sound line in music only. Usually music in sound films is treated merely as a pure accompaniment, advancing in inevitable and monotonous parallelism with the image.

Had I intended to connect the music with the image of the scene just described in this usual way, this approximately is how it would have gone. A waltz during the portrayal of the streets of Hamburg; a rousing, cheery march tune in association with the aggressive forward march of the demonstration; the introduction of a danger and disquiet theme when the police appear; the enemy theme strengthened each time the banner falls and rousing fanfares each time it rises during the struggle; music dropped to the uttermost depths of despair when the demonstration is defeated, and lifted to triumphal victory chords when the banner once more soars above the crowd.

The composer—Shaporin—and I decided to follow another road. The score was written, played, and recorded for the whole of the sequence as a single-purposed unity, a workers' march tune with constantly running through it the note of stern and confident victory, firmly and uninterruptedly rising in strength from beginning to end.

What was the significance of this line? We rendered in this second line, that of the sound, the subjective attitude to be adopted by the spectator towards the content of the happenings in the image.

Marxists know that in every defeat of the workers lies hidden a further step towards victory. The historical inevitability of constantly recurring class battles is bound up with the historic equal inevitability of the growth of the strength of the proletariat and the decline of the bourgeoisie. It was this thought that led us to the line of firm growth towards inevitable victory which we follow in the music through all the complications and contradictions of the events shown in the image.

The music guides the line of portrayal of the inner content representation of this historical march to certain victory, consciousness of which cannot, for us, be separated from perception of a worker marching into battle. What results on the screen ? As we pass along the quiet streets of Hamburg, we hear in the music, softly yet at the same time firmly, the sounds of the tune of the marching workers. The spectator derives rather an odd feeling from the incongruity between this music and the sight of the gleaming motor-cars as they glide past the windows of luxury shops. By the time the banner of the demonstration appears, the music has grown more and more definite, its significance is clear to the spectator, and it drags him into step with the workers' mass now firmly marching along the wide, suddenly emptied streets.

The police hurl themselves at the demonstrators, the battle begins, but the brave music informed with the revolutionary spirit that moves the workers and links them to the spectator continues to grow. The banner falls, but the music rises to crescendo. The position of the workers becomes more and more desperate, but the music grows. The demonstration is beaten, the hero perishes, but the music grows.

The defeat of the workers and the victory of the police overwhelm everything, but the music grows. And suddenly, at the very last moment, the banner that blazes up above the crowd synchronises in the finale with a maximum strength of emotional intensity in a musical phrase crowning in one topmost flight of sound the whole sequence and the whole picture.

When this sequence has been shown, especially when separate from the rest of the film, I have had the opportunity to observe cases of great emotional upheaval, particularly among persons whose lives have been devoted to the tasks of the working-class struggle. It has been clear to me that the emotion of such spectators cannot be attributed to the component elements separately, such as skilful editing of the image or the high quality of Shaporin's musical score. The crux of the matter is, of course, that the emotion derives from far deeper elements integrated as a result of the combination of the two lines—the objective representation of reality in the image and the revelation of the profound inner content of reality in the sound.

Though the example we have dealt with here does not relate directly to the actor's work, it yet is important for him, for he is one of those who must understand particularly clearly the significance of treatment of sound and image, not in their primitive naturalistic association, but in a more profound—I should term it realistic—association enabling the creative worker in the cinema to portray any given event, not merely simply in direct representation, but in its deepest degree of generalisation. Only then when, for each given event, we have found the independent rhythmic lines of sound and image appropriate to it, and thereby endowed its expression with the dual nature that opens the path to its dialectical understanding, shall we obtain the realistic and exceptionally forceful impression that the so numerous technical means of the cinema make possible.

We must not in our work for one moment allow anything to stand in the way of fullest realisation of this possibility. This is why we must seriously tackle the question of broadening the understanding and share of the actor.

Though it might pass that in silent film the actor was completely separated from editing, both during shooting and during the subsequent cutting-bench work, yet in sound film such a practice becomes a serious source of weakness.

In sound film the actor's possibilities in his means of organising the form of his work to be presented to the spectator are extremely widened, and at the same time there has come greater need for precision and point. He is able to control without mistake the emotions and interest of the spectator, if, of course, he understand properly the art of editing. The fact that realisation of those possibilities involves editing of diverse separate angles means that the proper understanding of them will bring him to an appreciation of the reason and necessity for splitting his acting during shooting. New possibilities always create new complications.

Full realisation will make actors and theoreticians of film acting at last understand that this problem, like any other, cannot be regarded only from one side. To be influenced solely by the desire to make the best and easiest opportunities for the actor to remain longest in his part will mean that we shall bring into our work the theatricalisation of cinema in its worst form. Long pieces, the shooting of films in shots of long duration in which two or more actors remain on the screen throughout, playing the scene through as though on a stage and forcing the spectator himself to pick out and choose what he has to look at or listen to at any given moment, just as though he were a member of a theatre audience—all this leads to development of cinema along a false and erroneous path, for in following it we follow a line of least resistance and renounce use of all the good which the cinema gives us and which alone the cinema can give.

The actor will only appreciate the technique of his work correctly when he understands it as a weapon for his creative struggle. Struggle for what? I reply: for the realistic unity of the acted image. The discontinuity of acting in the cinema which enables as a result an edited image that can deeply affect the spectator must not be destroyed by mechanically long scenes, but, by means of the actor's technique, by finding method for his work, we must enable him to destroy discontinuity's possible bad influence on the unity of the acted image. Discontinuity of floor work must be counteracted by unity of rehearsal work.

The unity the actor discovers within himself during the rehearsal period must serve to avert mechanical isolation of the separate pieces he has to deal with in actual shooting.

CHAPTER IX

INTONATION, MAKE-UP, GESTURE

On the stage there are three main matters for the actor's technique to deal with: voice, gesture, and make-up. Each of these matters is determined, as we have already seen, by considerations of what is meant by 'stage technique'; that is, as we have already defined, the means used by the actor to overcome the harsh limits imposed on him by the mechanical basis of the stage, and to achieve realistic unity in his image.

When the actor works on his voice production and his intonation, he is guided not by the dictates of his rôle, but by the distance separating stage from audience. Actors on the stage whisper loudly, thereby contradicting the very meaning of the act of whispering. What matter that the dramatic situation demands that a given actor's whisper be not heard by his colleague standing near? Not a scrap. The whisper must at all costs be heard by the spectator sitting in the back row of the balcony.

When the actor works on the plastics and expressiveness of his gestures, he strives to make them wide and generalised, eliminating minuteness not because the character whose image he is representing would have made such wide gestures, but because they must be perceived by the most remote spectator.

Still again, the actor puts on vivid rouge and draws a line of make-up for the purpose of making the shape and movements of his face clearly visible from that maximum distance which is mechanically conditioned by the dimensions of the theatre. Thus gestures, voice, make-up all constitute technique. It is implicit in this technique, we should understand, that the actor, in increasing the volume of his voice, yet strives not to let his lines degenerate into false declamation; in broadening the sweep of his gestures, yet strives to retain their realistic shape; in working out his make-up, remains yet oriented upon the realistic features of the human face.

The sum total of the stage actor's work on his voice, gesture, and make-up is covered by the formula: theatricalisation of the external shape of the acted image. This process cannot, of course, be considered as actor's technique by itself. It forms also a particular element in the general craft of the stage. But, speaking generally, in any art the technique of giving external shape to its elements cannot be treated as something separate, independent, and isolated from the creative process as a whole.

In emphasising it as ' technique,' I only desire to emphasise its direct dependence on the specific conditions of theatrical performance, distinct from the conditions of cinema.

The ' theatricalisation ' of the actor, his technique in response to theatrical conditions, cannot be treated separately as an art in itself. It is conditioned by the actor's striving to make his creation as vivid and effective as possible, and, in presentations of realistic style, it links up with the general struggle of the artist to preserve in the image the maximum complexity and vividness of the real-life event being reproduced in stage conditions.

The term ' theatricalisation ' of the actor's image should be paralleled in the cinema by a term ' cinematicisation.' I regard this term as worth inventing, because it corresponds to a definite content in our film work.

While ' theatricalisation ' involves a strengthening of the vividness and effectfulness of his voice delivery, gesture, grimace on the part of the actor himself, by deliberate effort transforming his normal non-stage delivery, gesture, grimace, the cinema achieves the same result of strengthening vividness and effectiveness by the use of a camera moved from place to place, change of angle, perspective, lighting, nearer or farther microphone, which means, in other words, that ' cinematicisation ' is mainly bound up with editing and the knowledge of its methods. Every expressive movement of man is always conditioned by the dialectical conflict of two elements: the inner urge to widen the movement as much as possible, and the volitional brake restraining the movement, the two by their interaction thereby resulting in an expressive form for the movement.

There exists a definite norm determining the shape of human movements in the ordinary conditions of real life. On the stage this movement shape is

altered by means of slackening somewhat the restraining tendency of the will. By this means, by
unbraking, weakening the restraint of the will, the
stage actor, preserving the inner meaning of the
gesture, preserving its inner urge, yet increases its
sweep and thus makes it clearly and distinctly
visible to the spectator in the theatre.

The cinema does not require this unbraking from
the actor. The least movement, inwardly stimulated
and restrained to the utmost degree, can yet be seen
and heard by the spectator through the agency of
closely approximated camera and microphone.

We are familiar, even in the theatre, with
efforts to approach realism in acting, the principal
being those that characterised Stanislavski and his
school.

These efforts were realised in their most marked
form in the early works of the First Studio of the
Moscow Art Theatre, where the theatre was no
bigger than a fair-sized room and the actor thus
maximally approached to the spectator. But this
method in the theatre immediately and inevitably
results in a degree of intimacy that contradicts the
basic requirement of every art—to embrace and
excite the maximum number of spectators.

The policy of changing the theatre into an intimate ' emoting circle ' inevitably resulted in a reaction and a demand for theatricalisation of the acting
and the whole performance as such, a reaction
which, in fact, was led by Stanislavski's closest
pupils, among them Vakhtangov.

INTONATION, MAKE-UP, GESTURE

As we have already seen, the close-up in the cinema removes the contradiction between the desire for realism in the actor's acting and the requirement of a maximum audience.

What are the changes resulting from this in the tasks that confront the film actor? First of all, resulting from the possibility of approximation of camera and microphone to the actor, disappears the need artificially to raise the volume of the voice and increase the scale of the movements of the body and face. In practice disappears from the actor's work the element of special study of voice production and strength of tone, which, in the film actor, need only be strong enough to cover the distance separating him from his colleague; in other words, as strong as would be requisite in the conditions of actuality.

(We recall that on the stage the actor must endow his voice with a strength determined not by the distance separating him from his colleague, but by that separating him from the spectator seated in the gallery.)

The elementary crudity of theatrical make-up becomes, also, entirely purposeless. In the cinema the quality of make-up, where this be necessary at all, is estimated by its efficaciousness in preserving all the finest complexities of expression of the given human face. An artificial expression—a cheek pasted on, a line drawn to represent a non-existent furrow—are simply idiotic in the cinema, inasmuch as, deprived of their theatrical purpose of helping the actor to establish an expression at a distance, they simply become a hindrance damaging that expression, particularly destructive in close-up.

If a film actor were made up in a theatrical way, one would have to put the camera in shooting far enough back not to see the details of the made-up face, so as not to show them to the spectator.

Stylised make-up automatically forces the cinema to renounce its own methods of work and change to a simple recording of a theatrical performance from the distance and angle of the audience seated in the theatre. Everything ' theatricalised ' is wasted or even harmful in the cinema.

The actor's work, at that moment of it which takes place in front of the camera, can be as near real life as is imaginably possible. The film actor playing in an exterior, in a real garden, by the side of a real tree or a real river, must not feel himself alien and apart from the reality around him. The formalisation of his work is expressed in that formalisation demanded by cinematic acting. Creative work in these conditions demands no less effort, no less technique, than the ' theatricalised ' acting of the stage actor, but of an entirely different kind.

In his book *My Life in Art*, Stanislavski relates how, on an occasion during one of their provincial tours, a group of actors taking a walk in a park happened by chance on a spot that reminded them of the stage setting of the second act of Turgeniev's play *A Month in the Country*.

The actors decided to try playing impromptu in the natural background.

INTONATION, MAKE-UP, GESTURE

Stanislavski thus tells of the attempt: " Came my entry; Olga Knipper and I, as required by the play, walked along the long tree-bordered avenue speaking our lines. Then we sat down on a seat exactly as in our stage business, started talking—and stopped because we could not continue. My acting seemed false to me against the background of real nature. And people say our theatre has brought simplicity to the point of absolute naturalism! How stilted and formalised seemed everything we were accustomed to do upon the stage."

I believe that the main element in the acting of the film actor has to be precisely the opposite of this, has to be, in fact, precisely the ability to walk with a colleague, without the slightest feeling of falsehood or awkwardness, along a real garden path and continue the conversation thus begun sitting on a real bench under a real tree.

Shooting in exteriors has always characterised the style of really cinematic productions, and, in my view, it will continue to do so in the future.

It is interesting to note that the theatricalised style of the film *The Tempest* transforms the few exterior shots used in it to the appearance of mere painted backcloths.

Stanislavski got his feeling of falsehood probably because the feeling of the natural background surrounding him forced him back upon feeling in all its fullness the living reality of his colleague, the impulse to speak and move in such a way as he would if connected with her alone, to raise his voice no higher than necessary from the point of view of a person standing close to him, to sit down on the bench in such a way as to be turned comfortably towards the person he was talking to without consideration of an audience looking at him from a definite viewpoint and demanding not merely the fact of a given movement but its emphasised portrayal.

Despite the fact that Stanislavski had striven with all his might towards the creation of actuality in the theatre, by means of transplanting naturalism on to the stage, training himself as an actor precisely into the scheme of a complete separation of himself from the audience and inclusion of himself into a separate life, with his colleague, on the stage, subduing the feeling of special ' portrayal ' of his behaviour—yet at his first contact with the surroundings of real life he felt the inevitability of the influence of stage conditions on the form of the actor's creative work.

When we speak of the ' unnecessary staginess ' of a film actor's performance, we so term it not because staginess necessarily involves anything of itself wrong or unpleasant. We simply register an unpleasant sensation of incongruity, and therefore falseness, as though at the sight of a man striving to negotiate a non-existent obstacle.

An elocutionary distinctness in an uttered word, theatrical loudness in a voice, even a slightly emphasised or generalised gesture, conflicting on the screen with the nearness of the huge close-up that is the nearest approach of spectator to actor, inevitably creates a sensation of unnecessary and foolish falseness.

But the same artificiality, the same gesture, in theatrical conditions, and therefore realistically directed towards the overcoming of obstacles really existing, becomes a high form of art deeply moving to the audience.

In a theatrical school, work on voice production and intonation forms the basis of the lessons on acting technique. In sound-film training, efforts are now made in the same direction, but unfortunately they are too often based on a mere mechanical transplantation into the cinema of stage practices.

I believe that the Americans, who have devoted all their attention to the perfection of recording apparatus, and the invention of apparatus that can correct speech defects recorded on the film by modification in cutting or re-recording of the film itself, are on a much more promising path.

The whole idea of elocution and voice production in sound film reminds one of the hoary and idiotic concept of ' photogenic faces,' and how film technicians used to declare in the old days that an actor could possess special facial and bodily qualities capable of creating a perfect and expressive screen image. Nowadays, at all events, we know that cameras and lighting have shown that any human being can give a beautiful image; all we have to do is to find out how to photograph him.

CHAPTER X

REALISM OF THE ACTED IMAGE

FROM all we have said so far, it might be concluded that the technique of the film actor must be oriented around two basic elements: first, the mastering of, and subordination by him of his acting to, the creative problems of the art of editing; second, the absorption of the acted image, organically and wholly.

But we come now to the question—what part is played in the film actor's work by what in ordinary parlance is called sincerity, spontaneity, naturalness? We know that in the cinema, in contrast to the theatre, there are frequently instances of actors who act their own selves. There are cases of supporting or minor rôles played by persons who have never studied acting in any conceivable way, yet who not only create strong and impressive images, but also fall in perfectly with the general style of the film, although professional actors also take part in it.

This would be impossible on the stage. A real live dog in *The Eccentric*,[1] the thundering of the hooves of real steeds on the wooden boards in *Hamlet*, either is revolting and entirely out of key with the whole performance. Yet one could hardly name

---

[1] Play by A. Afinogenov.—TR.

a film in which, alongside real actors, one does not see animals and children, who in no wise damage its sense of stylistic unity.

Plenty might be said against the contention that a casual man from the street, a ' non-actor,' could act a big and complicated rôle in a film. But it is impossible, without theoretical trickery, to argue that such a casual ' non-actor ' in a small scene or simple ' bit,' even placed next to a good film actor, would necessarily create in a film the same feeling of disturbance and out-of-placeness for the spectator that he feels at the sight of non-theatrical behaviour on the stage, such as in the already cited cases of dogs and horses, or, for example, the children who are sometimes introduced into a stage show.

Stanislavski himself, who, from the very beginning of his dramatic career, strove to attain naturalness in acting, was forced to abandon the idea of introducing into a theatrical performance an old peasant woman, in spite of the fact that she seemed to him to be the embodiment of truth and expressiveness.

It is, of course, not suggested that a film actor should limit himself to the possibility of once or twice playing his own self. Even if he play his own self, he must none the less modify his behaviour to some degree, in subordinating it to the task set out by the film as a whole; the rôle, even if himself, must be given some basic ideological directional characteristic. In no case, of course, will or can the image appearing on the film be a simple copy of the given person who acts, with the whole sum of his individual characteristics. In the end even a casual ' non-actor ' (wrongly called ' type ' [1]) in some measure follows the editing instructions of the director, in other words, does some acting.

The film actor, in the course of a protracted career involving work in several films, is bound to work on the creation of various images some of which at least are not identical with his own individual characteristics. Thus, inevitably, is bound to arise the question of working over himself, embodiment in an image outside himself, howsoever it may be dealt with.

The actor in his creative process first learns reality; then, together with the spectator and by means of the specific peculiarities of his art, he expresses externally the results of his knowledge in the form of a newly organised artificial behaviour composed by himself. In this work he invariably strives to preserve in live undestroyed shape his personal existence, he strives to continue to feel himself in front of the camera a whole, living person and not a mechanised likeness of one, and if, as we have already seen we do, we deny the mechanical conception of the construction of the actor's work, then already we acknowledge the necessity in this process for ' incarnating oneself into ' the image.

I shall not here analyse the process of ' living into,' or appropriating to one's person, the image. A

[1] Pudovkin uses the word ' type,' not for the non-acting material, to whom it is sometimes applied in the West, but for a stylised figure, who always plays a given rôle and none other—villain, hero, policeman, mother-in-law, etc.—Tr.

whole series of methods to this end, assembled even into a complex methodology, has been worked out by stage craftsmen. We have and will again later discuss its importance.

Let us now note only and essentially that this process of appropriation of the image, the transmutation by the actor of his personal behaviour into the behaviour of the rôle-man, is indispensable for the transmission to the spectator of an organically whole, realistically impressive live image. Having accepted this principle, we then note that, in the theatre, the person of the actor inevitably comes into conflict with the element of theatricalisation in the external forms of the image he appropriates. In the cinema these elements of theatricalisation are made unnecessary by the presence of the non-stationary camera and microphone that make possible an edited shooting of the actor. The actor in the film, being thus freed from the element of theatricalisation, is left with, as sole preoccupation, maximum approach of himself to realisticness.

By what process do we gather knowledge of a phenomenon as more and more real ? By the process of approaching it, studying it, in all its depth, in all its richness, in all the complexity of its linkage to other phenomena.

In art we term an image realistic if it be a representation of objective reality imaged with maximum exactitude, maximum clarity, maximum profundity, and maximum embrace of its complexity.

The frequent use of the word ' maximum ' in this

description suggests to us that naturalism is the highest form of the realistic tendency in art.

But again and again it is necessary to repeat that naturalism, realism, and idealism in art are not separate and independent forms, capable of existence unconnected with one another.

Naturalism and idealism are both hypertrophied forms, divorced in their development from the proper course of apprehension of reality, which always returns from abstract generalisation to living actuality, in order, having generalised living actuality once again, thereby to advance forward.

Naturalism, idealism, and realism in art stand in the same relation to one another as do mechanism, idealism, and dialectical materialism in philosophy.

Those of the naturalist school, in copying a phenomenon of actuality and not generalising it, create a mere cold mechanism, without the inner links that exist in actuality within the phenomenon, and without the outer links that bind it to other phenomena as a part to the whole.

The realism of a representation increases as its approach to the complexity of an actual object and as its deepening by detail, but at the same time it must portray the object as part of a whole.

Realistic work, then, only escapes from naturalism when in its representation of a phenomenon are present both the general external linkage and the inner generalising elements that (together with the outward appearance) make the given phenomenon in actuality a part connected to a whole.

Applying this principle to the work of the actor, it is clear that the realistic tendency in art will urge him towards the necessity for assembling, at some stage of his work, the separate discontinuous pieces of his acting in front of the camera into a whole inseparably linked with the whole of the show and, in general, with the place of the show in our constantly developing social life.

The old paradox of Diderot, which pointed out the possibility of the actor during a show being able to make the spectator cry by the excellent playing of his rôle and, simultaneously, his colleague laugh as he stands in the wings, by a comic grimace, and which thus apparently established the possibility of a mechanical split in the actor's behaviour into behaviour of a living person and behaviour in the play—none the less in no way contradicts the necessity, at some stage or other of the actor's working on his rôle, for a whole and organic unity of these two behaviours.

In this sense the teaching of Stanislavski is in its premises profoundly true and honest. Let it be that the actor on the stage does not, during the performance, live the life of the character he acts. But if the audience gets, in the impression it receives, a feeling of living realistic unity in the image, then this unity must come from somewhere.

This unity must emerge somewhen during the

creative process of the actor's work on the character. Coquelin and Karatuigin,[1] who both used to ' put something over ' in their acting, somewhere and sometime in their work must have created the content they portrayed.

The example of the cinema makes this contention even more clear. Actually, the grey-white shadows that flicker across the screen do not feel anything. They are there, technically fulfilling the part once and for all allotted to them, a series of fragmentary, separate movements—yet none the less the spectator receives the impression of a unified image. Why? Because as the basis of the selection of these separate movements has been made the organic unity of the real phenomenon recorded on the film.

It is interesting that it is characteristic of the cinema that it can allow the actor to stop his work before the form found for embodying his rôle has yet become a habit learned by rote and mechanically repeated.

We know that there exists in the theatre the peril of ' getting stale,' as it is called.

Stanislavski, giving in his memoirs a comparative valuation of his acting in the rôle of Dr. Stockman in its earlier and later phases, writes as follows: " Step by step I look back through the past and realise more and more clearly that the inner content that I put into my rôle at the time of first creating it and the outer form into which the rôle has degenerated in course of time are as far apart from each other as

[1] A Russian Garrick.

heaven and earth. At first everything came from a beautiful and moving inner truth, and now all that is left of it is empty husks, rubbish, and dust left over in body and soul from various casual causes that have nothing in common with real and true art."

I incline to think that this weather-beating of Stanislavski's inner truth was not solely due to the frequency with which he repeated his rôle. Surely it was due to the fact that Stanislavski himself underwent changes, and the inner organic elements, which at first linked him to the image of Stockman he had found, later no longer existed.

I cite this example because its sharpness underlines the contrast provoked by the film actor's work, the feature of which is that its living real link with the acted image ceases much earlier than does that of the stage actor, and, in the main, ceases at that conscious and deliberate moment of choice which the artist in any given art except the stage art uses to place a limit to his polishing of his creation.

The film actor must be truthful, sincere, and, in his striving for realism of the image, natural. This naturalness is not destroyed in him by the demands of theatricalisation. But, on the other hand, to find the right content for the acting image does inevitably require a great deal of important preliminary work on the inner absorption of it.

Here we see converging the fundamental claims of the Stanislavski school and the basic desiderata we set out for the film actor.

FILM ACTING

In my view, many of the methods adopted by the Moscow Art Theatre school are closest to what is wanted and most useful to bear in mind when setting up a school of film acting. Of course, one must be able to recognise and separate out from all the basic rules promulgated and introduced by Stanislavski those elements of theatricalisation which are suitable only for a theatre school.

The right course, I fancy, is to imitate the Moscow Art Theatre school, not in the form in which it actually exists to-day, but in the form in which it would exist based upon Stanislavski's ideas of verisimilitude of acting which, in the last resort, he could never realise because, so long as he worked in the theatre, he could never rid himself of its conventions.

Extremely interesting are those passages in Stanislavski's memoirs where he speaks of the necessity for ' gestureless ' moments of immobility on the part of the actor, to concentrate on his *feelings* all the attention of the spectator.

Stanislavski felt that an actor striving towards truth should be able to avoid the element of *portraying* his feelings to the audience, and should be able to transmit to it the whole fullness of the content of the acted image in some moment of half-mystic communion. Of course, he came up against a brick wall in his endeavours to find a solution to this problem in the theatre.

It is amazing that solution of this very problem is not only not impracticable in the cinema, but extreme paucity of gesture, often literal immobility, is absolutely indispensable in it. For example, in the close-up, in which gesture is completely dispensed with, inasmuch as the body of the actor is simply not seen.

CHAPTER XI

WORK WITH NON-ACTORS

IN speaking of realistic work by film actors, it is necessary to point out the tremendous importance of the experiments carried out in the cinema in work with so-called ' non-actors ' (I deliberately refrain from using the misleading term ' type '). I am far from the intention of providing excuse for any theory affirming that the cinema does not need specially trained actors. The formulation of such a theory has in the past been carefully ascribed to me, regardless of the obvious fact that all my practical experience in the cinema, in literally every film, has been connected not only with specially trained film actors, but also with former stage actors.[1]

I shall not delve into these ' theoretical exaggerations,' which I have already referred to elsewhere, but simply recall the facts, which are, that, in individual cases of work with non-actors, we have discovered in practice that, and sought in theory the reason why, elements of the real behaviour of a person not trained in any school are not out of place in a film and, indeed, at times can serve

[1] Pudovkin has, it is true, never specifically advocated the *exclusive* use of non-actors. But how far his enthusiasm for each problem-of-the-hour has laid him open to the ascription he complains of may be judged by the reader of his lecture to the Film Society, included in *Film Technique.*—TR.

as an example to be followed by experienced actors.

It seems to me that these experiences point first and foremost to the fact that the film actor, both in the whole and in every fragment of his work, should always orient his behaviour on the real concrete feeling of the purpose he follows in each separate piece. It should be recalled here that, in the cinema, this purpose nearly always has real, and in all the fullness of their reality sensible, forms. The whole atmosphere of exterior work, so characteristic for films, shows this.

In what manner have I used casual persons, non-actors, in my own films ? My method has been to create in the given pieces those real-life conditions the reaction to which of the non-actor was bound to be precisely that element I needed for the film.

Let us take as example the Young Communist and his piece of acting at the meeting in the last reel of *Deserter*. The boy photographed in this rôle was a naturally self-conscious subject, and, of course, the atmosphere of shooting and his anticipation of the requirements the director was about to make from him combined to render him excited, self-conscious, and tie him generally into knots.

I purposely strengthened and increased the atmosphere that was making him self-conscious because it gave me the necessary colouring. When I made him stand up in response to applause, and then began to praise his acting unstintedly and flatteringly, the youngster, much as he tried, was unable to hold back a tremendous smile of complete satisfaction, which gave me as result a gorgeous piece. I regard this piece as one of the most successful in the whole scheme, if such a term is legitimate in this case, of the film's acting.

In this case all the real conditions of shooting did in actual fact happen to coincide with the conditions that later invested the scene on the screen. They fitted both the confusion of the Young Communist on being unexpectedly elected to the presidium of a huge meeting, and his uncontrollable pleasure when the huge meeting greeted the announcement of his name with unanimous applause.

Certainly it was not the acting of an actor, for the element of conscious creation was not present in the lad who portrayed the Young Communist. But this experience can be turned inside out and applied on its practical side to help any actor wanting to find, in concert with the director, a realistic prop to bolster up his mood.

In the theatre, of course, as we have already seen, a real-life prop of this kind has either to be imagined or replaced by the magic 'just suppose' invented by Stanislavski.

About this 'just suppose' Stanislavski writes as follows: " The actor says to himself: all this scenery, props, make-up, public performance, etc., is a complete lie. I know it and I don't care. These things have no significance for me . . . but . . . *just suppose* all this that surrounds me on the stage were true, then this is how I should react to this or that event."

WORK WITH NON-ACTORS

From this magic 'just suppose,' according to Stanislavski, derives the true creative existence of the actor. Maybe this is true, for the theatre, since the theatricalisation of the actor's behaviour is an indispensable aspect of his art. In the cinema, however, even if this 'just suppose' exist, it does so in an entirely different form, probably connected, as is nearly every element of generalisation, with the editing treatment of the rôle.

I recall another characteristic example of work with a non-actor occurring during the shooting of *The Story of a Simple Case.*

There was a scene as follows: a father and his small son, a Pioneer, who have not seen each other for a long time, meet. It is early morning. The boy is just out of bed. He is stretching and flexing his muscles after sleep. At his father's question, " How's life, Johnny ? " he turns towards him, and instead of an answer gives him a sweet, rather shy, smile.

The task set was complicated and, besides, the object to be shot had to be a boy about ten years of age, because in the cinema not even the most old-fashioned and stage-minded director would dare to use a grown-up actor, or a girl made up to represent a boy, as is possible and has often been done on the stage.

In working with a non-actor it is impossible to count on rehearsals. Mechanically remembered movements are nearly always useless in such cases. To find the necessary form creatively and then, having found it, get it repeated is, of course, in work with anybody not specially trained also impossible. Therefore it is necessary, even in a case of such complex action, to be able, taking into account as finely and sensitively as possible the character of the person playing, to establish for him such conditions as will produce the movements required by the director in natural and inevitable reaction to a given external stimulus.

I therefore planned as follows: I decided, first and foremost, to make the boy experience a real pleasure from the process of stretching, more even, feel a need for it. To achieve this, I bade him bend forward, grip his feet with his hands, and hold them in this position until I gave him permission to straighten up.

" Then," I told him, " you'll feel a genuine pleasure in stretching and straightening your muscles, and that's just what I want."

I deliberately explained to him the content of the whole problem, reckoning that he would be interested in the experiment. This interest I needed for the success of point number two of my task.

The boy was really interested; I felt it. Now I further reckoned thus: when I give him permission to straighten out, and he stretches with genuine pleasure, I shall interrupt his movement with a question: " Well, Johnny, isn't it grand to stretch ? "

Talking during the shot was not allowed; the boy knew he had to keep silent. I knew his nature well, and I was convinced that he would answer me with precisely the smile I needed, acquiescent, and a little confused and shy at the unusualness of the situation.

I repeat: rehearsals would have been useless; I was all out for the spontaneity of the reaction I had foreseen might come.

The scene began. The boy stood bent downwards. I allowed him to straighten out, he stretched; I saw on his face a satisfaction both of physical pleasure and from his feeling that the game I had suggested to him was going without a hitch. I put my question and received in reply the beautiful and sincere smile I wanted.

Of course, it might have failed, but I was convinced that it would not, and I was right.

Work with casual persons, of course, requires especial fertility of invention on the part of the director. Equally, of course, it cannot be generalised into a principle suitable for work with all actors. Nor is it possible to schematise such examples of work with ' non-actors ' into a sort of scholastic system. But I do believe that, from the experience of such work, one might derive much that would be useful in practice for the process of absorption into the image, and the search for externally expressive methods of portrayal of inner states.

The creation of conditions that evoke a reaction naturally can sometimes be of great assistance in the search for forms for the acting even of professional actors, especially in circumstances of shooting in exterior.

In considering the question of the ' non-actor,' the

following should also be borne in mind: while it is idle to suggest the complete replacement of experienced and specially trained film actors by casual persons, it is equally impossible to attempt to produce a film with the whole colossal number of rôles taking part in it filled exclusively by professional actors. To refuse in any circumstances to use casual personnel without special training in acting is to abandon film-making altogether. A simple mathematical calculation will prove this: the number of big rôles in an average play is fifteen to twenty; in an average film there will probably be more like sixty, eighty, even a hundred separate scenes of different persons, each of whom has definite and considerable importance. Tiny bit rôles, occupying as small a time on the screen as twenty seconds to a minute, yet often solve highly important and serious problems and correspondingly demand a high level of expressiveness.

The mass, the crowd that remains on the stage of a theatre as something solid, general, undivided, splits in the film, as we know, into close-ups. The content of a crowd as a whole is revealed through the detail of its component human beings. In a close-up, each of these components of the crowd requires to be no less true and expressive than the actor who plays the leading rôle.

While on the stage a petty incident may be of only slight importance, turning out to be only a connecting link or, perhaps, just background atmosphere, in the cinema, with the continuous concentration of the attention of the spectator on each frame, these transitional, merely connecting elements do not exist.

In the film, every piece, even the smallest, must have a hundred per cent. content if the film is to be constructed clearly and rhythmically. The high standard that must be applied to the smallest incident should be considered in conjunction with the practical difficulties of concrete film production and the impossibility of keeping hanging around an indefinite number of small-part players. In Hollywood, of course, thousands of extras and small-part players live permanently in the film city. But this system could hardly be established with us.[1] With the correct development of cinema as an art maximally embracing and absorbing reality, with the consequent increase of exterior scenes causing location journeys of producing units to various parts of our country, one can hardly reckon upon carting about with one a huge crowd of actors for use only in one-minute-long scenes.

We shall always have to face the necessity for the director to know how to use for such scenes whatever persons he can collect on a location possibly far removed from his headquarters in the capital.

The position is further aggravated, I suggest, by the impossibility of using broad make-up, which on

[1] In the Soviet Union the general shortage of labour precludes film-extra-ing as a profession. Film crowds are called, in the main, from a roster of persons whose occupation is of such a nature as to enable them to snatch a few hours from their jobs at odd intervals. —TR.

the stage can transform a young Khmelev [1] to an old porter.

Of course, there could still remain open the course of adapting the scenario to the stock company the given studio has at its disposal. Kuleshov, who writes his scenarios with a meticulous eye on the size and composition of his producing collective, is inclined to favour this style of work. But this path, it seems to me, is not one that opens for exploitation the colossal possibilities of the cinema; on the contrary, it closes the way to real, profound development.

This is a matter that raises questions of the fundamental style of work. There is no reason why one should not take into account one or two leading actors, the better to adjust the content of the scenario, but it is out of the question to attempt it in respect to a hundred incidents. Such an attempt would even be objectless since experience has already shown, as we have seen, that ways can be found of fully exploiting untrained material in film acting.

The only barrier preventing such use would be scholastic maintenance of ' the cinema is for the actor ' as an abstract principle.

[1] Also a Russian Garrick.—TR.

CHAPTER XII

CÁSTING

I RETURN once more to the film actor's work on his rôle, and propose to pause at the very first stage— that of the choice of it. The film actor, like any artist in any art, bases himself on the profoundest absorption of the image in its teleology and in its ideology. In this process are inevitably present not only objective but also subjective elements.

If his only interest in the image planned is the task to be performed by the play or scenario as a whole, and if in the execution of this task he, as an actor, is not also interested in the image itself in the deepest degree, then no work of art will result.

If the play as a whole and the rôle in the play solve something that is alien to and divorced from the inner world of the artist himself, then no work of art will result. Only if play and rôle both speak in some degree about something that the artist himself desires to say with deepest sincerity and passion, only then can one be sure that his work will result in a real creative work of art.

I hold that from the very beginning, at the primary first encounter of the actor with his rôle, there must be present the element of deep inner interest on the part of the actor.

But apart from this general inner interest from the

very start of the work, the actor must infallibly feel and think out clearly the degree to which he himself is suitable for the perfect execution of the future work. It is no good the appeal of a rôle that interests the actor being limited to its ideological content. There must be an element of sympathy for characteristics in the rôle that will find an echo in the individual character and cultural background of the actor and can therefore become points of departure for the direction of his future work in appropriating the image.

From the first moment he encounters his rôle, the actor must feel an emotional sympathy with it in itself, apart from its links to the scenario as a whole. This primal moment of presentiment of the fullness and reality of the image may be personal to the actor, or may be discovered by him with the help of the director.

But in either case, this element of the actor being deeply moved by the possibilities of his proposed future work should determine the choice of casting.

It will be advisable to dwell a little more fully on this question of casting, because our present practice is still the mechanical allotment of rôles to actors, sometimes without taking into consideration their personal individual qualities, and always ignoring their creative interestedness.

It is clear that an actor's work in a given rôle will only give good results when it is preceded by an element of choice in his acceptance of the rôle—the outcome of an urge within him to play the particular rôle.

The film actor is far less favourably situated in this respect than the stage actor. The cinema knows no, or, more strictly speaking, few, established acting collectives, and the scenario, although as a rule written for a specific director, usually ignores the question of the cast, which is only later assembled and fitted into the rôles.

The opportunity for a film actor to choose a rôle is non-existent, and limited in practice to the possibility of saying yes or no to the offer of a given rôle.

I must say that the fault lies not only with the present organisation of the film industry and the lack of initiative obtaining among scenarists and directors. A large share of responsibility, permit me to say, for this sad state of affairs lies at the door of the lack of film culture among the actors themselves.

Let us analyse carefully the meaning of the element of being carried away emotionally by the rôle, which alone should decide the actor in his choice of it.

Before he begins his work on the image, the actor must (else he is no artist) be able to size up all this future work generally, as a whole. On the one hand, he must see in it his own interest in and emotion at the general task; on the other, and paramountly, he must sense in it clearly those possibilities in the external treatment of the image that are linked, first, with his estimate of the personal qualities of the proposed character, second, with his knowledge of the technical means he possesses to express them.

A rapid sizing up of all the possibilities the future rôle can give him is essential for the actor. It is this necessary, first-line general planning associated with every task and taking fully into account the problems with which it will confront him which should decide a man in taking on a job or refusing it. To this preliminary sensing of the rôle, the actor must bring, as I have said, not only a general ideological interest, but a complete summary review and feeling over of his own abilities and possibilities, his acting talents, the technical methods he possesses, his character, temperament, and background; in short, the sum total of his psycho-physiological characteristics.

A stage actor, when approaching the task of general feeling of the image, and weighing up the pros and cons of accepting or rejecting it, makes use of his knowledge of the specifics of stage work.

As we have seen, in his system of training, the film actor should approach the Stanislavski school. Therefore the basic elements of his primal liking for a rôle should be founded principally on the inner content of the image. But none the less, it would be a gross error to divorce this content from the external forms by means of which it will be transmitted to the spectator from the screen.

Unfortunately full knowledge of these forms has hitherto been the exclusive possession of the director, and the actor has either possessed such knowledge not at all or only in small, highly insufficient degree.

CASTING

The liking of a film actor for a given rôle has been primitive, in most cases quite disorganised, and often the mere desire of a comedian to play Hamlet. In case of an organised liking, the actor sympathetic towards a rôle is attracted by it because, even in the primary sensing of it, he already appreciates that every element in it that interests him not only does excite and interest him, but also is perceptible to him as one he can form and shape. The tasks may be as difficult as can be, but they will be accomplishable—that is the main thing.

For a primal taking-to-the-rôle of this kind, it is unquestionably necessary that the actor possess full and all-sided knowledge of the technique of his art. He must be fully armed with technical knowledge in order to judge whether a liking for a rôle on his part will lead to a real, and the necessary, result.

The stage actor who knows his stage, his producer, and his colleagues, the technical bases of the theatre, can bring this primal sizing up of his part to the pitch of imagining himself as he will appear on the stage in front of the audience.

The film actor, as a rule, does not imagine to himself the possibilities he has, or which can be put at his disposal, for the creation of the final form of his image on the screen, and without imagining this an actor cannot properly work. Hitherto this imagination has been the exclusive prerogative of the director. This is the man who hitherto has visualised in advance the actor's edited image, that is, the image that is to exist on the screen for the spectator, and it

349

has been his task to introduce this visualisation into the subjective compass of the living actor.

Of course, the film actor is not responsible for the fact that the general organisation of our film industry prevents and hinders his opportunities of sufficiently mastering the technical culture of film art. But, for whatever reason, he has been placed in such a position as to be unequipped to exercise full responsibility in his choice of a rôle. He has been mechanically separated from the sphere of editing, which has been kept as a preserve for the director, whereas in truth knowledge of it is the first and foremost condition of full film-culture for the actor most of all.

In conclusion, therefore, we see that the question of an actor's primal liking for a rôle comes back in practice in the end to the fact that the actor must be in possession of a much wider and deeper technical knowledge of the cinema, so that his liking for a rôle will be not just based on a primitive hunch, but an element, obeying definite laws, in the full creative process of work on the image.

CHAPTER XIII

THE CREATIVE COLLECTIVE

To deal with the question of the necessity for active participation by the actor in the choosing of his rôle, it was at one time thought to find a solution by organising a system of actors putting in ' claims ' for their rôles. These ' claims ' were to be based on complicated discussions about the schedules of themes planned by ~ach studio, which were supposed to be the concrete expression of the creative hopes, over the given period, not only of scenarists and directors, but also of actors who were supposed to choose and stake ' claims ' for definite images that appealed to them. In my view such a system is only likely tc result in an unnecessary and foolish mechanical competition of claims. Obviously no reading of claims, reports, or memoranda could possibly replace for the director and scenarist an essential acquaintanceship with and feeling of the given actor himself.

Memoranda and meetings are no use for a real understanding and estimate of the actor by his prospective director; what is required is profound mutual study. To speak the plain truth, the majority of directors and actors of to-day, despite the fewness of their numbers, have hardly ever met each other. The question of the producing collective has, in fact, not even been taken as far as the very first step of its possible development.

In recalling my own experience, I noted to what degree of inner contact a director's intimacy with an actor should reach in order to ensure the progress of shooting in that atmosphere of mutual help and trust that is so necessary for fullest advantages in creative work.

Our producing collectives are not together long enough to be able to organise themselves for the proper carrying out of even one film.

At present we are so organised that a director has no real contact with even the leading members of the cast until just before the actual beginning of shooting.

I must quote again my experience with Baranovskaya, when our contact only reached the real inner stage about half-way through work on the film. With the actor Livanov it was much worse—we only reached a mutual creative understanding right at the end.

Such a degree of lack of contact with and knowledge of an actor is, of course, impermissible and unpardonable, and indicates the need for immediate and most drastic reorganisation.

I cannot see the formation of permanent creative collectives being a practical full solution to the problem. One must repeat again and yet again that the colossal and unwieldy size of acting staff involved by any such attempt, in view of the limited possibilities the cinema affords the actor of radically changing

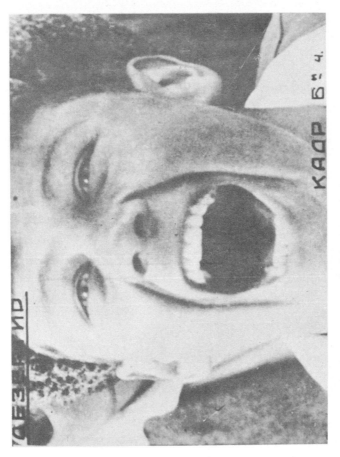

Non-professional in small part.
" DESERTER," *Pudovkin*.

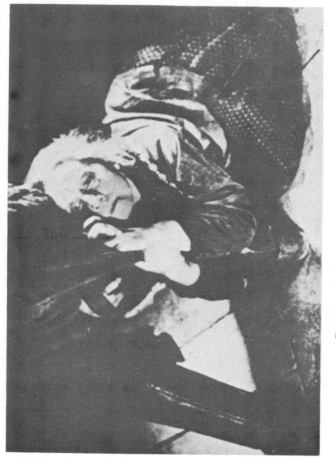

Baranovskaya, actress, as the mother.
"MOTHER," *Pudovkin.*

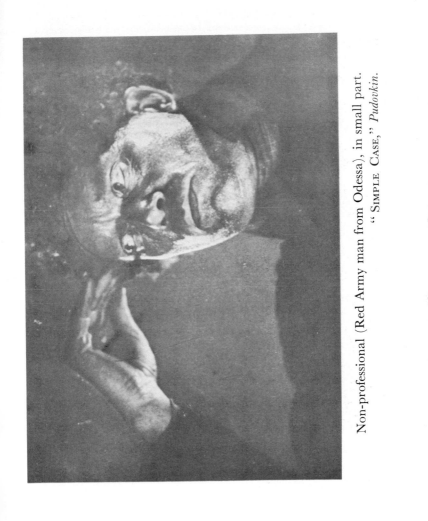

Non-professional (Red Army man from Odessa), in small part.
"SIMPLE CASE," *Pudovkin.*

Unnamed player as a jail officer.
" MOTHER," *Pudovkin.*

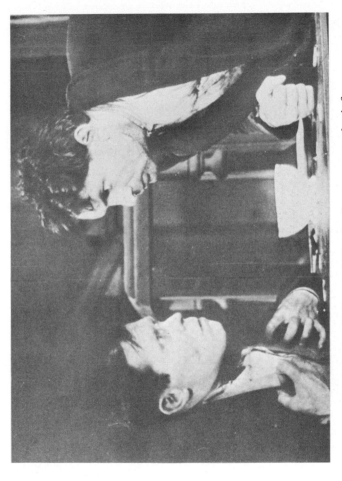

Pudovkin as Fedya and Vvedensky, actor, as the informer.
" LIVING CORPSE," *Otsep*.

Pudovkin as Fedya and Nata Vashnadze, actress, as Masha, the gipsy.
" LIVING CORPSE," *Otsep.*

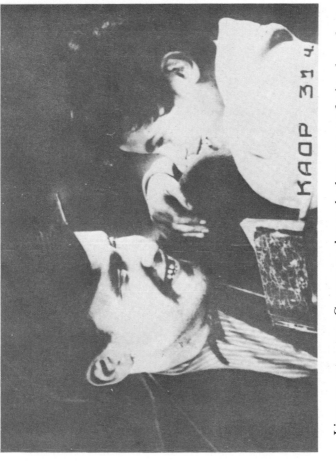

Livanov, actor, as a German worker and a boy, non-professional, as the son of a slain German worker.

"Deserter," *Pudovkin.*

Pudovkin as Fedya and Vvedensky, actor, as the informer. "LIVING CORPSE," *Otsep.*

his appearance, would inevitably cramp the creative sweep of the scenarist's imagination, in other words strike a blow at the most vital and characteristic essential of the film—its idea content.

On the other hand, of course, one should obviously support, develop, and encourage to the uttermost and in every possible way the organisation of permanent collectives in such cases as do find it feasible to transform the weight of their efforts into the welding of a creative unit out of their component workers, if only for instructional purposes, to raise the general cinematic culture of the actors concerned.

But I think that, apart from the creation of permanent collectives, we should also face up to the problem of bringing about circumstances which would enable an actor and director who have joined forces only for one or two films to achieve a profound inner mutual understanding and a linkage to one another of maximum extent.

The one and only basis for the formation of a collective with such an understanding is: first and foremost, the organic collaboration in the creative process of all its component workers; next, agreement in viewpoint, agreement in methods of work, in general cinematographic culture.

Work by such a collective, to go further—the very existence of such a collective in any real sense—is conceivable only in circumstances where all the workers of a producing unit collaborate in as close contact as possible from their very inception as a unit. Immediately and inevitably arises the question of the participation of the actor in scenario work. We have already noted that the common experience is for an actor to be confronted with a scenario already written, containing a rôle cut and dried and ready for him, when he should be engaged in investigating the rôle for elements that move him and could condition the fullness and content of his subsequent creative work.

There also occur examples of a scenarist writing his script with a given actor in view. This, of course, happens when the scenarist knows the identity of the actor to be cast, as would be the case in the circumstance of existence of a permanent collective.

But yet a third method is possible, and in this the actor, invited by director and scenarist, would be introduced into the work during the actual process of writing of the scenario, and therefore actually exercise a certain influence on his rôle. The contact resulting would be complex—scenarist, scenario, rôle, actor, director. This method would and should be adopted before the scenario is actually plotted definitely into its edited shape of shooting script. It is my regret that no practice any way approaching this has ever been known in our film history to date.

Though one might legitimately say that there have been instances of contact between a director and his actors or between a director and his scenarists, one can with equal certainty state there has never been, in the whole of our film history, an instance of close contact and co-operation between actor, scenarist, and director.

In my own experience, I have never had a collective, and I must confess that during my work I have admitted actors to creative collaboration only grudgingly and to a miserly extent. This has, of course, principally been due to the general atmosphere of production, which never leaves time for mutual intercourse of a really deep creative nature between the workers in a producing collective.

When the actual process of production of the film has started, it is already late to begin to set up real contact, and in some cases is quite impossible. One can still rouse a greater or lesser interest and keenness on the part of an actor in his work, but one can never hope for a really welded linkage with him. It is therefore not difficult to appreciate that it is quite taken for granted that the actor should fall out altogether when the most important stage of work on the film begins—that of editing. He steps aside, and returns only to see the film in completely finished state when he has no chance whatever to modify anything the director has done.

Why is the period of production marked with such excitement and nervous strain? Chiefly because one has always to work with an incomplete scenario and insufficient preliminary preparation. Too often nearly the whole of a director's energy during the shooting of a film is spent on working over the shooting script, and he only has a chance to familiarise his collective with the most vital and important elements in their creative work a day, or even an hour, before shooting.

This is a hopeless and essentially bad method of introducing the actor into the creative work of the collective. No collective can possibly be created during the production stage of a film; the good and only proper time for its creation is, of course, the preparatory pre-shooting period.

It is only during this preparatory period that the conditions suitable for mapping the general lines to mutual understanding obtain. It is only during this preparatory period that the general orientation of the film can be felt, schools of thought agreed, a real growth of utmost fullness take place.

We have already made clear the handicapped status of the film actor in our industry. While the director has the chance to say as clearly as he likes what he wants done, to choose the scenarist most suitable for the carrying out of what he plans, to pick his own cast, the film actor has hitherto had no possible means enabling him to express a desire for working along given lines of his selection.

One school has suggested as way out the giving to film actors of the opportunity to try themselves out in duplicate during the preparatory period, thereby giving them a chance to convince the director of their comparative suitability and advantages for the given rôles. But to have a possibility of choice, one must have enough alternatives to choose from. Do our actors have this possibility? Of course not, because the actual process of writing the scenario, the writing that establishes the final shape, fixing sharp and pointed characteristics suitable to a given particular actor, is done apart and away from all the actors. The moment the scenarist and director leave synopsis and treatment, which only generally sketch the outlines of the future characters, and start to develop and work out the actual scenario and shooting script, they, in fact, take away from the actor all chance of choosing his rôle.

If only the planned scenarios while still in their primary form of synopsis and treatment could be spread broadcast among the acting personnel, then at last the actors, considering and weighing their own possibilities, could express a choice of director and scenario, and then, by further contact, have the definite possibility of joint creative work. This would be the first real step towards setting up a real creative collective.

But the practical solution of this problem will, I fear, encounter serious difficulties. The acting staff of a given studio is usually in definite degree limited. The directorial staff is usually also limited. When one proposes a solution envisaging wide use of all forces for establishing creative collectives, one should probably begin by considering how to overcome tendencies towards separation in the various separate studios.

In my view a film-producing unit should be entitled to claim sovereign and separate status only if it has some definite and individual creative 'face,' that is, if its separately welded collectives together comprise a collective of higher degree, also welded to creative purpose. But we have no such producing units. Acting and directorial staffs are distributed casually, without any relation to their style of work or so-called ' school ' of art. This being so, pending some sort of regrouping on the basis of common style or artistic tendency among proposed collaborators, I think we must envisage, as practical possibility, exchange on a wide scale of their respective creative elements between the various units.

The wide broadcasting of synopses and basic treatments of films planned for production must be effected not within the limits of one unit, but among several, so that mutual choice of director and actor will have the chance to operate under conditions of real fairness.

In direct relationship with all this is the question of the so-called ' range ' of the actor, that is to say, the limits of his type, which, in the cinema, are, in fact, purely physical, connected with the external expressiveness of his acting elements. The possibilities of changing the physical appearance of the actor are far more limited in the cinema than on the stage.

For purposes of realistic work in film, the possibilities of artificial make-up entirely disappear; for example, it is quite impossible to alter a three-dimensional shape with a two-dimensional line. To draw or paint the relief of a face, as on the stage, is impossible in the cinema because the vacillating contrasts of light on movement will invariably expose the false immobility of a painted shadow and show it up just for what it is—a dirty mark. The painting of non-existent relief on a face in the cinema being impossible, to be effective it must be constructed tri-dimensionally, but even so, such an artificial and stuck-on protuberance will cease to be lifelike if it exceed a relatively tiny size, for it will fail to take part in the live and subtle interplay of the muscular system of the human face.

Make-up is possible on the stage only because the relatively constant footlights and stage lighting yield no shadow, and the spectator, seated relatively distantly, thus fails to remark and be disturbed by its immobility.

Variety in an actor's rôles in the cinema derives mainly from inner design, from variation in conduct in the novel conditions created afresh in each new film. In the cinema one and the same actor, with face and even character unaltered, can play many films.

We know, for example, how Chaplin, always staying in the same make-up and always preserving the same character, has created a tremendous generic image that passes through the whole series of his films.

It is in the light of these facts, I maintain, that we should study the question of the limits to a given individual's acting possibilities in the cinema.

At this stage, inescapably, the question of the so-called ' star-system ' comes out into the open. How is a ' star ' made and made use of in the bourgeois world ? If an actor has been accepted by the public in some film owing to his appearance, owing to his manner of acting, this latter being in most cases almost a trick, then the producing unit does all in its power to preserve, as carefully and rigidly as possible, all those properties in the actor that appealed to the public, and to adjust to them, by any makeshift, any material, so long only as that material is slick and catchy. In fact, the ' star system ' means no more than that the director presents the ' star,' in his given discovered form, against some background dictated by his employers. An example of the kind is Adolph Menjou, who acted brilliantly under Chaplin's direction. In a series of further, already desperately stupid films, mechanically preserving unchanged the appearance and general scheme of his behaviour, he has gradually become a less and less interesting empty doll.

I think that this method of repetition of appearance of an actor the public has once liked is neither acceptable to us, nor, indeed, is it in general acceptable as a form of art.

The repetition of an actor's appearance on the screen in a new film should not be effected simply for the sake of showing him once more unaltered in the shape the public liked, but in the course of making a new step forward on the path of his advance. He must somehow further develop the image on which he has begun to work, and carry this image through a new section of reality abstracted for the purpose.

Menjou, in contradistinction, has simply been shown repeating himself time after time, which has meant fundamentally no less than the collapse of his talent, because the film has just happened round him, instead of himself entering into the film.

Chaplin manages to preserve ever the same image, yet at the same time in each and every film of his he interests, because he is ever passing through new and still newer cross-sections of reality, thereby each time creating a really organically whole work of art.

A film with a ' repeat ' of an actor must represent some process in his development, some process obedient to laws, transforming the repeat into a step on the road towards wider and wider revelation of the image he has created.

CHAPTER XIV

PERSONAL EXPERIENCES

Now that I am drawing to a close, I should like to say just a few words about my own experiences in acting. It occurs to me that in these experiences are reflected all the unclarity and confusion about inner fundamentals, which are the reason why, to this day, the film actor has to all intents and purposes no agreed school of acting. My first rôles were associated with the methods of Kuleshov. The sole and only content of play-acting in that school is external expression, or treatment of the image only by a mechanical sequence of motions selected either by the actor or, sometimes, by the director.

The edited image of the actor on the screen was there constructed, exactly similarly, from a number of mechanically joined pieces, connected only by a temporal composition of schematised movements. Even the elements of the close-up, which, one would think, would require a greater degree of inner work from the actor, were usually restricted to the learning by heart of facial movements disintegrated into analysed components. Such director's commands as : jut out the chin, open the eyes wide, bend or raise the head, were a frequent part of the routine of the shooting process.

There used to be a certain amount of talk about

the possibility and necessity for basing all these movements on some inner something, though what this 'something' was no one quite knew or at any time defined.

At times, I remember, this 'something' was merely the satisfaction one experiences at the smooth and easy execution of a scheme one has memorised. At others one experienced an ecstasy difficult to distinguish from the sensation of general physical tension derived from consciousness of the importance of some deed one is accomplishing.

This is how I worked both in *The Adventure of Mr. West* and in *The Ray of Death*.

I must observe here that a tremendous feature of our work was the fact that Kuleshov, who possesses immense talent for teaching, did not neglect to steep us thoroughly in both scenario and editing work and gave me the chance, not only myself to act, but also to direct little scenes with other actors.

The completeness of this embrace of the whole process of creating a film on all its sides accustomed me to feel myself not only as a being working before the camera, but also in the continuity of the future images that were to appear as the result of editing.

I consider that Kuleshov's school, despite all the mechanism of his then approach to the actor, was immensely helpful to every member of his collective, and it is no accident that there emerged from it such fine actors as Fogel and Komarov.

I made an effort in my work at that time to base myself on inner mood, and to find some quality within myself that would enable me to feel, at the moment of shooting, a fully and wholly live being. But I had no possibility really to develop this during all the time I was with Kuleshov. Only when I went to Mezhrabpom and started work on my own did I get the chance to approach acting from a new angle, though admittedly this was in the course of my work as director. But every time I made a film, I always tried also to take a small part in it myself.

I regard as comparatively successful the little piece I played in *Mother*, where I represented an officer, a police rat, who came to search the dwelling of Paul. I remember that for this rôle, by habit of my old training, I based myself principally on the external traits of its image. I began by cutting my hair *en brosse*, grew a moustache, and put on a pair of spectacles, which, it seemed to me, by their contrast with the military uniform, which always lends a certain air of bravado and masculinity to the wearer, would especially emphasise the weak and degraded character of a typical police-officer rat.

I remember that the only inner mood on which I tried to base my acting was one of sour dreariness and boredom, such as seemed to me should cause the spectator to feel vividly the dourness of police mechanism, which impersonally and remorselessly mutilates every spark of living thought and feeling.

I remember that all the work on this tiny part was most closely bound up with its editing development. The somnolent, bored, and dreary figure of the police officer, mainly shown in long shot and medium shot, was purposely changed to close-up and big head when, in the course of the rôle, I began to show glimpses of interest in the chase as I scented the spoor.

My only big acting job was the rôle of Fedya in *The Living Corpse*. Here I was not the director. The task was big and complex. In every aspect of the development of the rôle the question arose of the teleology and directional aim of the image, of its place in the film, and its relation to the significance of the film as a whole. It must be admitted that not one of these questions was adequately solved.

My work on this film, owing to various attendant circumstances, took the form, on the whole, of a holiday from directorial work. I gave myself up entirely into the hands of the director, consciously deciding that I should not, in any given piece of film, make any attempt to transcend the limits of my own personal appearance and personal character.

What this meant was that in consequence I surrendered to the director the task of creating a united image. I never thought of the edited image as a whole. I had only an idea of the editing treatment of the individual pieces. As general linking-up element for formation of the whole, I provided my own self; in simpler language, I played this man as myself.

In each individual moment of the acting, by means of various methods of strictly individual kind and applicable only to myself, I brought myself into a mood suited to enable me, in all personal sincerity and the unity of my own character, to make the various movements and go through the various actions required of me by the scenario and director.

I recall a scene in which, revolver in hand, I stand behind a stove, peering round its edge, displaying to the spectator the half-crazed face of a man on the verge of suicide.

I remember that, to act this piece, I hid from the camera behind the stove and, pressing the revolver against my heart, repeated without a break the words of Kirillov in Dostoievski's *The Demons*: " At me, at me, at me. . . ." When finally this had brought me into an almost fainting condition, I peered around the edge.

I recall another scene typical of the same principle. In an empty hall, just before leaving my home and abandoning my wife, I take leave of my sister. I remember that it was quite easy for me to summon up in myself a feeling of extreme care and tenderness towards the girl who played the rôle of the sister. She appealed to me in life as a person. To feel that, on going away from her for ever, on leaving her alone in this empty house, I should call forth from myself sorrow and a desire to help her, a caress that at the same time would be a parting gesture putting her away from me, was simple and easy: it was not alien to, but actually accorded easily with, my real-life characteristics.

Speaking in general, my work in *The Living Corpse* was carried out to an extent with considerable and profound inner feeling and was heavily charged emotionally, but it never gave me the feeling that I had it in me to play any other rôle, one based on an image not fully reproducing my own and usual character as manifested in life.

My experience in playing in *The Living Corpse* can, of course, in no way serve.as a proper example of acting work.

The inner linkage, the inner organisation of the character, was built up not by the path of transmutation of self, but by that of direct manifestation of self. In each given piece, I remained in the fullest literal sense of the word myself. Any element new and alien from myself appeared solely as the result of editing. In other words, the screen image of Fedya appeared solely as the result of dictates laid down by the scenario; it was never constructed creatively by acting the character.

I incline to think that the basic and decisive factor in this work was precisely my personal indifference to the image as a whole, which made me approach my work as a mere journey across the film, without striving to subordinate my actual self to the teleology of the image, which alone can give the actor not just the satisfaction that comes from the accomplishment of a technical task, but the sense of a solution of the ideological tasks posed by the film as a whole, living, growing, full of content, not only for the spectator, but also for the actor as well.

I hold that, in the present state of our cinematic theory and practice, it is still impossible to speak of any definite system of work or system of training for the actor. Such a system has first to be created, and to begin with, as the point from which we must depart, we must take the establishment of the indispensable conditions that provide the possibility of organising such systems.

At this stage all I can do is to limit myself to the simple narration of the empirical experiments in my own and other people's work.

CHAPTER XV

CONCLUSIONS

1. THE new technical basis of cinema (non-stationary camera and microphone) renders not only unnecessary but senseless for the actor all the technique connected in the theatre with the wide distance actually separating the actor from the stationary audience. The following are therefore eliminated: stage-specialised voice production, theatricalised diction, theatricalised gestures, painted features.

2. In consequence of this the theatrical sense of an actor's ' range ' becomes altered. The variety of rôles he can play in the cinema is dependent: either on the variety of characters he can play while preserving one and the same external appearance (Stroheim), or, alternatively, on his development of one and the same character throughout a variety of circumstances (Chaplin).

3. Having lost the possibility of creating a ' type ' with the aid of theatrical methods: stylised make-up, generalised gesture, emphasised voice expression, and so forth, the film actor in exchange acquires possibilities, inconceivable in the theatre, of closely realistic treatment of the image, maximal approach in his acting to the actual behaviour of a living man in each given circumstance. A ' type ' is created in the cinema largely at the expense of the general

action, at the expense of the wealth of variety of human behaviour in various situations. (Compare the development of the ' type ' in the novel form and in drama—the cinema here is nearer to literature than to the theatre.)

4. From the culture of the stage actor is taken over into the cinema everything connected with the process of creating a united image, and its ' absorption ' by the actor, everything that precedes the search for ' stage ' and ' theatricalised ' forms for the acting. (Of course, in practice no sharp division between these two periods exists. A feeling of ' stage ' form will always be present with the stage actor, yet it is possible to some extent to draw a line.) For this reason the Stanislavski school, which emphasises (more truly, emphasised) most particularly the initial process of deep ' absorption ' by the actor of the image, even at the expense of the ' theatricalisation ' of its content, is nearest of all to the film actor. The intimacy of acting of the Stanislavski school actor, leading sometimes to an overburdening of the performance with little-noticed details and thus a loss by that acting of theatrical ' panache,' is inevitably and remarkably developed in the cinema.

5. All the means theatrical culture has created to help the actor wholly ' absorb ' an image scattered in pieces throughout a play must be taken over into cinema practice. In the first rank of importance is rehearsal work, developed paramountly along the line of creating for the actor every possible condition

for prolonged, unbroken existence in the image (the rehearsal scenario).

6. The editing treatment of the actor's image (composition on the screen of the separately shot acting pieces) is in no sense a directorial trick, taking the place of acting by the actor. It is a new, powerful, peculiarly cinematic means of transmitting this acting. To master it is as important for the film actor as it is important for the stage actor to master ' theatricalisation ' technique (stage delivery of his acting).

7. Hence it follows that the culture indispensable for the film actor will only attain the necessary heights when included in it is profound knowledge of the art of editing and its various methods. This desideratum has hitherto incorrectly been applied only to the director.

8. The growth of a film actor cannot be separated from practical work on his film, and accordingly he must be closely linked with it, beginning with the final polishing of the scenario in the course of rehearsals and not being discarded from it during the period of cutting.

9. In work in sound films, the actor equipped with this culture must strive to find examples of acting and its editing that will develop forms of powerful impressiveness, such as were found in its day by the silent film. He must not yield to the reactionary force that tempts both himself and the director—adaptation to mechanical use of theatrical methods alien to the film.

CRITICAL ICONOGRAPHY
OF THE
FILM WORK OF V. I. PUDOVKIN

REVISED AND COMPLETED

CRITICAL ICONOGRAPHY

PUDOVKIN was born in 1893, died 1953. His father, of peasant stock, was a commercial traveller in Penza, Volga region. The family moved to Moscow, where Pudovkin received his education, studying physics and chemistry at the University but leaving to join the army, when war broke out, before taking his degree. Serving in the artillery he was wounded and taken prisoner in February 1915, learning languages in a German prison camp during the next three years. In 1918 he escaped and returned to chemistry but, moved by seeing D. W. Griffith's *Intolerance*, applied in 1920 to join the film training college G.I.K. (State Institute of Cinematography). The students here made films in the course of training under G.I.K.'s first principal, Vladimir Gardin.

IN THE DAYS OF STRUGGLE (*The Struggle for Peace*), (G.I.K. and V.F.K.O., 1920), 3 reels, 1970 ft.
Directed by I. Perestiani. Pudovkin played a Red Army officer.

HAMMER AND SICKLE (*In Difficult Days*), (G.I.K. and V.F.K.O., 1921), 5 reels, 4921 ft.
Directed by Gardin with Tisse as cameraman. Pudovkin was chief assistant director and played Andrey Krasnov, a poor peasant, afterward a Red Army man.

HUNGER . . . HUNGER . . . HUNGER . . . (G.I.K. and V.F.K.O., 1921), 2 reels, 1640 ft.
Pudovkin co-directed with Gardin, Tisse again cameraman. The film is described as an "agit-poster".

The same year Pudovkin assisted Gardin in staging a dramatization of Jack London's *The Iron Heel* at the Theatre of Revolutionary Satire. He refused an invitation from Gardin to co-direct with him for the Ukraine film producing organization but collaborated on the scenario.

LOCKSMITH AND CHANCELLOR (Vufku, 1923), 6 reels, 6965 ft.
Gardin directed. Scenario, adapted from the play by Lunacharsky, jointly by Gardin and Pudovkin.

Pudovkin next studied for two years with the group called "Kuleshov's Workshop", which produced and acted without film owing to shortage of raw stock; eventually the R.S.F.S.R. film producing organization supplied them with imported film.

THE EXTRAORDINARY ADVENTURES OF MR. WEST IN THE LAND OF THE BOLSHEVIKS (Goskino, 1924), 7 reels, 8530 ft.
L. Kuleshov directed. Scenario by N. Asayev, Kuleshov and Pudovkin. Pudovkin worked as art director and played the "Count", Zhban, an adventurer who seeks to despoil U.S. Senator West, a tourist in U.S.S.R.

THE DEATH RAY (Goskino, 1925), 8 reels, 9505 ft.
Kuleshov directed. Pudovkin worked as his assistant and as art director, and played the chief villain, Father Revo, a fascist priest

Pudovkin then accepted an invitation from Mezhrabpom to make a documentary film illustrating Pavlov's work on conditioned reflexes. This was the real beginning of his *personal* creative work. It began an association with Anatoly Golovnya, his cameraman, that lasted almost unbrokenly for 25 years. Mezhrabpom was the film unit of the Russian section of the "International Labour Defence", and a great rival of the Moscow state film studio until the merger of its staff in 1934. For technical reasons connected with its subject, the documentary took two years to complete, and he broke off for other work meanwhile, this first film not being released until after *Mother*.

THE MECHANISM OF THE BRAIN (Mezhrabpom-Rus, 1926), 6 reels, 6070 ft.
Scenario and Direction—V. I. PUDOVKIN. Photography—A. N. Golovnya. Technical scientific direction—Prof. L. N. Voskresensky. Physiological experiments and operations—Prof. D. S. Fursikov. Animal-life direction—L. Danilov and S. Averintsev. Conditioned reflex experiments with children—Prof. V. I. Krasnogorsky. Child-life direction—A. Durnovo.

In Britain the censors refused a certificate; the film was first shown here, privately, to the Royal Society of Medicine (Neurological Section), in March 1929.

LITTLE BRICKS (Mezhrabpom-Rus, 1925), 6 reels, 5905 ft.
Directed by L. Obolensky and M. Doller, on the theme of a famous popular song of the day. Pudovkin played a workman.

CHESS FEVER (Mezhrabpom-Rus, 1925), 2 reels, 1312 ft.
Direction—V. I. PUDOVKIN and N. Shpikovsky. Scenario—N. Shpikovsky. Photography—A. N. Golovnya.

A comedy made as a sort of glorious lark in connection with the chess congress of that year in Moscow. By an experiment in cutting and editing, Capablanca —who posed politely for newsreel shots—was made to appear to play a part reconciling the cross-starred lovers. The girl was played by Anna Zemtsova (Pudovkin's wife), and minor roles are played by "Workshop" groupers—Barnet, Raizman, Protozanov, later famous as directors.

MOTHER (Mezhrabpom-Rus, 1926), 7 reels, 5905 ft. Direction—V. I. PUDOVKIN. Scenario, based on the Gorky novel, by N. Zarkhy. Photography—A. N. Golovnya. Art direction—S. Kozlovsky. Chief assistant director—M. Doller.

Cast—Pelageya Nilovna Vlasova, the "Mother" (Vera Baranovskaya), her husband, a workman (A. Chistyakov), her son, Pavel (Nikolay Batalov). Anna Zemtsova plays a revolutionary student, friend of Pavel, and Pudovkin plays a mild, bespectacled police officer. The cast were nearly all professional actors, mostly of the "Workshop" group. Kuleshov is said to have helped in the direction of the crowd scenes.

In Britain the censors refused a certificate; the film was first shown, privately, to the Film Society in October 1928. A sound version, with musical arrangement by D. S. Blok, was issued in U.S.S.R. in 1935.

It was during the making of *Mother* that Pudovkin wrote and published the two booklets comprising, under the title *Film Technique*, the greater part of the present volume. With Eisenstein *(October*)* and Barnet *(Moscow in October)*, Pudovkin made his next film as

* In English-language countries: *Ten Days that shook the World.*

part of a triad in celebration of the 10th Anniversary of the Revolution. Just as *Potemkin* is expanded from its original conception as an episode in a wider canvas *1905*, so *The End of St. Petersburg* is expanded from its original plan as part of a history *Petersburg-Petrograd-Leningrad.*

THE END OF ST. PETERSBURG (Mezhrabpom-Rus, 1927), 7 reels, 8202 ft.

Direction—V. I. PUDOVKIN. Scenario, by N. Zarkhy. Associate-director—M. Doller. Photography—A. N. Golovnya. Art direction—S. Kozlovsky.

Cast—Chistyakov again plays a worker and Baranovskaya his wife. Ivan Chuvelyev is type-cast as a peasant lad, and his real brother, V. Chuvelyev plays his brother, a new recruit to industry who becomes a strike-breaker. Tsoppi plays a "patriot" agitator. Pudovkin has a small part as a German officer. Non-acting material, type-cast for example in stockbroker parts, is used much more than in the previous film.

First performed in England, privately, to the Film Society in February 1929. Later shown publicly.

THE HEIR TO JENGHIZ KHAN* (Mezhrabpomfilm, 1928) 8 reels, 10,170 ft.

Direction—V. I. PUDOVKIN. Scenario—O. Brik, from a story by I. Novokshenov. Photography—A. N. Golovnya. Art direction—S. Koslovsky and N. Aronson.

Cast: Bair, a Mongol huntsman (Valery Inkishinov), Bair's father (I. Inkishinov), A. Chistyakov (a partisan leader), A. Dedintsev (a British colonel), L. Byelinskaya

* Known outside the U.S.S.R. as *Storm over Asia.*

(his wife), A. Sudakevich (his daughter), K. Gurnyak (a British soldier with a loose puttee), B. Barnet (a British soldier with a cat), V. Tsoppi (Mr. Smith, agent of a British fur company). Much more "non-acting" material was used in this film than in any other of Pudovkin's dramatic subjects. The Mongolian scenes were filmed on location, the tsam (religious dance drama) was actual.

In Britain the censors refused a certificate; the film was first shown, privately, to the Film Society in February 1930. A dubbed version, with music composed by N. Kryukov, was issued in U.S.S.R. in 1952.

For a time after these two films, Pudovkin travelled abroad. This is the period of his lecture in London to the Film Society; his visa was prolonged after questions in the House of Commons. For a time he acted before returning to direction, playing the most important role of his career in a joint production by the film companies of the Soviet and German sections of the I.L.D., made in Berlin.

THE LIVING CORPSE (Mezhrabpomfilm and Prometheusfilm, 1929), 7 reels, 7327 ft.
Directed by F. Otsep from Leo Tolstoy's play. Pudovkin played the chief part, Fedya Protasov. Golovnya was cameraman and Sergey Kozlovsky one of the two art directors.

THE GAY CANARY (Mezhrabpomfilm, 1929), 6 reels, 6562 ft.
Kuleshov directed. Pudovkin played a charlatan conjurer.

CRITICAL ICONOGRAPHY

NEW BABYLON (Sovkino, 1929), 8 reels, 7218 ft.
The second picture directed by G. Kozintsev and L. Trauberg. Pudovkin had a tiny part as a salesman in the Oriental Department of the huge general store in Paris of 1871 that gives the film its name.

The next three films marked a period of comparative failure. The first was the worst. It was conceived in terms of sound film, but had to be made silent because adequate apparatus was not available in U.S.S.R. at that time. The result was that many ideas just did not come off, and the relationships in the story—of two married couples in the post-revolution period—were incomprehensible to the audience.

THE STORY OF A SIMPLE CASE (*Life is Very Good*), (Mezhrabpomfilm, 1932), 8 reels, 8638 ft.
Direction—V. I. PUDOVKIN. Scenario—A. Rzheshevsky, from a short story of Mikhail Koltsov. Associate director—M. Doller. Photography—G. Kabalov and G. Bobrov. Art direction—S. Kozlovsky.

Cast—The chief parts (Pavel Langovoy, his wife Mashenka and his second wife, a worker and his wife) were played by A. Baturin, Y. Rogulina and M. Byelousova, A. Gorchilin and A. Chekulayeva respectively. Chistyakov had a part (Uncle Sasha) and non-acting material was still used in several important roles (*e.g.* Baturin and Byelousova).

When first issued in 1930, the obscurity of the film raised protests on the part of the public which led to its withdrawal after a few days. Two years later it was re-issued in revised form under the present title, but it was hardly more successful. The film was first shown in England, to the Film Society in May 1933.

The next film was to have been another joint Soviet-German production with Prometheus, but Hitler's advent to power caused the plans for a German version to be abandoned and the scenes begun in Hamburg were finished in Odessa and Leningrad. Though muddled and inconclusive, the film contains sequences of great power and gives greater expression than any other to the ideas on counterpoint in sound entertained at that time by Eisenstein, Pudovkin and Alexandrov.

DESERTER (Mezhrabpomfilm, 1933), 7 reels, 8746 ft. Direction—V. I. PUDOVKIN. Scenario—M. Krasno-stavsky, A. Lazebnikov, Nina Agadzhanova-Shutko. Photography—A. N. Golovnya and Y. Fogelman. Art direction—S. Kozlovsky. Music—Y. Shaporin. Sound arrangement—D. Blok. Sound recording—Y. Nesterov.

Cast—Boris Livanov played the lead (Karl Renn), Tamara Makarova and Yudit Glizer had parts (Greta and Marcella). Chistyakov and Gurnyak were in it. S. Gerasimov and M. Shtraukh had tiny parts as trade union "right-wing" officials and Pudovkin as a porter.

The film was first shown in England, privately, at the Film Society in November 1933.

Pudovkin had by now revised the views on "non-acting" material expressed in *Film Technique*, and his new ideas had formed the subject of a lecture to G.I.K. in 1930. In this last film and henceforward he used actors almost invariably. The State Academy of Art Research invited him to expand his revised views and this he did in a lecture lasting four days that forms the second part of the present volume. In 1935 Zarkhy, who had rejoined Pudovkin as writer, was killed in a car accident in which Pudovkin was injured. After long convalescence he proceeded, not very successfully, on the theme of air adventure, family love and sacrifice, on which they had been engaged.

VICTORY (*The Happiest*),* (Mosfilm, 1938), 9 reels, 7655 ft.

Direction—V. I. PUDOVKIN and M. Doller. Scenario by N. Zarkhy, under literary supervision of V. Vishnevsky. Photography—A. N. Golovnya. Art direction—V. Ivanov and V. Kamsky. Music—Y. Shaporin. Sound recording—Y. Nesterov.

Cast—The mother, her son Klim Samoilov and his brother Sasha were played by Y. Korchagina-Alexandrovskaya, V. Solovyev and A. Zubov. Not shown in Britain.

The growing threat from Hitler gave rise to a new genre in the Soviet cinema, the patriotic-historical. Pudovkin found new energy with these themes, and his contributions were two: the first, dealing with a united popular revolt against the Polish occupation of Moscow in the early seventeenth century, has tremendous fighting scenes but is somewhat overwhelming; the second, about the extraordinary and unvanquished Russian military commander of the late eighteenth century, was one of his finest successes.

* Issued in U.S.A. as *Mother and Son*.

MININ AND POZHARSKY (Mosfilm Studio, 1939), 15 reels, 12,140 ft.

Direction—V. I. PUDOVKIN and M. Doller. Scenario— V. Shklovsky. Photography—A. Golovnya and T. Lobova. Art direction—A. Utkin and K. Yefimov. Music—Y. Shaporin. Sound recording—Y. Nesterov. Lyrics—N. Aseyev. Consultants—V. Picheta, V. Lebedev and N. Protasov.

Cast—The name parts were played by A. Khanov (Kuzma Minin) and Boris Livanov (Dmitry Pozharsky). V. Moskvin had a part and a reappearance was made by Ivan Chuvelyev (Vaska). Awarded a Stalin Prize, 1st Class, in 1941. Not shown in Britain.

20 YEARS OF CINEMA (Mosfilm, 1940), 10 reels, 8038 ft. Part-documentary film for the 20th Anniversary Festival of Soviet cinema, jointly directed and edited by Pudovkin and Esther Shub. The plan of the film and its sub-titles were by Yuri Olesha and A. Macheret.

SUVOROV (Mosfilm Studio, 1940), 12 reels, 9680 ft. Direction—V. I. PUDOVKIN and M. Doller. Scenario— G. Grebner. Photography—A. N. Golovnya and T. Lobov. Art direction—V. Yegorov and K. Yefimov. Music—Y. Shaporin. Sound recording—N. Timartsev. Consultant—N. Levitsky.

Cast—The actor who gives the wonderful performance in the name-part (N. P. Cherkasov), and whose sole venture this is outside the theatre, must not be confused with the famous film actor N. Cherkasov who played Nevsky and Ivan for Eisenstein. The "N" in each case is Nikolay. They were not related. Awarded a Stalin Prize, 1st Class, in 1941. Released in Britain by Anglo-American during the war.

At the opening of the war, those film directors who remained in Moscow turned to producing the so-called *Cine-Battle Magazines*, a series of compilations of short dramas, comedies and documentaries on topical themes. Pudovkin's contribution was the editing of an item from British Ministry of Information material on the W.A.A.F. and a short melodrama of peasant revenge against the German occupationists.

FEAST AT ZHIRMUNKA (from *Cine-Battle Magazine No. 6*), (Mosfield Studio, 1941), 2 reels.

Direction—V. I. PUDOVKIN and M. Doller. Scenario— L. Leonov and N. Shpikovsky. Photography—A. N. Golovnya and T. Lobov. Art direction—B. Dubrovsky-Eshke. Music—N. Kryukov. Sound recording—N. Timartsev.

Cast—The chief part is that of Grandmother Praskovya (A. Zuyeva). Released in Britain by Anglo-American during the war, as part of a re-arranged selection of items from the series.

The Moscow studios were bombed, and the film colony evacuated to Central Asia to continue its work. Here Pudovkin made a rather flat, straight adaptation of the great popular patriotic theatrical success of the day, acted a small part for Eisenstein and began the third of his great historical films—on the famous Russian naval hero of the Crimean war—completing it after the general return to Moscow.

IN THE NAME OF THE FATHERLAND (Alma-Ata Studios, 1943), 10 reels, 8614 ft.

FILM TECHNIQUE AND FILM ACTING

Scenario and direction—V. I. PUDOVKIN and D Vasilyev. Photography—B. Volchek and E. Savelyeva. Art direction—A. Wechsler. Trickwork—A. Ptushko. Musical arrangement—B. Volsky. Sound recording— K. Gordon.

Cast—N. Kryuchkov played a leading role (Safonov), also M. Pastukhova (Valya Anoshchenko). Pudovkin played the considerable role of the German general.

The film was shown in Britain during the war by Anglo-American; the play—K. Simonov's *Russian People*—was also performed in Britain, first at the Palace Theatre, London.

IVAN THE TERRIBLE (*Part I*), (Alma-Ata Studio, 1914), 12 reels, 9006 ft.

Eisenstein directed. Pudovkin plays the tiny part of "Nikolay Big-Fool, a madman".

ADMIRAL NAKHIMOV (Mosfilm Studio, 1946), 12 reels, 8337 ft.

Direction—V. I. PUDOVKIN. Scenario—I. Lukovsky. Chief assistant director—D. Vasilyev. Photography— A. Golovnya and T. Lobova. Art directors—V. Yegorov, A. Weissfeld and M. Yuferov. Music—N. Kryukov. Sound recording—V. Zorin and N. Shmelev. Consultants—Academician E. Tarle and Naval Captain N. Novikov.

Cast—The name part is played by Alexander Diky. Napoleon III, Osman Pasha, General Pelissier and Lord Raglan are among those portrayed, the last by P. Gaideburov. N. Brilling plays Captain Evans and Pudovkin plays Prince Menshikov.

386

CRITICAL ICONOGRAPHY

The film was sharply criticised by the authorities on its first appearance for alleged unhistoricity and imbalance in the portrayal of the central character. Several sequences were re-made. Eventually, in 1947, it was awarded a Stalin Prize, 1st Class. Not shown in Britain.

THREE MEETINGS (Mosfilm Studio, 1948), 9 reels, 7467 ft.
Directed in combination by Yutkevich, Pudovkin and Ptusho, with Tamara Makarova, Boris Chirkov and N. Kryuchkov in the chief parts and music by N. Kryukov.

The next, penultimate, film was Pudovkin's contribution to the series of film-biographies of Russian scientific innovators. It makes rather heavy weather of its subject, the mathematician and pioneer of aeronautics.

ZHUKOVSKY (Mosfilm Studio, 1950), 9 reels, 8117 ft.
Direction—V. I. PUDOVKIN and D. Vasilyev. Scenario —A. Granberg. Photography—A. Golovnya and T. Lobova. Art direction—A. Weissfeld, A. Goncharov and V. Kovrigin. Music—V. Shebalin. Sound recording—V. Zorin. Scientific consultant—Academician S. Khristianovich.

Cast—Y. Yurovsky plays the name part.

The film received a Stalin Prize, 2nd Class, in 1951. Not shown in Britain.

Prior to *Zhukovsky*, Pudovkin had attended the Wroclaw "Conference of Intellectuals for Peace" in 1949. From now on he was to spend more time in the peace movement, touring India, attending conferences and congresses abroad, writing articles. He completed only one more film, based on a best-seller about a man who returns from the war to find his wife has married again. In it he accomplished what had eluded him so long, a story of personal relations which, while no masterpiece, yet succeeds in being simple and touching.

THE RETURN OF VASILY BORTNIKOV (Mosfilm Studio, 1953), 11 reels, 9725 ft.

Direction—V. I. PUDOVKIN. Scenario by G. Nikolayeva and Y. Gavrilovich from G. Nikolayeva's novel *Harvest*. Chief assistant director—Y. Silberstein. Photography—S. Ursevsky. Art direction—A. Freidin, B. Chebotarev and O. Vereisky. Music—K. Molchanov. Sound recording—V. Bogdankevich. Lyrics—M. Isakovsky.

Cast—The chief parts are those of Vasily Bortnikov (S. Lukyanov), Avdotya, his wife (N. Medvyedeva) and Stepan Mokhov (N. Timofeyev).

Released in Britain, but only on 16 mm., by Plato.

Note—For further iconographical information see *An Index to the Creative Work of Vsevelod I. Pudovkin*, by Jay Leyda (Special Supplement to Sight and Sound, Index Series, No. 16, London, November 1948) and *V. Pudovkin: Izbrannyiye Statyi;* ed. I. Dolinsky (Gosudarstvennoye Izdatelstvo Iskusstvo for G.I.K., Moscow, 1955).